Good News For Today We Are Not Alone

---

*A Layman's View
Of The
Christian Faith*

Frederik H. Jonker

*Fairway Press
Lima, Ohio*

GOOD NEWS FOR TODAY WE ARE NOT ALONE

FIRST EDITION
Copyright © 1994 by
Frederik H. Jonker

The Scripture quotations in this publication are from the following translations:

The *Good News Bible*, in Today's English Version. Copyright © American Bible Society 1966, 1971, 1976. Used by permission.

The *Holy Bible, New International Version*. Copyright © 1973, 1978, 1984 International Bible Society. Used by permission of Zondervan Bible Publishers. All rights reserved.

The *King James Version of the Bible*, in the public domain.

The New English Bible. Copyright © the Delegates of the Oxford University Press and the Syndics of the Cambridge University Press, 1961, 1970. Reprinted by permission.

The New Jerusalem Bible. Copyright © 1985 by Darton, Longman & Todd, Ltd. and Doubleday, a division of Bantam Doubleday Dell Publishing Group, Inc. Reprinted by permission.

Library of Congress Catalog Card Number: 93-73833

7999 / ISBN 1-55673-836-6   PRINTED IN U.S.A.

This book was written, not because the author thinks he is a good Christian, but because he thinks that being a Christian is a particularly good thing.

— *Hans Küng in, "On Being A Christian"*

To Marijke, my granddaughter, who has Down Syndrome and is the most successful person I know. She gives and receives more love and affection than any other person I know.

Table Of Contents

Foreword

This book is about the Christian religion. The book, I believe, is easy to read, and states in simple, everyday language what I, a layman, understand the Christian message to be for the people of the world today. Contrary to what most people outside the church believe, the teachings of the church are not cast in stone. Especially, in today's fast changing world, it is the task of the church to interpret again and again the Christian message so that it is relevant for the people of today. Despite these changes in interpretation, the main message remains the same as reflected in the title of this book, The Good News For Today (is) We Are Not Alone. In fact, we all live in God's world and have a glorious future ahead of us.

The purpose of the book is to inform the reader about the basic teachings of the Christian religion, and why I believe the message of Jesus today is more important than ever for the continued well-being of the average person; I would even go so far as to say for the continued existence of this world. Without religion, and I include here the non-Christian religions, the world would be a much poorer place to live in. I believe that only when we see our existence as part of a much larger overall plan for this world can we give our lives true meaning and direction. That belief is based on the firm conviction that we live in a world for which there is a long-range plan — a world that is governed by the love of the Creator for the people created in his/her own image. It is my hope that this book clearly conveys that message to everyone who reads it.

I would like to thank the people who have helped me in the writing of this book and who have given me so freely of their time. In particular, I want to thank the minister of Trinity United Church in Beamsville, the Reverend Gerald Brown, who read the chapters as they were written and who gave me the much needed encouragement to continue. I also thank Dr. Peter Morris who made many valuable comments and suggestions. I want to especially thank my wife, Barbara, for her support, her many useful suggestions and her tireless efforts to make my English conform to the rules, and who made sure that nothing but inclusive language was used throughout the book. Thank you all.

Note On The Use Of Inclusive Language

Most references to God in the Bible use the father figure. As a result, Christians, up to recently, have generally used male terms, such as father, him and his, when referring to God. However, it has always been realized that God is Spirit and therefore neither male nor female. More recently, it has been increasingly recognized that using only male terms limits our understanding of the qualities of God, which include many attributes more readily associated with the female gender. Since I find it difficult to refer to God as "It," I have used inclusive language throughout the book which recognizes both male and female qualities of God.

1

Why This Book Was Written

Some time ago, my sister and I, while on a joint holiday, had a rather heated discussion about the meaning of life. She, being a Freudian psychiatrist, had lost much of her faith in God, and argued that you did not need the concept of God and of a life hereafter to give meaning to life on earth; while I, an engineer, tried to explain that to me the concept of God and a continued life after death were the only things that could make any sense of this world and could provide a real meaning to our earthly existence.

We were both brought up in a traditional Christian home and while her psychiatric practice had made her lose much of her traditional faith in a personal God, my engineering career had actually reinforced my belief in a personal God who is close to us and who is present with us every day of our lives.

This discussion reminded me how difficult and ill-prepared most Christians are, including myself, to express our deepest feelings in terms that are meaningful to others who do not share the same beliefs. In my particular case, I have always had great difficulty in explaining why I, a practical engineer and business-man, call myself a Christian, that is a follower of Jesus Christ, in this modern age of science and technology.

I realized during the discussion with my sister and with others as well, how many terms we use in the church, words like sin and grace, that have lost much of their original mean-ing. The result is that it is sometimes difficult to explain in simple terms what Christianity is and what it stands for. The readers who are used to working with specialized equipment, such as computers, know how difficult it often is to explain what they are doing to outsiders who are not familiar with their specialized language.

So, in some ways this book was written to explain some of the tenets of the Christian religion, and to make the ideas and thoughts behind it more accessible to persons who were not brought up in a Christian family environment and who are not familiar with its traditions.

One additional reason for writing this book is related to the fact that, in the last two or three decades, there have been a number of scientific discoveries which have resulted in a different appreciation of religion by science, something that is only now beginning to be recognized by the public at large. It is my hope that by including some of this new thinking, the reader will get an idea of how profoundly some of these dis-coveries are changing our outlook on God, the universe and the ultimate reality behind it.

You may ask, as many people have asked, "Where do you, an engineer, get the nerve to write a book about the basics of the Christian religion?" Sometimes I have asked myself that question. My answer is very simple: I believe that a book on this subject, written from the perspective of a professing Chris-tian, who is at the same time a practical and informed mem-ber of our technical society, may be helpful to other people who are searching for a meaning to life. In particular, I be-lieve the book may be of help to those fellow travellers on life's journey who are grappling with some of the problems, controversies, and seeming contradictions which the acceptance of the Christian faith invariably brings with it.

So, this book is written from the perspective, and based on the experiences and background of an informed layman and not of a professional theologian. For this reason, I believe that it may be helpful for the proper understanding of what follows to know something about the messenger who is writing this message.

I was brought up in Holland in a fairly strict Christian family. As a result, I was, from an early age on, steeped in the beliefs and doctrines of the orthodox protestant church. During my high school years, and later at university, I was exposed to views of life that were in many ways contradictory to those taught to me by my parents and by my church.

This was the age of the controversy over the creation story: the story of creation as told in the Bible versus the story of evolution as proclaimed by science. Of course, I found it hard to accept that God would have created the earth some 6,000 years ago with all the fossils neatly in place in their appropriate layers of rock and sandstone. So it was, that at an early age, I had to come to grips with the seeming contradictions between science and religion.

At the same time, my youth was shaped by the effects of the Second World War which was very much part of my everyday life between the ages of 12 and 17. I found the belief in a loving God, who is in control of this world, hard to justify in the light of the systematic extermination of the Jews, the senseless bombing and killing of millions of civilians, and the equally senseless killing of millions of young men on the battlefields.

Later as an engineer, I travelled widely on all continents and came in close contact with other cultures, religions, and value systems. I met people who as earnestly believed in their gods as I did in mine; and the God whom I believed to be the creator of the entire universe was certainly not their God, nor did my God seem to have a great impact on the lives of these people.

13

All these experiences profoundly influenced my own thinking and affected my own interpretation of what God's message was for today's world. So, my personal faith, and therefore the contents of this book, is to a considerable extent shaped by my own struggles with these three ideas:

•the apparent contradictions between science and religion;
•the apparent absence of God in a suffering world;
•the existence and validity of other world religions.

It is clear from the world literature that others have struggled with these problems as well. The apparent incompatibility of science and religion has prevented many people from taking the Christian religion seriously because they believe that the findings of modern science are not compatible with the message contained in the Bible. At the same time, the apparent absence of God from a suffering world has turned many away because they cannot believe in a benevolent, caring God who allows the senseless suffering of so many people and does not interfere in the evil things that happen, even if earnestly approached in prayer to do so.

On the other hand, the continuing co-existence of Christianity with four or five other world religions, makes one ask: Who is right? Which one is the true revelation of God? or, Are they all in some way, manifestations of the same Spirit?

In struggling with these questions and searching for answers, I have found it necessary to go back to the roots of the Christian religion and search for revelations of God that would provide an insight and, if possible, provide answers to these eternal concerns and questions. So, starting with chapter two, that is what this book is attempting to do.

At this point you may well ask, why should I continue reading this book, especially if you are not particularly interested in hearing about these old religions in the first place. My answer to that question is simply that I believe it to be absolutely essential for the peaceful, and maybe even the continued existence of this world that we find answers to a number of fundamental questions which concern all of us, such as:

- how do we develop a value system that will make it possible for our children and grandchildren to live in a peaceful world and safe from extinction?
- how do we transform our present-day society to get rid of our indifference to the injustices which are so prevalent in our society?
- how do we find meaning to our individual lives in this materialistic and technological society?

Whether you are a Christian, or seeking a religious home, or are not in the slightest bit interested in religion, the fact is that finding answers to these questions is crucial to the continued well-being of this world and its inhabitants. This book, if nothing else, attempts to suggest answers to these questions. This is not to say that there may not be other religions and cultures that can provide meaningful answers to these questions as well, but this book is about finding answers from a Christian perspective.

As far as adherence to a set of values is concerned, it is important to realize that in the last decades, the membership in the various mainline churches has decreased considerably. Fewer people attend church and fewer children go to Sunday School. At the same time, our public education system has long ago abandoned any type of religious education, and makes no attempt to teach anything that remotely resembles moral values or ethics. The almost inevitable result has been a decreasing appreciation of what moral values are, and a decreasing adherence to values in the conduct of our daily lives. The natural outcome of this has been that the last decades have seen a sharp increase in lawlessness, in materialism, and generally in egocentric behavior which puts the "I" in front of everything.

Today, one of the main challenges the churches of all denominations face is to combat the general feeling that the old message has lost its relevance in this century of scientific and technical achievements which have so dramatically changed the lifestyles of many people. On the other hand, I am convinced that today more than ever before, we need the values and ethics which Jesus told us to live by. Without these constraints, modern technology will almost certainly cause the destruction of the world as we know it. It may happen through ignorance, it may happen by accident, or it may happen by a deliberate attempt of one group to dominate another group without regard for the consequences. Whatever the reasons, it is sure to happen if we do not temper our quest for scientific achievements and material well-being by considerations of ultimate values, and a sense of responsibility for the earth we have inherited.

At the same time, it must be clear even to the most biased person, that the material wealth and the scientific discoveries of the industrialized nations have not been able to come up with solutions for the most desperate situations which this world faces. Despite all our scientific achievements, we still are unable or unwilling to prevent the starvation of millions of people, who were just unlucky enough to be born in some of the poorest countries of this world. Hand-in-hand with this goes our inability to stop the increase, let alone decrease, the number of people who have to live under the most inhumane conditions of poverty and disease.

Also, our achievements have not been able to provide answers to humankind's eternal questions such as, "Who am I? Where am I going?" and "What can possibly be the importance of my life?" It is of course possible that people do not ask these basic questions any longer and are content with accepting life as they find it, but somehow this does not seem probable. It is more likely that the questions are buried under a horde of concerns for the immediate future, most of them the direct result of our inflated lifestyles. One thing is certain, our achievements are not making people happier or more content. For confirmation of that it is sufficient to read only one issue of any daily newspaper.

I am firmly convinced that the only way we can stop our destructiveness is by adopting a lifestyle which is less based on materialism and more on Jesus' message of love and compassion for our neighbour and even for our enemy. If we all agreed to live in accordance with that simple message, there would be no more war, there would be no more starvation, no more hunger and no more crime: In short the world would be transformed. I believe that there are few people who do not long for such a transformation and who would not do everything in their power to make this transformation a reality. Unfortunately, most of us probably feel that we are helpless and unable to make a real contribution to seeing this come true. But this is not so. In this case, as in so many others, we must start with ourselves and take the first step in this process of renewal by changing both our own value system and our own lifestyle.

So, in answer to the question why should I read this book I can only say that it may just possibly be of help to you if you are, like I am, concerned about:
- the value system the world lives by today;
- the lack of justice in this world;
- finding meaning to life.

If you are not concerned about or interested in these subjects, you should stop reading right here and now, because you will only get frustrated by this, essentially one-sided, view of life. Before doing so, however, you might consider what others have to say in this regard. For instance, in a recent book, *The Great Reckoning*, the authors make these somewhat surprising statements:

"Religion adds the crucial exponents to the cost-and-reward calculus that influences human beings to comport themselves in a civilized way ...

"The breakdown of the justice system in the USA has made crime so profitable and pervasive as to make a strong comeback of religion almost inevitable."

At the very end of this long and rather depressing book they list 15 steps to survive this economic calamity. They recommend that the first step one should take is to, Get Committed. As they write:

"Your choices remain the biggest single factor that control your destiny. Seek to strengthen your moral commitment and religious faith ... A Bible is not a bad teacher of history and guide to survival in hard times."[1]

To make it easier for the reader to judge whether what follows is of interest, I have briefly summarized each chapter below. However, before continuing, I would like to make a general comment about the order in which the various subjects are presented. In general, I have tried to present what follows in a logical sequence, but that, unfortunately, is not always possible. The main reason for this is what I have, somewhat irreverently, called the chicken and egg situation which arises when talking about God. We believe that God is the beginning of everything, but we can not really know God except through the revelations of the Son, Jesus Christ. Thus to talk about God, you must know who Jesus is, but you can not talk about Jesus until you know who God is, and so forth.

The chapter which follows immediately after this one contains a very abbreviated history of the world as we understand it today, and how the most recent scientific developments have influenced our thinking about the meaning of life. My assertion is that if you believe that there is no God, then you are saying at the same time that there is no real future for this world, because everything points to the fact that, one way or the other, this world will come to an end. Science and technology can not help because, by their very nature, they can not provide answers to the ultimate questions of human existence, nor can they provide a value system for humankind to live by. The point is that, unless you believe in a life hereafter, there is no future and the only thing you can do is to make the best of the situation you find yourself in. But, this is not the message of this book. I believe we have a future, a glorious one, and an eternal one.

The next chapter (3) is about the God of the Christian religion; how God was revealed, first to the Jews and later to all people through the son, Jesus Christ. I realize that in this chapter I am basically trying to do the impossible, because God is so different from us and exists on such a different level that it is impossible for us to ever fully comprehend what God is like. Nevertheless, I believe that God has revealed enough of his/her nature that the qualities of God that are important to humans can be understood. The chapter ends with a section dealing with the question that confronts everyone, including the writer, namely: Does God exist or is God just a figment of our imagination, and/or is it merely a concept invented by humankind to give it a sense of security and fill the awesome void that would otherwise exist?

Chapter 4 concerns itself with the forces that appear to exist in the universe which seem to oppose God, such as evil and its personification, the Devil. You may ask yourself if these evil forces exist, where do they come from? Did God create them as well?

I think that there are very few people in the world today who can deny that there is an evil force at work in God's creation. For that you only have to think of the Holocaust in which 6 million Jews were massacred, or the killing fields of Cambodia, or the atrocities that, at the time of writing this, are being committed in the former Yugoslavia. There is, I believe, only one explanation for this and that is that there exists an evil force that makes humans do things that are, by any standard, inhuman, and completely against God's will.

The next chapter (5) contains an account of the life, death and resurrection of Jesus Christ, whom we believe to be the Son of God; the mediator between God and humanity. It includes that almost unbelievable story of his crucifixion, his burial, his resurrection and the effect this had on his closest followers, the disciples. For Christians, the resurrection changed everything because it proved that death can be overcome, and that death is not necessarily the end. The chapter closes with an evaluation of the proof and the evidence we have that Jesus was indeed a historical person and that the resurrection actually took place.

19

Chapter 6 is in many ways the most difficult because it deals with the two aspects of life that have, more than anything else, tended to separate us from God, namely sin and suffering. In it the question is asked, What is sin? Am I a sinner? — I don't feel like one. The question I believe is easily answered by focussing our attention for a moment on all the things that are going wrong in our world today, and which we could fix easily if we just wanted to do that badly enough: such things as hunger, poverty, war, and so forth.

The other subject of the chapter, suffering, is divided in two different categories: suffering of which we humans are the cause, and suffering that is beyond our control and which appears to be completely senseless. The question we must seek to answer is, How can God, whom we believe to be the personification of love, allow this suffering of innocent people?

The next chapter (7) contains a discussion on how we as imperfect people can be reconciled with God who is perfect. In it, consideration is also given to the question how the suffering of an innocent person can possibly cause us to be reconciled with God? The chapter ends with a section dealing with the question, Who is reconciled with God? Is it only the relatively small band of believers and faithful? I think not. I believe that we should look at Jesus' life, death and resurrection as a reconciliation with God, in one form or the other, for all the people of the world.

In Chapter 8, a complete review of all Jesus' teaching is presented. His teaching about who God is; who he is himself; what our importance is; what the meaning of life is; how we should live our lives and, finally, how we should communicate with God.

Chapter 9 is in some ways the culmination of all that went on before. In it the question is asked, What does God demand from us today? What should we be doing in today's society to make God's message heard and to make our society live in accordance with the simple rule God gave us. How do we do this individually, as a church, and as a society?

In the last chapter (10) the question is asked, Where do we go from here? To some extent the answer to that question depends on whether you agree that the Christian message of love for your neighbour has any relevance in this day and age. If you are looking for a value system that just may be able to save this earth and its inhabitants from self-destruction, then you may want to take the next step and get to know more about this religion and become involved yourself.

This is very briefly what you will find in the next pages of this book. I certainly do not claim to have all the answers. But I am firmly convinced that something needs to be done to reverse the trend of sinking further and further into complete chaos. At the time of writing this, it appears that by far the greatest majority of Italy's politicians are being indicted for serious wrongdoing. Unfortunately, this is not the only example of immorality by our political leaders. One thing is clear: they do not provide the example that we should be following.

Most probably you do not agree with all that I have written, but I think we all can agree that something has to be done. For me, what needs to be done is to follow the teachings of Jesus and apply these teachings in our own life and in the life of our society.

So, in some ways this book is a journey of discovery in which we are trying not only to find a meaning to life but also to find that high road from where we may be able to begin to re-orient and redirect the path our society is taking.

I hope that you will join me on that journey, always remembering that we have this Good News that we are not alone and that God is with us wherever we go.

2

Life Without God
(Humans In The Universe Alone)

Introduction

The long history of civilization shows that ever since humans emerged as creatures with a capacity to think and to reason, they have had religious beliefs and have followed religious practices which were very much part of their daily lives. Living in very close contact with nature, their lives were completely controlled by forces entirely beyond their control and comprehension. But, being humans much like we are today, they naturally began looking for ways and means by which they themselves could exercise some control over these forces of nature.

An early example of this are the rock paintings which were discovered in some of the caves in Europe and Africa and which show signs of occupation by the earliest human hunting societies. Most of these paintings depict hunting scenes or show just the outline of the animals on which they depended for their daily survival. Some of these paintings are found in the most inaccessible places, so they most likely did not paint these pictures for their artistic enjoyment alone. Today, it is generally agreed among scholars that the main purpose of these paintings was to influence the outcome of their hunts for food which, of course, was for them a matter of life and death. In making these paintings, they must have felt that there was something or someone who could help them if they just appealed to that entity by making a graphic depiction of the thing they most needed or that concerned them most.

Also, recent excavations have shown that at a very early stage in human development, people began placing tools, weapons and, in some cases, household utensils in the grave beside the buried person. Since these implements were, in many cases, difficult and time consuming to make and could have been used by the survivors to great advantage, placing these implements in the grave obviously meant that they expected the dead person to have some use for them in the future. At the same time, they must have known from bitter experience that the body itself would decompose and would eventually become dust and bones. Thus, the placing of these implements in the grave must have meant that they expected the dead person to somehow survive in another life where he might have use for these tools, weapons and household utensils.

Yet other archeological excavations have shown that, at an early stage in their development, humans began to follow certain religious rituals and ceremonies, such as the sacrifice of animals, the performance of fertility rites, and so forth. These rituals and practices had the clear objective of trying to influence the deities and spirits, which they believed surrounded them, to improve their ability to survive in what must have been a very harsh and hazardous environment.

For me it is clear from these and similar discoveries that no matter how primitive these early societies may have been, humans believed at an early point in their development in at least one or two of the three concepts on which much of our religious thinking is based:

- First of all, they recognized that there was some supreme being or beings in charge of their world to whom they could appeal through certain rituals and sacrifices.
- Secondly, they must have had some feeling that there was something outside their physical bodies that could survive death.
- Thirdly, they must have had some conception that there would be a new physical life after death in which they might need the tools they had been using in their everyday life here on earth.

These feelings, expectations and beliefs of early humans led eventually to a wide variety of religious practices which were observed in virtually the same form for hundreds of succeeding generations. Eventually these early religious practices evolved into the major religions of today.

An interesting sidelight on this is provided by Richard Leaky, who in his recent book, *Origins Reconsidered*, quotes the Harvard biologist Edward O. Wilson as saying:

> *The predisposition to religious belief is the most complex and powerful force in the human mind and is in all probability an ineradicable part of human nature. It is one of the universals of social behaviour, taking recognizable form in every society from hunter-gatherer bands to socialist republics.*[1]

It is important to remember that these religious beliefs were shared almost universally among all people and were part and parcel of their daily lives. I imagine life then must have been something like it is still lived today on the island of Bali outside the main tourist areas. Sometime ago, my wife and I visited this beautiful island and we were impressed to see how much the Hindu religion of these people was an integral part of their every day life. For instance, every morning a very small, symbolic offering of rice and flowers was placed in the front of each house, including our hotel room, as an offering to the spirits which they believe surround them. Temples are everywhere and are used for a wide variety of rituals and ceremonies. These, and other outward signs of their religion, surround them from the day they are born, and successive generations grow up accepting their religion as an integral part of daily life.

I am sure that there are sceptics in Bali, people who question certain aspects of their religion as, no doubt, there were sceptics in the early primitive religions, but they are at best a small minority. It is only in the last few generations that a large segment of humankind has started to question the validity of the basic concepts of religion and, in fact, has come to believe that they could do without them. They believe that religion is irrelevant to life in today's society, and that it hinders a person's full development as a free and independent human being.

Life Without God —
Our Apparent Loss Of Value And Direction

It would seem logical to assume that humans, having rejected religion and thereby the belief in a meaning to life that transcends death, must have found a meaning to life somewhere else; or, alternatively, they may have come to the conclusion that life has no meaning and is in fact absurd. Absurd, because when we deny the existence of God and of a life after death, we say in effect that we are alone in this universe. We imply that there is no plan and that there is no final destination, not for our own lives, not for the lives of our children, and not for our civilization that has taken so long to develop. The best we can hope for then is that life on earth will be shaped by an ongoing evolution which could eventually culminate in a better adapted human being, operating in a better adapted environment. But even this society will eventually disappear, and there will be nothing left of all that humans have struggled so hard to achieve over all these centuries.

It would be reasonable to assume that, since people have now lived for some considerable time with this concept of "going it alone," there should be some signs that would begin to justify this confidence they have in this evolution, and in their own abilities to shape their future and to make the world a better place to live in. I believe that most people will probably agree with me that these signs are hard to find: In fact, many people are of the opinion that the world is regressing instead of progressing. The world seems not only not to be improving, but to many people conditions seem to be getting worse.

For example, if you were to ask the average person in the western world in which way s/he perceives his way of life today to be different from that of previous generations, the answers you would get would probably vary widely, but most likely the list would include the sense of uncertainty and confusion which they believe past generations did not have. As an example, they might quote the change in basic economic principles. In the past, people worked hard in the prime of life in order to save enough for their old age, and when they could not look after themselves any longer they moved in with one of their children who would care for them much as they had looked after their parents when they were old. Today, this is simply not so anymore. The idea of moving in with one's children in old age is in many ways impossible for any number of reasons, all good and sufficient on their own, but the result is nevertheless that most parents today end up in old-age residential or nursing homes separated from their family and loved ones.

Far worse than this is the situation with the thousands of people who cannot find adequate housing and who obviously have no one to turn to. Recently, I saw a sign above an air vent on a major downtown Washington street which read, "When I get here, I am home." Others live in corridors or under bridges and viaducts. No doubt, something like this has always existed, but not to the extent we see it today. The truly horrifying thing is that we seem not to be able to do anything about it. Actually, most of us now seem to have accepted this situation as a fact of life for the downtown areas of our cities.

Also, a person might say that there used to be a more or less general understanding on what was considered good conduct and what was considered bad conduct. Moral values, if not strictly adhered to, at least were generally acknowledged and, in principle at least, supported. Today, there does not seem to be that general basic agreement any longer. The main principle which seems to govern the conduct of a large segment of the population is the one that dictates: What is good for me is good, and what is bad for me is bad, and everyone for him/herself. This new set of moral rules is the direct result of our new-found scientific and materialistic philosophies. From a purely scientific point of view, there is simply no distinction between good or bad, something is either true or false, it is either proven or not proven, and that is all that matters.

Similarly, in a purely materialistic society, moral values are simply not relevant. As someone once said, "In a materialistic society one might as well make a moral appeal to the Atlantic Ocean than to expect a purely materialistic society to come forth with a set of moral values." A recent newspaper article, using the results of a survey of businessmen, found that most business people said that they would place profits before ethics. Since our modern society is so much influenced by crass materialism, these results should not surprise us in the least. Also, today we live in a society where the streets of almost all the North American cities are unsafe at night, and in many cases they are unsafe during the middle of the day. At the same time we are forced to protect our homes with all types of electronic security systems.

One of the other major differences, between now and then, is what we believe science can do for the human race. The attitude used to be that ever-increasing knowledge and understanding of the natural phenomena that surround us would give us ever-increasing control over our bodies, our minds and our natural environment. Eventually, this was supposed to give us complete fulfillment as a mature person, who had complete control over his/her own destiny. Religion, one believed, was obsolete and science and technology had taken its place. As someone expressed it, ''If enough scientific facts are known and are made available to the people, religious notions will disappear of themselves like phantoms of the night disappear when the day breaks.''

At this point, you might ask yourself whether you believe that further scientific development will ever be able to give you a sense of fulfillment and can possibly give meaning to your life. I believe that today very few people, including the most optimistic, believe this to be the case. Today, very few, including the most optimistic and dedicated scientists, would make this type of statement any longer. Experience has taught us that behind each problem solved another set of problems and unknowns take their place. But, more important, today we are beginning to seriously question the value of much that has been accomplished. For instance, it will be for later generations to decide whether the discovery of the atomic substructure and our ability to split the atom will be a blessing to humankind or whether it was one of the most disastrous discoveries ever made. The same holds true for many other areas of science such as genetic engineering, and even the invention of an artificial heart may cause more problems than it solves. Some years ago, the ''green revolution'' which was responsible for the doubling and tripling of rice and other crops, and long considered to be one of humankind's greatest achievements, was found to have so many harmful side effects that we are even beginning to re-evaluate the overall benefit from this great achievement.

But probably the biggest change of all has occurred in our perception of what the future of our earth will be. Today, we have arrived for the first time in human history at a point where we have serious doubts and misgivings about the continuing existence of the human race on this planet. Not because of things beyond our control, but because humans have discovered not just one, but several ways of destroying all life on earth. The chances are that someday, either purposely or by accident, these new powers will be used to extinguish life once and for all. We can do it the relatively slow way through industrial pollution or the fast way through atomic warfare. This power in the hands of mortal humans is something so new in the 50,000 years of human development that we have not really had time to adjust our thinking. In the past civilizations came and went, but there was always a new civilization appearing on the horizon ready to take on the intellectual and materialistic development of the world. Not so today. If we use this awesome power in the wrong way we finish it once and for all, for all humanity and for all life on this earth.

It is in this atmosphere that today's searching mind must find answers to questions regarding the meaning of human life here on earth and about its final destination. For some people, the inability to find an answer is so unacceptable and agonizing that they seek a way out by rejecting life altogether. For many the only answer to this sense of alienation is suicide or a complete mental breakdown. Carl Jung, the famous psychiatrist, once said that about one third of his patients were suffering from no clinically definable neurosis, but from the senselessness and emptiness of their lives.

This sense of isolation and alienation is often further aggravated by the difficulty people have to effectively communicate with one another. It is rather ironic that this seems to be the case at a time when new ways of communicating, in a technical sense, are invented almost daily, and at a time when the communication industry is one of the fastest growing segments of the economy. We find that even with people with whom we have a close personal relationship such as husbands, wives, parents, children and friends, we often have insurmountable problems in expressing our deepest feelings. Even if we are lucky enough to have a close relationship with one other human being with whom we can fully and openly communicate, we soon discover that no matter how close we are to the other person, he or she is different from us, different often in some real and essential way. We find that our thoughts, desires, anxieties, fears and hopes are not necessarily of the same importance to that other person.

Modern science tells us that we are shaped and fashioned by the genes our parents provided to the new embryo. Since there never was, and never will be, an identical set of genes, there never will be another person in the whole universe like us. In fact we are isolated from everyone else by our own, distinct and unique personality, and this unique person is going to exist for what is astronomically speaking only a very short period of time. As everyone very well knows, one's life comes eventually to an end. No matter what value we may have been able to find for ourselves, the final answer to where we are going must always be the same. Whether we are cremated, or whether we are buried with the greatest pomp and circumstance, whether our ashes are scattered to the wind, or whether the biggest headstone money can buy is erected on our grave, in a very short time we will become dust and the memory of our existence will fade away. If we are lucky our grandchildren will remember us, but at the very best two generations later we will be remembered only as some feeble old man or woman on some faded colour photograph, probably wearing some funny, outdated clothing. One thing is sure, that offspring is very unlikely to know anything about the struggles, accomplishments and defeats which made up our lives. Just ask yourself for a moment how much you know about the lives and struggles of your grandparents. Most likely not very much and most of what you know is probably very superficial.

Of course, the memory of some people, famous people, great contributors to society, will linger on, maybe we will even have to memorize their names and birthdates in school. But even they, be it after 50, 500, or 5,000 years will eventually be forgotten and, compared to the billions of years by which we measure time in the universe, even that remembrance span is totally insignificant. They, like us, came from dust and returned to dust, and the memory of their achievements will fade away and eventually be forgotten.

Some years ago a Chinese peasant stumbled purely by accident on one of the most imposing funeral arrangements ever made, that of the first emperor of China. The burial chamber contained hundreds upon hundreds of lifesize clay soldiers, their weapons and horses arranged by battalions. Since that first discovery the place has become one of the main tourist attractions of China today. Historians have researched the history of this person. As it turns out this man, after countless battles in which thousands upon thousands of people lost their lives, established for the first time a united China and became its first emperor. After establishing this far-flung empire he set upon the task of building a better society. He built roads, irrigation systems and schools. In his later years he was consumed by the ambition to become immortal, and he employed vast numbers of people to find for him that elixir of life that would give him immortality. Of course, after a great number of failures, it became clear to him that even he, in all his might, was subject to the same fate as all his other subjects. So, he decided that he would achieve some sort of immortality through his funeral monument, and he employed whole armies of craftsmen to build this most impressive tomb.

Yet, in a comparatively short time, his fame and achievements became so irrelevant to the people of that time, that his carefully constructed tomb was allowed to be covered by the sands of time and his name was forgotten except by historians working in dusty libraries. He, like us, came from dust and returned to dust. This is not to say that people such as this emperor have not made great contributions to improving the lives of many people, but in the end they will be forgotten and their achievements, which may have enriched our culture, will be forgotten as well and become irrelevant when the end of time comes.

It is clear from the above that life without God has, so far at least, not given us a sense of value or direction. Neither has it given our lives the sense of lasting importance that we all are searching for.

Probably one of the best descriptions of what it means to live without the belief in God was given by Max Horkheimer, a Jewish philosopher, who was not sure how to think about God. Nevertheless he writes that he is convinced:

- *that without God, there is no meaning in life that transcends pure self-preservation;*
- *that without religion no valid distinction can be found between true and false, love and hate, readiness to help and lust for profit, morality and immorality;*
- *that without God, the longing for perfect justice must remain unfulfilled, and in the end the murderer must finally triumph over the innocent victim;*
- *that without God, our "need for consolation" remains unsatisfied. Philosophy can not console; consolation is a religious function.*[2]

This I believe, is as good a summary of what it means to live a life without a belief in God as I have seen anywhere. If, however, we still want to live without religion, we may be justified in thinking that meaning for our life and for the universe can possibly be found in that branch of human endeavor where humans have attained some of their highest achievements — science and technology. Surely, one may be justified in thinking that this highly successful undertaking of humankind will be able to give meaning to life and, maybe even, give it value and direction, if not now, then perhaps in the future.

Human's Value And Importance According To Science

Science is in essence our ongoing, and hopefully never ending, attempt at trying to discover the laws, rules, and processes which govern the behaviour of the universe and everything in it. It assumes that everything in this world and beyond follows a set of rules that, if we try hard enough, can be discovered and through applied technology can be used by humanity for its own purposes.

This definition of science has a number of interesting implications:

First of all, it indicates that science itself is founded on a belief, a faith, something that cannot be proven, namely, the belief that the universe is open to rational explanation and exploration. In other words, it rests on the belief that there is order in the universe and that there are laws to be discovered which govern the behavior of everything in this universe.

Secondly, it is precisely this belief in the apparent established order of things in the universe that others have used as a proof that God exists. So, both science and religion believe that there is an order in the universe and that it is therefore open to exploration and explanation. Christianity believes it because it believes the world to have been created by God for a specific purpose. The scientist believes it because it is one of the basic premises without which science becomes a fruitless and meaningless endeavor. In any case, so far this basic premise seems to fit the facts. So, we ask, what does science, as distinct from religion, tell us about our origin and our final destination?

Current scientific thought is that it all started with a very tightly packed ball of matter. Where this ball came from in the first place has never been explained. It somehow was there. It is interesting to note in this regard, that modern science talks of space and time having been created as well at the time this first ball of matter appeared on the scene. Thus, time and space did not exist before that and it is useless to ask where it was located and where it came from. If this is true, then the answers to these questions lie obviously outside the domain of physics. In any case, because of the extremely high temperatures and internal pressures, this ball of matter became unstable and exploded forming immense clouds of the most basic elements. Eventually these clouds condensed into individual stars which then grouped themselves into immense clusters of stars, the galaxies.

Some of the stars, like our sun, attracted material that did not become part of the star itself but kept circulating around it in fixed orbits. This material, after some time, condensed into solid matter and eventually formed satellites or planets of which our earth is a prime example.

To some scientists and philosophers the idea of the universe being created on a specific date is untenable. For one thing it comes too close to the biblical account of creation in which God created the universe out of nothing.

In any case, the galaxies, once created, continued on their outward flight away from the center. In fact, according to this theory we are living in an ever-expanding universe with the outer edges at present some millions of light years away.

Some scientists have begun to question this concept of an ever-increasing universe, and believe that they have found evidence which would suggest that gravitational forces will eventually overcome this outward momentum and reverse the direction of movement. Ultimately, this would cause the universe to collapse again into this tight ball of matter. The theory is then postulated that this ball will eventually explode again because the material in this ball will become too tightly packed to be stable for any period of time. And so on, and so on.

For some, this theory fits better with what they consider to be proper and fitting. It does away with this idea of a definite beginning of the universe since this process of expanding and contracting could have been going on forever, and they believe therefore that no definite beginning or end is necessary to explain the existence of the universe.

However, regardless of the way our galaxy was formed, among the millions of galaxies there is one that is of special importance to us, the one we are living in. You can see it on a clear night as a streak of light across the sky, The Milky Way. This streak of light is made by the millions upon millions of other stars that are part of our galaxy. Somewhat to the side of the center of this galaxy there is a fairly small star which we know as our sun. Its nearest neighbour, Alpha Centauri, is some 4.3 light years away; that is at such a distance from us that it takes a light beam from earth 4.3 years to reach this star, or put in more understandable terms it would take a rocket, flying at a speed of 30,000 miles per hour, 25,000 years to reach it.

Twirling around this sun of ours are nine satellites, the third from the inside is our earth, held in its orbit around the sun by the forces of gravity. Thus, the center of our own little universe is the sun, a medium sized star which through its continuous conversion of matter into radiant energy (sunlight) makes life on earth possible. Unfortunately, no matter how huge the sun's reservoir of energy is, eventually it will be exhausted and life on earth will come to an end.

However, even that is unlikely to be the cause of our demise. Life as we know it, is possible only within a very narrow range of temperatures. A very small change in the average temperature on earth will make it impossible to grow food on very large parts of the earth. This temperature range, which makes life possible today, is governed by the precise path of the earth around the sun and the tilt of the earth's axis. The smallest interstellar accident which knocks our planet the tiniest amount out of that path will have disastrous consequences. If we get too close to the sun we fry, and if we get too far away we freeze. Not a very enticing long term prospect!

However, since we are dealing with cycles of billions of years, it does not really matter to us from a practical point of view whether the universe is in a stable condition or whether sometime in the far future we are participants in an interstellar accident. What is important, from our point of view, is that you and I are living on a small satellite of a small star which is part of a medium sized galaxy of which there are billions of others around in the universe. It is clear from this that, as far as size is concerned, our earth is of no importance whatsoever in the overall scheme of things. A grain of sand on a beach is of greater significance to our earth than the earth is to our universe.

In any case, the earth is our habitat and there is very little we can do about it. All the expectations we had at one time that it would be possible to transfer life to another planet, or another star, if life here becomes impossible, are fast fading away. The space explorations have clearly shown that we can forget the idea of ever being able to immigrate to one of the other planets of our solar system if and when the earth cannot sustain life any longer. They are either too hot or too cold or are covered with poisonous gases.

As far as the satellites of other stars are concerned, we are even more unlikely to find a safe haven there. As indicated before, the nearest star is 4.3 light years away. Even if we could reach it somehow in a reasonable timespan, it is very unlikely to have satellites which are able to sustain life as we know it. It has been estimated that the closest star with satellites, that could possibly have conditions anywhere near to what we need to survive in our present form, is at least 60 light years away. That is so far away that a radio signal sent from earth in 1940 will still not have arrived there today.

Considering all this, it is clear that we must do with what we have today. As far as science is concerned, the earth is not the center of the universe, it is a minuscule speck in a gigantic universe, and, although probably unique in the universe, it is a temporary uniqueness that will eventually disappear. Human's importance in this scheme of things is most likely to be very small indeed and probably irrelevant in the long run.

After having looked at what science tells us about the origin of the earth, it will be interesting to find out what science tells us about humankind's own origin and destination. According to the latest theories of evolution, that beginning was not a very spectacular event. An accident really! Millions of years ago, we learn that conditions were just right, in some of the mudflats and estuaries of the world, for some chemical processes to take place which eventually resulted in the formation of the first living cell. We were apparently literally pulled out of the mud! Once this first living cell was formed there was no holding us back. We progressed very slowly at first from single cells to multiple cell systems, which eventually developed through evolution and mutations into plants and animal life. Ultimately, there occurred the most important mutation of them all, an animal became a reasoning and

37

thinking being. These thinking and reasoning beings began to walk upright, thus freeing their hands for other activities such as carrying things and making tools and other implements, most of them related to their main concern of gathering food for themselves and their families. Soon these implements were not only used for hunting but also to bash fellow humans around with as well. This aggression, towards their own kind, appears to be one of the characteristics that distinguishes humans from animals. There appears to be no other animal that kills its own kind just for the pleasure of it.

In any case, humans began to learn to speak and some 5,000 years ago they learned to communicate through the written word. Ever since then, humankind's ability to control its own environment has grown at an ever increasing pace. We have learned to fly, we have learned to go to the moon and even to send spacecraft to far away planets. Finally we have discovered that ability which really puts us in the driver's seat, the ability to destroy not only ourselves but everything that is living on this planet. All that, we have learned to do in the last 60 or 70 years, most of it through my lifetime. If you are like most of us, you will not have the faintest idea of what may develop over the next 50 years during the life span of your children and grandchildren.

In his book *Sacred Eyes*, L. Robert Keck[3] divides the development of humankind into three stages or epochs. According to him, in Epoch I, which he calls our childhood stage, we develop physically. This stage came to an end some 10,000 years ago when humans started to practice agriculture and began to live in permanent settlements. In Epoch II, our adolescent stage, we developed our mental capacity. This stage is now coming to an end with its final achievement, our scientific development of the last century. He believes that we are now in a transition stage to Epoch III, what he calls our stage of maturation. In this epoch we will develop our spiritual capacity which will eventually lead the world to some sort of earthly paradise. He is, however, realistic enough to point out that we may never reach this stage because we may well have destroyed ourselves at the end of Epoch II by the misuse of our scientific discoveries.

Much debate has been going on over the last decades about the question whether life, as we know it, exists in other places in the universe among the billions and billions of stars that make up our cosmos. There appear to be many arguments both for and against the possibility that intelligent life may exist outside our earth. However, in recent years there seems to be a concensus building up that it is very unlikely that this is so.

In his book, *Paradigms Lost*, John L. Casti made a detailed assessment of the probability that man is unique in the universe. He approached the problem from seven different points of view. The first question he asked was, "Is the particular way in which life arose here on earth a statistical fluke, unlikely to be repeated anywhere ever again? Or is the combination of steps leading to earth's life forms an almost inevitable outcome given similar environmental conditions?" His conclusion is that it is very unlikely that life on earth, as we know it, would re-emerge if it ever were destroyed, and that there is indeed something special not only about humans, but also about life in general as we see it here on earth today.

He next asks the question, "As living, intelligent, communicating entities, are humans unique in the galaxy?" After investigating this question in detail, he comes to what he calls, "The sad conclusion that we are probably alone in this galaxy and that we could very well be alone in the entire universe."[4]

It is clear from these and other considerations that it is indeed very unlikely that we will find intelligent life anywhere else in the universe. But, even if life existed outside our solar system, the distances, even in our own galaxy, are so enormous that unless we find some way to communicate at a speed that far exceeds that of light, it still would be impossible to contact them and exchange ideas and knowledge.

So, there we are. According to science we are created more or less by accident, existing for a limited period of time only, and living in a planetary system which is none too stable and is bound to come to an inglorious end either by our own hand or from natural causes. As far as size is concerned, we are somewhere to be found between the minuscule microcosmos of the atomic substructure with its whirling electrons and protons, and the vast macrocosmos of the galaxies and stars many of them with their own whirling planets and moons. It is difficult to see that humans in this scheme of things have any importance at all.

But humans are optimists by nature and so they are not going to accept this state of affairs without a determined fight. To many, that value of ourselves which we are looking for can only come about by scientific endeavors and further basic discoveries about the nature of the universe. Thus, for some people without a faith in a supreme being, the pursuit of science has become a religion. Someone expressed this most forcibly as follows:

> *My grandfather preached the gospel of Christ,*
> *My father preached the gospel of socialism,*
> *I preach the gospel of science.*

One could reasonably ask what he thinks his children and grandchildren are going to preach. Another statement by someone else proclaims:

> *Probably the greatest gift to posterity is that we have*
> *released our children from the fear of the supernatural.*
> *The concept of God is still available for those who need*
> *it; those who do not, have no longer to be ashamed and*
> *need no longer to be afraid.*

It might be thought that, with science having governed our thinking and with technology having transferred its findings into an ever increasing array of practical and sometimes highly beneficial applications, we should now be able to detect an increase of general well-being, happiness and contentment. As was already mentioned in chapter one, this does not seem to be the case. The following quotations, from some of the best minds of today, seem to go one step further and indicate that we may be going backwards rather than going forwards. Linus Pauling, twice winner of the Nobel Prize for science, said recently in an interview that he is afraid that within the next 25 to 50 years there will occur the greatest catastrophe in the history of the world. Nevertheless, he is optimistic that the human race will survive, to quote:

> *The looming catastrophe might well result from a world war which could destroy civilization and might well be the end of the human race. Or it might take the form of mass starvation among a world population that has doubled every 35 years. Or it might be the result of the collapse of the systems on which we depend, ... I am forced, as I think about what has happened in the world in my lifetime and as I observe governments in their process of making decisions, to conclude that the coming century is probably going to be one in which the amount of human suffering reaches a maximum.*

Alvin Toffler, the author of *Future Shock*[5] sounds equally pessimistic about the outlook for our society. He points out that it is not only technology that seems to have broken loose, but that many other social processes, such as urban development, crime, violence, ethnic conflict, and so forth, have run loose as well and that they defy all our best effort to guide them, let alone control them. His concern is further deepened by his impression that, while the rate of change seems to be accelerating, there is no evidence at all of a corresponding acceleration in the rate at which we can respond to these changes. This being so, he believes that we may well be on the threshold of losing all control over our future development and destiny.

A final quotation from Hans Küng in his book, *On Being a Christian*:

> *The progress of modern science, medicine, technology, industry, communications, culture surpasses the boldest fantasies ... And yet this evolution seems still far away*

> *from leading us to some sort of paradise and often leads away from it . . . The longer we consider the situation the less we can avoid the disturbing observation that something is wrong with this fantastic quantitative and qualitative progress. In a very short time the sense of not being at ease with technical civilization has become universal.* [6]

The feelings expressed in these quotations clearly indicate that we cannot expect the application of more and more science to result in greater human happiness, or that it will lead to a brighter future for our children and grandchildren and for the world in general. Not that there is anything wrong about most of our scientific and technological achievements. What is wrong is to have an unbridled faith in science as a total explanation of the ultimate reality, and in technology as a cure-all for all our problems. Above all, the expectation that science will give final answers to our questions about the meaning of life and the final destination of the human race is completely unrealistic. Furthermore, as we said in the beginning, we should not expect science to provide guidelines for our moral values. Splitting the atom in itself is neither good nor bad, but what we do with that invention must be governed by considerations that are not scientific but moral.

Before closing this chapter, it may be well to reflect for a few minutes on how we expect the relationship between science and religion to develop in the future. Of course, this is almost impossible to do given the rapid, and sometimes unexpected, turns modern science has made in the last decades. However, one or two recent developments seem to indicate that the apparent incompatibility of science and religion is becoming more and more a thing of the past. Or, if not quite that, the controversies seem to be becoming less and less sharply defined.

For instance, as already mentioned, the postulation of the "Big Bang" theory for the formation of the universe is in many ways less incompatible with the creation of the universe by a Creator than previous scientific theories. The other significant recent development in the history of science, the formulation of the Quantum Theory has, I believe, similar implications. This theory is terribly difficult to understand, because it violates some of our most cherished ides of how things ought to work. It is based on a number of observations which, in the physics we all know, make no sense at all. In particle physics, it was discovered to everyone's astonishment that a particle could be here, or there, or it could be at the same time at both places. Furthermore, it was discovered in examining the nature of light, that light is both a wave of energy and a stream of particles, depending on the observer and the type of experiment.

John Polkinghorne, in his book, *reason and reality*, concludes from these and other observations that "The world conceived by the new physics seems more amenable, or at least less intractable, to a religious interpretation than was the world of the older physics." Further along in his book, he uses these astonishing theories and discoveries to conclude: "If the physical world is so perplexing, we can scarcely expect the divine world to be any less complicated or easier to understand."[7]

It is entirely possible that further developments of scientific theory along these lines will reinforce Polkinghorne's assertion that "the physical universe seems shot through with signs of mind." Similarly, Paul Davies, a mathematical physicist, states in his book, *The Mind Of God*, that through his work he has come to believe more and more strongly that the physical universe is put together with such an ingenuity that he cannot simply accept it as the result of an accidental evolutionary process. He has come to believe instead that there must be a deeper level of explanation behind its development. He then goes on to say that he cannot accept that the mind is an incidental quirk of nature either but that instead it must be a fundamental part of the nature of things.[8] Other scientists, trying to describe the origin of the universe and what can possibly be behind it, use such phrases as: "Knowing the mind of God" (Hawkins), and "Seeing the face of God" (Smoot).

These interesting statements seem to imply that science is beginning to give serious consideration to the possibility that there may, in fact, be a mind or creative force behind the creation and continuing development of the universe.

If it is true that science will eventually come to the conclusion that there is indeed a mind behind creation, it will have at least confirmed one Christian belief, that of the existence of a Creator. But that is about all it ever will be able to do. It can never fully discover the mind of God, nor will it be able to say anything about God's final plan for creation, the universe, and humankind.

To conclude, what is humankind's value and importance according to science?

1 — In terms of science, the earth and its inhabitants are a minuscule speck in the immensity of the universe.

2 — The evolution of human life happened by accident and, according to some, is very unlikely to have occurred anywhere else in the universe, nor is it likely to reoccur on earth if we destroy life here.

3 — Science and technology have given humans the ability to destroy that speck of life in the universe once and for all.

4 — It is unrealistic to expect science to ever provide answers to the meaning of life.

5 — According to science, the final destination of humanity is complete extinction, and if we are correct with our statement that there is unlikely to be life anywhere else in the universe, life on earth will have just been a brief glimmer of light in the cold darkness of an immense universe.

6 — After all life has been extinguished, the universe will continue in its complete meaningless way, there will be no final goal and no ultimate destination. It will just be what it has always been, a cluster of matter or energy subject to its four basic forces that will govern its behaviour for all eternity. The one and only perpetual motion machine!

This is the message of science, but the Good News for today is that we are not alone in the universe; on the contrary, there is a Mind, a Creator, behind it who not only created it but who has an ultimate plan for it.

3

The God Of The Christian Religion

The Word Of God, The Bible

In the following chapters, I will repeatedly make reference to the Bible and I will quote from it extensively. It may therefore be helpful, before proceeding further, to give a brief description of the Bible, what it contains and why I believe the Bible is important today.

In essence, the Bible is a collection of books in which the Christian believes God has revealed him/herself and, in some real way, is still revealing him/herself today. In other words, it contains God's message for all of humanity and for all times. It is for this reason that it plays such a central role not only in the individual life of each Christian but also in the life of the Church as a whole.

The Bible consists of two sections: the Old Testament which deals mainly with God's revelation through God's chosen people, the Jews; and the New Testament, which deals with God's revelation through the Son, Jesus Christ.

The Old Testament consists of 39 books starting with the Book of Genesis and ending with the prophesies of one of the minor prophets, Malachi. The best known book of the Old Testament is probably the first book, Genesis, because it contains in the first two chapters the story of creation — actually two stories of creation. This story of the creation of the universe and of humankind as told in the Bible is very different from that presently taught by science which is, of course, supported by a large amount of scientific evidence. This difference has caused a great deal of controversy over the years and has actually resulted in some great court battles. These battles were mainly fought over the issue of what should be taught in the public schools which are supported by people's taxes. In many ways, this was very unfortunate. Surely, it must be clear to everyone that the writers of Genesis could never have written an account, 4,000 years ago, of what we now believe to be the correct story of the creation of the universe, without using terms and concepts that were only invented recently. If they had, the story would have been completely incomprehensible to the people of that time, and it would not have been able to convey the message it was intended to convey. We believe that the story of humankind's creation, as told in the Bible, is there and in that form because of what it has to say about God and what it has to say about humankind. It certainly was never intended to give us a lesson in natural history or provide new scientific insights. Furthermore, it is clear that the people who actually assembled the Old Testament did not take this account as scientific evidence either, otherwise they would never have allowed two different creation stories to appear, side by side, in the first two chapters of Genesis.

Despite the fundamental differences between the Biblical and the latest scientific accounts of creation, it is rather astonishing to see the similarity in the sequence of creation in these two accounts. In the story of Genesis, God first created the heavens, then the earth, then he separated land and water. After that appeared, first the fish, then the birds, followed by the land animals and finally humans. I believe, that this is very close to the sequence of events as presently proposed by science. Truly remarkable, considering when the Book of Genesis was written!

After describing the creation of the universe, the Book of Genesis continues with the story of Adam and Eve, the first man and woman pair, and their expulsion from the paradise God had created for them because they did not follow the rules that God had given them for living in this paradise. The Old Testament continues with the accounts of the descendants of Adam and Eve, eventually reaching the time of the patriarch Abraham, who probably lived some 4,000 years ago. Abraham and his family lived originally a semi-nomadic life in what is now southern Iraq. At quite an advanced age, Abraham was called by God to leave the land of his forefathers and move his entire household to a place in what is now called the State of Israel. This man, Abraham, is one of the most fascinating figures ever to arrive on the world scene. This head of an obscure nomadic tribe became the founding father of three of today's five major religions. He is not only the founder of Judaism and therefore of Christianity, but he is also considered to be the founding father of Islam. (see also Appendix 1)

The remainder of the Book of Genesis, and much of the other books of the Old Testament, relate what happened to this tribe started by Abraham, between the settlement of Abraham in Israel and the birth of Christ, some 2,000 years later. To the Christian, it is not this history itself that is important, but the way God revealed him/herself to a chosen people, the Jews, and how God made an agreement (covenant) with them that they would be God's special people and that s/he would be their God.

In addition to this historical account, the Old Testament contains a number of books describing in great detail the laws and regulations that the Jewish people were told to observe. Then there are the books that contain the prophesies of the special messengers God sent when the Israelites wandered away from God and started to worship other gods.

Good News For Today

Outside the Book of Genesis, probably the best-known book in the Old Testament is the Book of Psalms. This book contains some 150 psalms or songs which were used by the Jews mostly during their many religious events. These psalms are still very much part of the Jewish and Christian tradition and are, even today, regularly used in almost every church and synagogue service. They obviously have a quality that transcends time. The best known of these psalms is no doubt number 23. I suppose, that almost everyone in the western world has heard this psalm at one time or another during a funeral service:

> *The Lord is my shepherd; I shall not want*
> *He maketh me to lie down in green pastures:*
> *he leadeth me beside the still waters.*
> *He restoreth my soul ...*
>
> *Yea, though I walk through the valley of the*
> *shadow of death, I will fear no evil:*
> *For thou art with me ...*
>
> *Surely goodness and mercy shall follow me all the days*
> *of my life: and I will dwell in the house of the Lord*
> *forever.*
>
> — *King James Translation*

The Old Testament also contains three books that have no explicit religious content, but they contain much wisdom and some very exquisite poetry. They are the Book of Proverbs, Ecclesiastes, and the Song of Songs; the last one is entirely made up of love songs and the joyful exchanges between two lovers. Not many people, who are not familiar with the Bible, would have thought of finding the following poem among its pages:

> *How beautiful you are, my darling!*
> *Oh, how beautiful!*
> *Your eyes behind your veil are doves.*

Your hair is like a flock of goats descending from
Mount Gilead
Your teeth are like a flock of sheep just shorn.
Your lips are like a scarlet ribbon.
Your neck is like the tower of David,
built with elegance ...
Your two breasts are like two fawns, like twin fawns of
a gazelle that browse among the lilies.

— *Song of Songs 4, New International Version*

Unfortunately, in addition to this joy and happiness, the Old Testament also contains a number of horrible stories filled with great cruelty. As reported in the books of the Old Testament, the Israelites were ordered by their God to perform acts of savagery which are beyond our comprehension. That these were not isolated cases is clear from the fact that in chapter 20 of Deuteronomy (the fifth book of the Old Testament), Moses, the leader of Israel at that time, commands his armies to kill the inhabitants of the cities they have conquered. The reason given by Moses for this savagery is that otherwise the Israelites may be tempted to "follow all the detestable things they do in worshipping their gods, and sin against the Lord your God." (Deuteronomy 7)

It is difficult, if not impossible, for us to accept that this cruelty was ordered by God. Even the defense that this was how conquering armies generally behaved at that time, or that, in settling North America we did the same, is no real excuse. The only fact we have that may throw some light on these strange commands quoted above, is that the Israelites apparently did not follow these commands to the letter, because the cities they were commanded to destroy continued to exist according to later chapters in the Old Testament.

In the end, we can only admit that we do not know what the truth is about these and other atrocities that appear in some of the chapters of the Old Testament. We can only say that the God we know is the personification of love and does not ask people to act in this way. On the contrary, the God we worship told us to show kindness and compassion to others as he had told the Israelites to act just a few chapters before this:

> *He, the Lord, defends the causes of the fatherless and the widow and loves the alien, giving them food and clothing. And you are to love those who are aliens, for you, yourselves, were aliens in Egypt.*
>
> — *Deuteronomy 10, New International Version*

The other noteworthy fact about the accounts in the Bible is that the people who are depicted there are very human figures. All, including some of their most cherished heroes, are shown to have serious flaws in their characters and they repeatedly forget about God's laws that are supposed to rule their lives. For instance, one of the great heroes of the Old Testament, King David, who was a great warrior, a strong person in many ways, a God-fearing person, a man who wrote the most exquisite poetry, is also known to be a weakling, a man who could not control his sexual passions, a man who stole the beautiful wife of one of his junior officers. The result of this realism is that the Bible, and especially the Old Testament, is a book crammed with fascinating personalities and with interesting real life stories.

The New Testament is made up of 27 books; the first four are the gospels written respectively by Matthew, Mark, Luke and John. They give an account of what happened during Jesus' life on earth, and they contain much of what he taught during that time.

The gospels are followed by 21 epistles, or letters, written by the disciples of Jesus to individuals and to the churches they had established during their travels to spread the message of Jesus across the then known world. The last book is called Revelation and contains the visions of a follower of Jesus while he was exiled to a lonely island. This book is very difficult to understand because of the many allegorical descriptions it contains.

Together, these 59 books are called the Bible or sometimes The Holy Bible or Holy Scriptures. These books were written mostly in Hebrew, Aramaic and Greek and were eventually all translated into Latin, the official language of the church for many years, and later into almost every language of the world. For the English language, the most widely used translation for many years was the Authorized or King James version, which was made in the early 1600s. Over the years, the language used in this translation became outdated; at the same time new discoveries were being made, and are still being made, that throw new light on some of the circumstances and conditions that prevailed during biblical times. As a result, over the years, new translations were made; the best known of these are: The Good News Bible, The New English Bible, The New International Version, The New American Standard Bible and The New Jerusalem Bible.

The attitude of Christians toward this Bible varies widely from accepting the Bible as infallible, that is believing that every word in the Bible is absolutely true and correct, to accepting the Bible as a book that contains much good advice and should be read by everyone if for no other reason than its literary value.

Of course, it is not difficult to prove that the Bible contains a number of mistakes and errors regarding geography, history and the natural sciences. But, as we said before, the writers of these books never intended to teach geography or to provide new insights about the nature of things; instead they were concerned with transmitting a message to the people of that day.

So, it is this fallible book that we believe to contain God's message for humankind. You may ask, how can I find God's message in a book that is so full of errors and mistakes? How do I know what is true and what is not? The answer is simply that we believe that God is using the Bible as a vehicle through which s/he speaks to us. It has been the Christians' experience when reading the Bible, that they receive different types of messages at different times. That is why the Christian Church is not a static institution, but changes with what it believes God's message to be for a changing world. The plain fact is that we believe that God has a message for us, the emphasis, but not the essence, of which may change with time. So, in reading the Bible, we believe we hear God's word speaking to us today. It speaks to us through the printed word and through the inspiration we receive through the reading of these words. For instance, the Reformation was started by Martin Luther after reading some passages in the New Testament and realizing, for the first time, that salvation could be obtained through faith only. This was a new insight, at that time it was generally thought that salvation could be obtained by doing good works and especially by giving liberally to the church. In other words, people could buy themselves into God's grace. Today that idea has completely disappeared. We believe instead that faith is the essential requirement for being reconciled with God and that as a result of that faith we will try, as a matter of course, to do whatever needs doing.

On a more personal note, like most Christians, I have always had problems with accepting that Jesus' saving grace was only for the relatively few true believers. One day, when searching for a passage in the Bible for this book, I was struck by what the apostle Paul wrote in his letters to Timothy and Titus. In these letters Paul writes: "God's grace has been revealed to save the whole human race." To me, that was a new message, a new insight, which I have found to be very helpful in that it opened up for me a whole new perspective of God's plan for the entire world.

So, it is clear that the Bible is not a religious book that can be analyzed by a computer or of which a useful, permanent summary can be made of what God is and what God wants us to do. Instead, we believe that it is a book through which God speaks to us individually. Therefore, in order to hear God's word for us, it must be read and listened to individually. That is why Christians everywhere read and reread this book. That is why they treasure it as something very special which does not lose its value and significance with time; after all, we believe it to be God's word for us, even after all these centuries.

Before closing this section on the Bible, it may be useful to once again emphasize that the books of the Bible were written between 2,000 and 3,000 years ago by Jews who were very much products of their time. Their world view was entirely different from ours today. They used imagery and refer to conditions and customs that are unfamiliar to us and they wrote these books very much from a semitic, male perspective. So, when reading the Bible, especially if you do so for the first time, I recommend strongly that you use a good Bible commentary to help you in understanding some of the more difficult and obscure passages. See also Chapter 10.

God As Revealed In The Bible

In Chapter 2, we have seen that the idea of the existence of a supreme being, who controlled or influenced people's lives directly, occurred fairly soon after the emergence of humans as thinking and reasoning beings.

Over the centuries, these early concepts of the existence of a higher being or deity, as well as the concept of the continued existence of a soul or spirit after death, slowly led to the formulation of a number of primitive religions. While the practices and rituals of these religions varied considerably from place to place, they do however appear to have had a number of basic beliefs in common. For instance, they all believed in the existence of good and evil spirits, both of which could be approached by humans through various sacrifices and rituals to make life easier for them or, if not that, at least to help them to survive such calamities as droughts and infertility.

That early civilized humans did not take this lightly is clear from the enormous temple complexes, pyramids and worship centers that were erected by these people without the benefit of modern tools and equipment. For example, the Mayans in Central America and the Incas in Peru, although their civilizations occurred much later around 500 to 1,200 A.D., built the most astonishing pyramids and temple complexes for the worship of their sun and moon gods. It must be remembered that this was accomplished without the benefits of metal implements, horses or even wheels. Everything was done by simple muscle power over long periods of time. Obviously the dominance of their gods over their daily lives was such that they were willing to spend, what we would call today, a very large percentage of their G.N.P. (gross national product) on the worship of their gods.

Out of this great variety of religious thoughts and practices eventually emerged a number of main religions: Hinduism, and its offspring Buddhism, in the Far East; and Judaism, Christianity and Islam in the Middle East. (For a brief description of these religions see Appendix 1.)

It is interesting to note that considering the long period of evolvement of these religious feelings, literally over tens of thousands of years, most of these religions were founded at approximately the same time, that is speaking in historical terms. Buddha lived approximately 500 years before Christ and Mohammed about 600 years after Christ, while the founders of the two great religions of China, Confucius and Lao Tzu, were born respectively around 550 and 600 B.C. Since the appearance of Islam no new major religion has appeared on the world scene. It must be remembered, though, that Judaism and Hinduism existed long before that. Modern research has indicated that the great flood described in the Bible probably happened around 3,000 B.C. and that Abraham, who is considered to be the founding father of the Jewish nation, lived somewhere around the year 2,000 B.C. On the other hand, the earliest manuscripts of the Hindu religion appear to have been compiled around 1,200 to 1,500 B.C.

Of course, the main reason Judaism is so important to the Christian religion is that both have the history of the Jewish people as told in the books of the Old Testament as a common heritage, and to a certain extent this is also true for Islam.

According to both the Jewish and the Christian religion, God made him/herself known, in first instance, through a pre-selected people — the people of Israel, also known as the Hebrews or the Jews. These Israelites started off as a wandering nomadic tribe, led by such patriarchs as Abraham, Isaac and Jacob, in what is today called Iraq and Iran. Eventually they settled in parts of, what today is, the State of Israel and the Kingdom of Jordan. The son of Abraham, Isaac, became the father of the Hebrews, while another son, by a servant girl of Abraham, became the father of all Arabs. As a result, Abraham is considered by both Jews and Arabs to be the founding father of their people, and the history of the Jews is therefore very closely linked with that of their Arab neighbours. As a consequence, there are many ties and shared customs between the Jewish religion and that of the predominant Arabic religion, Islam. Even to the extent that in Islam, Jesus is considered a major prophet, second in importance only to Mohammed himself. Also, after Mecca and Medina, the city of Jerusalem is one of their most holy places. Unfortunately, this has led to one of the most difficult international situations of modern times in that both sides claim the city of Jerusalem to be an essential part of their religious heritage.

As Christians and Jews then, we believe that God has made him/herself known to humankind slowly over the centuries through a pre-selected people, the Jews. This makes the Jews, God's chosen people, a people set aside and different from all other tribes and nations. God might have chosen a tribe in Africa, or one of the states of India, or one of the provinces of China. He might have, but he didn't.

In some ways this is an interesting choice. From a geographic and cultural point of view, the people chosen by God were located in a very central position within the then known world. To the South was the Egyptian civilization, to the East were the civilizations of Persia and India, and to the West and North

55

were the emerging cultures of Greece and Rome. It is difficult
to believe that this location was chosen purely by accident. Today we would say that it was probably the optimum location:
a location that greatly helped the spread of Christianity in later
years.

The books of the Old Testament describe how God revealed
him/herself slowly, step by step, to the chosen people.
However, from the very beginning it was made clear to the
people of Israel that their God was a very personal God who
was involved, not only with Israel as a nation, but also with
each one of them personally. This belief in a personal God
is most clearly expressed in one of the Psalms, probably written by King David, around the year 1,000 B.C., which reads
as follows:

> *Lord, thou hast examined me and knowest me.*
> *Thou knowest all, whether I sit down or rise up;*
> *thou hast discerned my thoughts from afar.*
> *Thou hast traced my journey and my resting places,*
> *and art familiar with all my paths.*
> *For there is not a word on my tongue*
> *but thou, Lord, knowest them all.*
> *Thou hast kept close guard before me and behind*
> *and hast spread thy hand over me.*
> *Such knowledge is beyond my understanding,*
> *so high that I cannot reach it.*
> *Where can I escape from thy spirit?*
> *Where can I flee from thy presence?*
> *If I climb up to heaven, thou art there;*
> *if I make my bed in hell, again I find thee.*
> *If I take my flight to the frontiers of the morning*
> *or dwell at the limit of the western sea,*
> *even there thy hand will meet me*
> *and thy right hand will hold me fast.*
>
> *— Psalm 139, The New English Bible*

It is clear from this passage that the writer very much believed
in a God who was much involved with him personally, so much

so, that he felt he could not go anywhere without God being at his side.

In the beginning the Jews were convinced that their God, the God of the patriarchs Abraham, Isaac and Jacob, was one God among many others and that other nations had other gods who might be just as powerful as theirs. At the same time, it is obvious from the context of the Old Testament writings, that they did not know the creation story as written down in Genesis, at least none of the prophets ever refers to it. So during much of this time they did not think of their God as the Creator of the whole universe, and as such the only one. This uniqueness of God is such an essential part of both Judaism and Islam that both recite the affirmation of this fact daily. For the orthodox Jew it is, "Hear O Israel, your God is one," while the devout Muslim repeats daily, "There is one God and Mohammed is his prophet."

It is interesting to note that God revealed him/herself slowly. In some ways one can see in this a confirmation of the evolution theory about the creation of humankind through a slow evolutionary process. It is exactly what one would expect to happen if God wanted to reveal him/herself to a slowly emerging humanity. A sudden complete revelation would be much more logical in the case of the creation of human beings in one instant as is described in the creation story in Genesis.

It should be noted that regardless which route we assume to be correct, the timing is about the same. The latest theories about the ascent of humans, place the discovery of the wheel, of writing, of agriculture, and a host of other essential elements that made it possible for humankind to fully develop its potential, at about 8,000 to 10,000 years ago. On the other hand, if one follows the genealogy of the Bible, the creation took place at about the same time. In other words, following the creation of humans through the evolutionary process puts a thinking and reasoning human being on the earth at about the same time as the Genesis story does. In the first case, it is through ages and ages of evolution, while in the second case the same result is obtained by the almost instant creation of the earth and its occupants. Considering that, according to present day science, the evolution process has been going on for literally billions of years, this is a truly remarkable coincidence.

After the awareness of the uniqueness of the God of Israel had finally taken hold, a parallel awareness grew concerning the Hebrews' special place in history and that God would accomplish his/her plan for all humankind through them. And so we see the prophets in the Old Testament begin to refer to a special messenger whom God would send to reveal him/herself more fully to humans. Throughout the books of the prophets this messenger is referred to by a wide variety of names. Anyone who is familiar with Handel's ''Messiah'' will remember the names: Emmanuel (God with us), Lamb of God, Wonderful, Counselor, Prince of Peace, and so forth. When that Messiah finally did come in the person of Jesus Christ, the religious leaders of that time largely rejected him and, in the end, even caused him to be crucified by the Roman authorities.

Humanly speaking, one would have expected that this would be the end of the special position the Jews occupy in the history of the world. Nothing could be further from the truth. The Jews have suffered more than any other people from persecution in almost every part of the world where they have tried to settle, but today their special place in history is even more evident than ever before. As a matter of fact, in some people's minds, one of the strongest arguments for the existence of God is the fact that today, 2,000 years after their dispersal across the world and after unbelievably cruel persecutions in every part of the world, they have maintained their identity. Not only that, but they have been able to regroup and survive in what is now called the State of Israel despite the most enormous odds against that survival. Maybe it does not prove that God exists, but it surely proves that the Jews are a people with a special place in history.

Before discussing what God is really like, it may be well for us to reflect for a moment on the difficulties involved in trying to understand what God is and how God acts. First, consider the different planes on which we operate. We, who are bound to this earth, who are mortal and finite, are trying to understand the One who is immortal and infinite, who created not only the minuscule sub-atomic particles but also the immense universe stretching millions of light years in all directions. In human terms, it must be something like us trying to explain to a microbe what human life is all about. The best we would be able to do is to try to explain life in terms of things it can understand, whatever these may be. But to explain what love is, or what compassion is, would be completely impossible because we would be talking on entirely different planes of awareness. And so, I believe, it is with humans. We will never be able to completely comprehend with our earthbound intelligence what God is and how God operates. At best, we can expect to be able to get only isolated glimpses of God's being.

Since God is so entirely different from us, we can expect that some of the glimpses we do receive of God's nature will be, or at least appear to us to be, quite contradictory. I believe we find ourselves in a similar situation as the four blind men in the Indian legend. This legend relates how four blind men were walking on a path in the jungle, and how they literally ran into a big elephant. The first one, who ran into the side of the animal said, ''I have run into a wall''; the second one, who had run into a leg said, ''I have run into a tree''; the third one, who was hanging on the elephant's tail said,

"I don't know about you two, but I am hanging onto a rope"; and finally the fourth blind man, who had run into one of the elephant's tusks said, "I am holding on to a piece of polished hardwood." Thus, while each blind man was giving a perfect description of what he was experiencing, the descriptions were so different and so contradictory that they would never be able to conjure up the image of an elephant without the help of a person who could see the whole, and who would explain to them how their widely differing observations nevertheless fitted perfectly into the overall picture of an elephant.

As Christians, we believe that we are like the blind men, we can only experience certain aspects of God's being, but we cannot see the whole picture. As Karl Barth, the famous Swiss theologian, once said, "The angels will laugh when they read my theology."

The Christian believes that the only one who can help us in putting that picture together is Jesus Christ, who is the only one who has ever lived in this world who has seen God. But even then we will only be able to get a faint glimpse of the true nature of God because we are still earthbound: we are still finite and unable to comprehend the things that are not of this earth and are infinite. It is only after our own entry in the infinite world that we will be able to see the whole picture. As the Bible puts it:

> *Now we see puzzling reflections in a mirror, but then we shall see face to face. My knowledge now is partial; then it will be whole, like God's knowledge of me.*
>
> — *1 Corinthians 13, The New English Bible*

The Attributes Of God As Revealed In The Bible

Who then is this God of the Christian religion? What distinguishes this God from the gods of other religions? How do we know that this God is the right one and the only one? And, if s/he is the only one, then what about the other religions — are they completely mistaken? These are all good and valid questions that everyone must answer for him/herself. In this book we are dealing with the Christian religion, with the God of Christianity because we believe in this God and have experienced him/her. This is not to say that we want to demean the other religions. Far from it. There is no doubt that the other major religions have had, and are having, a tremendous influence for the good on the lives of millions of followers. Most of these religions contain many elements that we can readily accept and ascribe to (see also Appendix 1). However, in this book we deal with the God as revealed in the Bible and it is this God we worship.

Since we believe that God has been revealed step by step in the Bible to his/her people, the Israelites, we will try to follow how knowledge of this God grew through the pages of the Bible.

The very first revelation is made right in the first sentence in the Bible which reads as follows:

> *In the beginning God created the heaven and the earth, and the earth was without form, and void; and darkness was upon the face of the deep. And the Spirit of God moved upon the face of the waters. And God said let there be light; and there was light.*
>
> — *Genesis 1, verses 1, 2 and 3, King James Bible*

So, God was revealed first of all as the Life Force and Creator: the creator of the whole universe created by God's word from nothing. It may be difficult to grasp how even God could create something out of nothing. Maybe we can think of it as God creating positive and negative matter out of nothing (a void). The positive part of this creation we then experience

61

as our universe. The end of the world we can then visualize as God putting the two together again, resulting in the same void with which we started. The only thing remaining which was not there at the beginning is the human soul or spirit which is eternal. This imaginary process closely resembles what happens when we go to the bank and borrow money to build a house. First there is nothing, no money and no house. Then after the loan has been made, there is something positive (the money in the bank which allows us to build the house) and something negative (the mortgage). At first they add up to nothing, but they nevertheless allow us to build the house and to live in it, much as we live on this earth.

The Bible story goes on to relate how God created all manner of living things, culminating eventually in the creation of human beings:

> *And God said, let us make man in our image after our own likeness to rule the fish in the sea, . . . So God created man in his own image, in the image of God created he them; male and female he created them. And God blessed them and said to them: "Be fruitful and multiply and increase, fill the earth and subdue it . . . "*
>
> — *Genesis 1 verses 26, 27 and 28, King James Bible*

The most astonishing revelation concerning humans in this passage is that God created us in his/her own image — a statement that is repeated four times in this short piece of text. This is, after the revelation of God as the creator of the whole universe, probably the most important statement as far as the ascent of humans is concerned. Whether human beings slowly evolved in accordance with the theory of evolution, or whether they were created in one instant with all the fossils in their appropriate places, is in the end quite immaterial. What is important is that when humans finally did emerge as thinking and reasoning beings, they were shaped in the image of God. Not by a fluke of natural selection, but by the will of God. It is this crucial truth that neither Jews, Christians, or Muslims can ever forget or discount, because it is one of the cornerstones of their faith.

Considering the importance that Christians attach to these statements, it will be no surprise to learn that over the years humans have tried to interpret what it means that humans are created in the image of God, and what it says both about God and about humankind. In considering this, I believe that it must include at least the following:

•First of all, it must mean that we can think and reason like God which is not the case for all the other things God created;

•Second, it must mean that we can distinguish between good and evil, again like God, but unlike the animal world which cannot make such a distinction;

•Third, it must mean that we have a free will which gives us the ability to choose between good and evil;

•Fourth, it must mean that we can respond to God and can communicate with God. In particular, that we can respond to God's love and to the love of other people;

•Fifth, it must mean that we can create, maybe not create things out of nothing like God can, but nevertheless create.

At this time, it may be well to consider the belief that some people have that God *is* the universe, or part of the universe, or that the universe emanates from God. We believe that nothing could be further from the truth. God, we believe, is entirely distinct and separate from the universe and is not even part of it. God was there long before the universe came into existence, and will still be there long after the universe has ceased to exist. God is not part of it, but stands far above it.

So then, the first quality of God, as revealed in the Bible, is that s/he is the Creator, not only of this earth but of the whole universe. God did not only create it, but also sustains it. No doubt, in the next decades, science will come up with new theories about the formation of the universe and about its eventual fate. While it is certainly fascinating to follow the further evolution of human's thinking in this regard, we must remember that, in the final analysis, it is an impossible task. Human beings, no matter how far they will be able to proceed with unravelling the mysteries of the universe, will never be able to overcome the handicap that their thinking must always be limited because they lack the capability to think on the plane on which God is thinking. Thus our knowledge will always be partial, "as through a mirror darkly." In any case, as Christians, we believe that God, the Creator, is all powerful, that God is both the beginning and the end, and that God is infinite and unlimited both in time and space.

The second quality is God's uniqueness — God is the only one. There may be other supernatural beings in the universe such as angels, but they are like human beings in that they were created by God and are subordinate to God. As was mentioned previously, for both Jews and Muslims the uniqueness of God is such an essential part of their understanding of God that they repeat this affirmation daily in their devotions. Of course, this uniqueness begs the question, If God is unique in the universe, where did God come from? It is a good and valid question but there is no real satisfying answer to it. We can only affirm what we said above, namely, that we believe that God is unlimited in both time and space; s/he is the beginning and the end of everything both on earth and in the universe.

The third quality that emerges from reading the Old Testament is that God is emotional. In the Old Testament, story after story tells of the emotions of God. God gets angry, is jealous and is sad when people do the wrong things. For instance, when the people went against God's rules, it is reported in Genesis 6 that, "The Lord was grieved that he had made man on the earth, and his heart was filled with pain."

The fourth quality of God relates to what we have commented on before: God is a personal God, who cares for us personally. This characteristic of God is hard to accept for some people who find it difficult to believe that the God who created the universe wants to have a personal relationship with them. Nevertheless, most of these same people have no problem praying to God most fervently when, for instance, one of their children becomes seriously ill. In other words, it may be intellectually difficult to accept but when we really feel the need of God's protection and presence, our intellectual problems disappear and we do not hesitate to ask for God's personal intervention.

In both the Old and the New Testament, this personal relationship is compared to the relationship a child has with its parents. Thus, we are encouraged to call God our Father, and we are told to think of ourselves as God's children. Not one of the other major religions comes close to teaching this relationship that exists between God and his/her people that is such an essential part of the Judeo/Christian religion. In describing this close relationship the Bible uses mostly the father figure, probably because of the dominant position the father occupied in the early Hebrew households. The Bible could just as well have used the mother image, since God is spirit and therefore neither male nor female. In some respects, the use of the mother figure is probably more appropriate in today's society, since generally the image of a mother is thought to project more closely the image of a caring and loving parent.

Some Christians have great problems with both the father and the mother image of God. Maybe they had parents who were not anything like the image we like to project of the perfect, loving and caring parent. For instance, for Bishop John Spong, the image of God as a person is not helpful at all. As he said, his own faith journey has led him more to think of God as the divine force, the life giver, the source of all being, and as such he sees God in life in the flesh, in himself and in other people.

For others, the problem arises from the fact that God is often thought of as a white, patriarchal man which, for men and women of another colour, is not something they can readily relate to. For example, for Chung Hyun Kyung, the well known Korean female theologian, God became only real when she thought of God as a Korean woman with the face of her mother.

The fifth quality of God, which is very clearly depicted all through the Bible, is that God is just and that humans will eventually have to give account of what they have done, or for that matter, what they have failed to do. This could not be otherwise since it is God who has given us the moral laws which are an expression of God's character. It is precisely this characteristic that makes it impossible for God to accept our imperfect nature and to condone our wrong doings.

The sixth quality of God is that s/he is the personification of love. Nowhere is this made clearer than in the life and death of Jesus. Emil Brunner, a Swiss theologian, puts it this way in his well-known book, *Our Faith*:

> *God's feeling towards us is infinite love. Fellowship is the one thing he absolutely wants. God created the world in order to share himself. He created us for fellowship.*[1]

Because I will use the word love all through this book, it may be well to define what exactly is meant by this term. Unfortunately, in our western languages we have basically only one word to describe the feeling of love. The Greeks, on the other hand, used at least three different words to describe the same feeling. They used eros to describe sexual love, filia to describe the love between parents and children and agape to describe the love between God and humans. In Webster's Dictionary this love is defined as "God's benevolent concern for humankind" and "human's devout attachment to God." It is the love described by Paul in his famous chapter on love in his letter to the Corinthians where he writes:

> *Love is always patient and kind; love is never jealous; love is never boastful or conceited, it is never rude and never seeks its own advantage, it does not take offence or store up grievances. Love does not rejoice at wrongdoing, but finds its joy in truth. It is always ready to make allowances, to trust, to hope and to endure whatever comes. Love never comes to an end . . . . As it is, there remains: faith, hope and love, the three of them; and the greatest of them is love.*

— *1 Corinthians 13, The New Jerusalem Bible*

In recent years, the concept that God is love has taken on a somewhat different meaning. It is said that love is indeed the very essence of life itself, that it is the essential energy of the universe, and that it is the core of all reality. As Robert Keck expressed it in *Sacred Eyes*: "Love is fundamental to everything that is."[2] By this way of thinking, love is not only an emotional feeling that cements personal relationships, but also a form of energy that governs the functioning of the entire universe. This I find personally somewhat difficult to grasp, but if God is the personification of love and in effect *is* love, then creation must obviously also be impregnated with that quality.

In listing these qualities of God, we must always remember what was said earlier about our earthbound mind and our existence in our particular time-space frame. Living within these limits we cannot possibly begin to understand what God is like in totality. We should therefore be prepared to accept the fact that God, in all likelihood, has other qualities which we cannot possibly imagine at this time. This being so, there are bound to be contradictions and things we cannot comprehend in our present state of existence. To name just a few:

- •If God created everything, God must also have created evil.
- •If God is all powerful, how come God has not erased evil from the face of the earth?
- •If God is love, how can God possibly tolerate all the suffering that is going on in God's creation?

We are bound to ask ourselves these and other questions because they seem to contradict what we have said about God and they, more than anything else, have driven people away from a faith in a benevolent God. As someone said, "I do not want any part of a God that lets a young child suffer, or a God that created a world in which half of the food supply depends on the killing of other creatures." These are all true and valid observations and questions, and no book dealing with the Christian faith can possibly be complete without considering these questions in detail. In this book I will return to these questions in chapter 6, which is entitled, "The Things That Separate Us From God — Sin and Suffering."

In summary then, the qualities that God has revealed to us in the Bible are:

God is the creator, the life force behind creation;
God is unlimited both in time and space;
God is unique, there is no other one like him/her;
God is emotional, God knows joy, grief and anger;
God is intensely personal and cares for us individually;
God is the personification of love.

It is interesting to see how most people have a preferred image of God, one that probably fits their own character best. So, today in the literature, we can find God depicted as:

The Creator, the Life Force, the Life Giver;
The Alpha and Omega, the beginning and the end of everything;

The Infinite One;
The Unique One — The Only One;
The Great Caring One;
The Father or Mother of Humankind;
The Personification of Love.

All these images are valid to a certain extent, but I believe we lose a great deal if we stress one at the expense of the others too much, because God is all of these and more.

Does God Really Exist?

Before continuing, it may be well to reflect for a moment on the question, "Does God, any God, really exist?" In thinking about this, it may be that we should rephrase the question, because existence of anything or anyone can only be proven if that existence has been experienced as a presence. For instance, we know that soil exists because we can dig it up and hold it in our hands. Similarly, you know that a person exists and is real only if you can see her, communicate with him or embrace her, in short when you experience his or her presence. So, when we ask does God exist, we are really asking, have I or someone else experienced God's presence?

Hans Küng, one of the best known modern theologians has written an 800 page book on this subject entitled, *Does God Exist?* with the subtitle, "An answer for today."[3] It is a very interesting book and I shall quote from it once in a while, but it is not always easy to read and it is very long. There are, naturally, scores of other writers who have tried to tackle this all important subject.

In a book titled, *The Survival of God in the Scientific Age*, Alan Isaacs poses the question as follows:

> *There are three simple questions which every member of the community should be encouraged to consider before*

> *he commits himself to a belief in the concept of God.*
> *The answer to these questions are, of course, not at all*
> *simple; but if intellectual integrity is to have any mean-*
> *ing, no one is entitled to say that he believes in God un-*
> *less he is able to answer at least one of the questions in*
> *the affirmative. The questions are:*
> 1) *Can the existence of God be established by unaided*
>   *reason?*
> 2) *Has God unequivocally revealed himself or his exis-*
>   *tence to me personally?*
> 3) *Can I, as an act of faith, accept the existence of God*
>   *on the strength of revelations experienced by others?*[4]

Let's look at the first question: Can God's existence be proven? In the past, the church had a number of so-called proofs that God did exist. However, today, very few people believe that they are valid. In addition, the problem with these proofs is that, at best, they establish that some sort of deity exists, but it does not say anything about that deity's character; and it certainly does not say anything about the God we call our Father/Mother. However because these "proofs" are of general interest and have some validity for some people, they are briefly described below.

•The first proof is generally referred to as the "cosmological" argument. It basically starts with the assertion that behind every effect there must be a cause. Thus, if we go far enough back in history we must eventually meet up with the very first cause that started the ball rolling. This first cause could then be reasonably called the Prime Mover or God, since God is by definition at the beginning of everything.

•The second is called the "teleological" proof. It is based on the observation that the universe, with its microcosmos and its macrocosmos, seems to be so perfectly organized, that there must be someone behind this structure who has put the order and organization in it. They argue that if one were to land on a deserted island and were to find a piece of complicated machinery clicking away, one would not say to himself: Hey! that is an interesting example of evolutionary development! Instead one would quickly come to the conclusion that the island is not uninhabited as originally thought, since it is clear that there must be someone around who has not only built the machinery, but who also maintains it.

It is interesting to note that this argument for the existence of God has recently re-emerged, this time, from a somewhat unexpected corner, science. For instance, Paul Davies, whom we have quoted before, writes in his book, *The Mind Of God*, the following:

> *Through my scientific work, I have come to believe more and more strongly that the physical universe is put together with an ingenuity so astonishing that I cannot accept it merely as a brute fact. There must, it seems to me, be a deeper level of explanation ... I cannot believe that our existence in this universe is a mere quirk of fate, or accident. Our involvement is too intimate.*[5]

•The third proof is based on the "ontological" argument and is probably the more difficult to follow. In its most simple form it postulates that if in this world we find that there exists the idea of a supreme being or a god who is the personification of perfection, then the idea would not have occurred to humans in the first place unless that Supreme Being (God) existed. And since almost all known societies have a belief in a Supreme Being, then it is obvious that God must exist.

Over the years, these proofs have been the subject of intense scrutiny and all have been found to have inconsistencies which make their validity, at best, dubious. In his book, *How To Think About God* with the subtitle, "A guide for the 20th century pagan," Mortimer J. Adler concludes that he has reasonable grounds for affirming the existence of God. He then goes on to point out that there is the world of difference between the God, who he has reasonable grounds to assume exists, and the God of the Jewish, Christian and Islam religions. He simply cannot bridge the gap between God, the Creator, and the God who concerns him/herself with human beings.[6]

Thus, going back to the first question, "Can the existence of God be established by unaided reason?", the answer must be: No, we cannot prove the existence of a God who is both the creator and the one who is concerned with us personally. At the same time, it is equally impossible to prove that this God does not exist.

Of course, for the Christian, his/her religion would undergo a radical change if it could be proven with mathematical certainty that this God did exist. It would completely dispense with the need for faith and trust on which the Christian religion is based.

This leaves us to answer the next question: "Has God unequivocally revealed his/her existence to me personally?" Unfortunately, not everyone, including the writer, can answer that question with a resounding Yes. The problem with the question is the use of the word unequivocal, meaning unmistakably, plain and clear. Many people, including myself, will readily affirm that they have experienced God's presence on many occasions; sometimes in very ordinary circumstances and through very ordinary people, and at other times the circumstances and the people were very special.

However, today, in our scientific age which looks at everything in a critical and inquiring way, we are naturally reluctant to ascribe spiritual values to feelings that psychologists can probably readily explain as being the logical results of emotionally charged events. As an example of these, I offer the following two very different occasions on which I felt strongly God's presence.

The first example happened during the Second World War when the village in which I lived found itself in the middle of a battlefield. Shells were exploding everywhere; machine guns were rattling beside the basement window where we were seeking shelter; tanks were lumbering up and down the street; and our greatest fear was that a soldier, be it friend or foe, would fling a hand grenade into our basement, just to make sure that there were no live enemies there. We were huddled together pressing ourselves against the outside wall of that basement, and we were afraid. When the noise of the battle was near its peak, my father got out the family Bible and read Psalm 23, the one quoted on page 48:

"The Lord is my shepherd, I shall not fear ...

Even though I walk through the valley of the shadow of death, I will fear no evil, for you are with me ..."

That was an almost magic, spiritual, moment; our fears were calmed; and we even felt at peace, because at that moment we felt God's presence there in that basement with the war raging all around us.

The second example I want to relate occurred almost 40 years later when my wife and I were travelling through Communist China. Driving through the city of Wuhan, we noticed a cross on a brick wall. When we went to look at what might lay behind this wall, we found a fairly large church. The door to the church was open and when we entered we found two young men inside — one was the assistant minister of the congregation, and the other was a student minister. Although we did not speak a word of Chinese and only the assistant minister spoke a few words of English, we were able to communicate and they proudly showed us the church and how it had survived the cultural revolution. In the end, we found a Chinese hymn book which also gave the titles in English. So, we ended up singing together the familiar hymn, "What a friend we have in Jesus" — the Chinese ministers singing in Cantonese and the two of us singing in English. Of course, I can not be sure about the two Chinese, but we felt God's presence there in the middle of Communist China, in a church behind a wall.

As I said, no doubt, a psychologist could explain our experiences of God's presence as something that can readily be explained in psychological terms without bringing God into it. But, as far as that second question is concerned, yes I have experienced God's presence, but not in such a way that it can be used as proof for others that God exists.

The third question, "Can I, as an act of faith, accept the existence of God on the strength of revelations experienced by others?" This can, I believe, be answered much more positively and unequivocally. The history of the church, and in particular the history as recorded in the Bible, is overflowing with the stories of people who have had this direct contact and, as a consequence, have changed the world. The best known example of this is probably the sudden conversion of the apostle Paul, who on his way to persecute the early Christians in Damascus, had a very personal encounter with the living Christ. (See Acts of the Apostles, Chapter 8.) As a result of this encounter he became a changed man who eventually became the foremost Christian evangelist of his time. He spread the message of Christ, whose followers he had first persecuted, to most parts of the Roman Empire often under the most difficult circumstances.

Another example of how the personal encounter with God can change people is the miraculous change that occurred in the disciples of Jesus after his resurrection. These first disciples were mostly uneducated simple fishermen. Yet this small band of unsophisticated people transformed the world with their message, and started a world-wide movement that 2,000 years later, in the sophisticated 20th century, is still very much alive and is a vital force in today's society.

Today, there are a number of well-known people, who have changed the world because they heard God's call. There are famous people like Mother Teresa, Martin Luther King, Bishop Romero, and so forth, but there are thousands of others, less well known, who have met the living Christ, heard his call and responded. So, to the third question of Mr. Isaacs, I believe we can most positively answer with Yes, we can without a doubt, because we can observe the difference the encounter with God has made in the lives of the people who have had this encounter.

In the end, the only way to convince people that God exists is the same way we convince others that it is possible to transmit images from a television studio to a living room without the benefit of a direct link. Most of us would fail hopelessly if we tried to explain in detail how the transmission process works. We might be able to talk about radio waves and transmitters, but if we were asked how this really worked we would most likely be stumped. However, if you have enough trust in the maker of the television set, all you have to do is switch the set on and all necessity for further explanation disappears. It works, and you can safely leave the explanation to the experts. So it is in many ways with the proof of the existence of God. You cannot prove it, but if you have the trust and faith to switch it on, you can experience it, just as with the television set.

As mentioned at the beginning of this chapter, Hans Küng wrote a book on the question, *Does God Exist?* At the end of this book he concludes that after:

- considering the objections raised by the philosophers and
- comparing the alternatives of the Eastern religions;

the question, "Does God exist?" can be answered by a clear, convinced "Yes." He then finishes his book with this statement:

> *Does God exist? Despite all upheavals and doubts, even for man today, the only appropriate answer must be that with which believers of all generations from ancient times have again and again professed their faith. It begins with, "You God we praise," and it ends in trust, "In you Lord, I have hoped, I shall never be put to shame."* [7]

The good news for today is that we have all the evidence we need that God is real and that this God is a God of love who cares for us personally.

4

The Forces That Oppose God

Introduction

In the previous chapter we have seen how God slowly revealed him/herself over the ages to the chosen people, the Jews. In the next chapter we will continue with the account of how God was revealed more clearly to all the world through the son, Jesus Christ. However, before we do so, we must pause for a moment and reflect on the fact that there appear to exist very strong forces in the universe that oppose God. Forces that try to separate us, human beings created in God's image, from the God who created us.

In chapter 3, it has been explained how God, according to Genesis, created the universe and, especially, how God created humans as separate beings in the image of himself/herself. In other words God created humans as perfect beings without flaws and blemishes. Humans lived in paradise and lived in close communion with God, their Creator. Whether we accept this story of paradise at face value or not, it is clear that what the story tries to tell us is that God had wanted us to live in perfect harmony, not only with him/her but also with the other members of the human family and with the other creatures God had created. Unfortunately, it is painfully clear to everyone living in this world today that we are not living in a paradise, that we are not living in close communion with God, and that we are not living in perfect harmony with our neighbours.

So what happened? Did God change his/her mind after creating humankind, or is there another power at work in the world, a power stronger than God, that is ruining his/her plans? If so, where does this power come from? These are some of the questions humankind has asked and must ask, because they are pressed upon it by what it daily sees and experiences. As Christians we must acknowledge that our response to these questions constitutes an enormous challenge which cannot be side-stepped with quick and pious answers.

It is clearly evident from what we see daily around us that there is something in this world that is opposed to God and God's plan for us. Over the centuries, this opposing force has been given different names. If we visualize it as a living spirit with an existence of its own, we call it Satan or the Devil. If we identify it more as an impersonal, all pervading attitude, we call it evil or an evil spirit. All known religions, from the earliest recorded onward, contain this element of two opposing forces — the good spirits and the evil spirits, the forces of dark and the forces of light.

Not only is there something interfering with God's plan for this world, but there also appears to be something that separates us from God our Creator personally: something that stands almost immovable between us, a rebellious attitude that makes us do the wrong thing, although we may want to do the right thing. In the general terminology of the church this rebellion against God's will is called "sin." Unfortunately this word, as so many others we will be using, is overloaded with misconceptions. If we hear it today we sort of cringe or snicker because we associate it with Bible thumping television evangelists or with sexual misdemeanors. However, most of us, no matter what our religious background, will acknowledge freely that we are less than perfect and that we often do not measure up to even our own standards, let alone to the standard Christ has set for us, to love our neighbour as ourselves.

In a later chapter I will come back to this subject of sin, and where and how we fall short both individually and as a community. For the present it is sufficient to note that we do not love our neighbour as ourselves, and that we find it almost impossible to overcome our own self-centeredness. This causes us time and time again to do the wrong thing, and not to take action when we know that we should do so. If you are like me, you can probably point to a good many occasions in which you did something that was entirely against your own better judgement. Maybe you even hesitated for a moment, but you went ahead anyway. That is sin. Similarly, each one of us can probably remember occasions when we saw someone else do something wrong or something that was harmful to others, but we did nothing. That is sin. That this is not at all an unusual situation is clear from what the apostle Paul wrote about similar incidences in his life:

> *So I find this rule: that for me, where I want to do nothing but good, evil is close at my side. In my inmost self I dearly love God's law, but I see that acting on my body there is a different law which battles against the law in my mind.*

— Romans 7, The New Jerusalem Bible

One other aspect of our lives, which cause many people to reject God as a loving Father/Mother, is related to the problem of human suffering. We all have to die sometime, and we all suffer at one time or another both physical pain and mental anguish. No one is exempt, not the good people nor the bad people, not the rich nor the poor, not the Christians nor the atheists. The question we must answer is, "How can we reconcile this suffering with the love of God for creation?"

Sometime ago, a well-known television evangelist of the 1950s was participating in a television debate about the belief in a loving God. This ex-evangelist explained that he had lost his faith in God as a direct result of his inability to reconcile the suffering in this world with the idea of a loving God. No doubt there are millions of others who have gone and are going through the same agonizing experience.

In the past, human pain and suffering were often associated with God's sense of justice. It was argued that humankind was not following God's commands and was doing the wrong thing continually, and so God's sense of justice demanded some sort of punishment. This brings in the difficult question of justice and retribution. On an earthly scale of things we are all for it, especially if some wrong has been done to us. But do we want God to operate on that same principle? Ask yourself, do you really want the perpetrators of atrocities, such as were committed in World War II concentration camps, to go without punishment in both this world and the next? I believe most people would say no, we want justice done, but that involves retribution and suffering. The question then is: Do we want God to operate on the same principle when it concerns us? I believe we should at least consider this when we think about suffering resulting from the application of justice. At the same time then, one may well ask: Can the suffering of one little innocent child possibly be justified as part of a sentence against all humankind for its wrong doings? Albert Camus, the French atheistic existentialist, who despaired about the suffering he found in the world, was nevertheless greatly distressed by the possibility that there was no justice for evildoers in this world. He wrote:

> *The certainty of the existence of a God who would give meaning to life has a far greater attraction than the*

knowledge that without him one could do evil without being punished. Confronted with this evil, confronted with death, man from the depths of his soul cries out for justice.[1]

The Christian proclamation has always been that:
- God made the world and it was good when it was finished;
- God is all powerful and does not lose control; and
- God is the personification of love.

If we accept these statements to be true, we can, obviously, not at the same time accept that God is the cause of, or the creator of, evil and human suffering since this would be in direct contradiction to these three axioms of the Christian faith. The only resort we have is to seek clarification in what the Bible has to tell us about these forces that separate us from God and that have caused so much suffering through the ages.

Before doing so, it may be interesting to note that other religions, besides Judaism, Islam and Christianity, also have similar beliefs in the existence of evil as opposed to good. In Hinduism, the evil forces are often thought of as gods and demons who are leading people astray and who cause suffering and pain. Some of these gods can even be both evil and good, depending on the form they assume at any given moment.

In Taoism, there is the principle of life's basic opposites: good-evil, active-passive, positive-negative, light-dark, summer-winter, as symbolized in Yang and Yin, the two interwoven figures inside a circle.

So, the distinction between good and evil, between evil forces and good forces, is something that seems to have been recognized from the earliest of times.

The Old Testament's References To Evil

The Old Testament starts with the creation of the world and then immediately follows through with the story of what has been called "man's fall from grace" or "original sin." It must be remembered that not many people today take this account literally. Certainly the Old Testament writers do not seem to have done so because, except for three minor references to Adam, the names of Adam and Eve are never mentioned by them in all of the 39 books of the Old Testament. On the other hand, Christians through the centuries have recognized that the story as told in Genesis has an important message to convey to all humankind.

As I have mentioned before, the creation story in Genesis tells us that humans were created in God's image. One of the things this most certainly means is that we were created with a free will whereby we can either accept or reject God. We, God's creation, were given the freedom to make the wrong choices or to make the right choices.

This is the account in the first book of the Bible of what happened to the first couple in the paradise God had created for them:

> *The serpent was more crafty than any wild creature that the Lord God had made. He said to the woman, "Is it true that God has forbidden you to eat from any tree in the garden?" The woman answered the serpent, "We may eat the fruit from any tree in the garden, except for the tree in the middle of the garden; God has forbidden us either to eat or to touch the fruit of that; if we do we shall die." The serpent said, "Of course you will not die. God knows that as soon you eat from it, your eyes will be opened and you will all be like gods knowing both good and evil." When the woman saw that the fruit was good to eat, and that it was pleasing to the eye and tempting to contemplate, she took some and ate it. She also gave some to her husband and he ate it. Then the eyes of both of them were opened and they discovered that they were naked; so they stitched fig-leaves together and made themselves loincloths. The man and his wife heard the sound of the Lord God walking in the garden at the time of the evening breeze and hid from the Lord God*

*among the trees of the garden. But the Lord God called
to the man and said, "Where are you?" He replied, "I
heard the sound as you were walking in the garden, and
I was afraid because I was naked, and I hid myself." God
answered, "Who told you that you were naked? Have
you eaten from the tree which I forbade you?" The man
said, "The woman you gave me for a companion, she
gave me fruit from the tree and I ate it." Then the Lord
God said to the woman, "What is it that you have done?"
The woman said, "The serpent tricked me, and I ate."*

— *Genesis 3, The New English Bible*

From this account it is clear that humankind exercised that
right to choose and used it to go against the few rules its Creator had set for it. In fact, humankind, in the persons of Adam
and Eve, chose to be, as the serpent put it, like gods, knowing
both good and evil. In other words, humankind wanted to be
like God. How this actually happened is somewhat of a mystery. If we follow the concept that humankind slowly developed from more primitive forms of life, then according to
Genesis there must have been a period of time during its development when it was in a state of perfection — the unfallen
state. However, as John Polkinghorne put it in his book, *reality
and reason*:

*The difficulty arises from picturing this situation as hav-
ing arisen subsequent to an unfallen state, with the associated notion that a radical change occurred as the
consequence of some disastrous ancestral act ... We detect no sign of a sharp discontinuity in the course of earthly or cosmic history, no indication of a golden age from
which our present plight descends by degeneration.*[2]

While there may not be any evidence in history of a "disastrous ancestral act" that could potentially have caused the
transformation from a paradise-like existence to a more vio-
lent sinful existence, there is, however, a great deal of evidence
to suggest that in the early, food gathering, stage of our

development, people lived a very peaceful existence. During this period, which came to an end roughly 10,000 years ago, there was apparently no warfare, people lived on fruits and seeds, and there was a great sense of cooperation and equality. Archeologist W. J. Perry, as quoted in *Sacred Eyes* by L. Robert Keck, states:

> *All the available facts go to show that the food gathering stage of history must have been one of perfect peace. The study of the artifacts of the Paleolithic age fails to reveal any definite signs of human warfare.* [3]

If we follow the archeological records further, it appears that this idyllic stage in our development came to an end when we became meat eaters and therefore hunters, and when we began to settle in agricultural communities. Archeological records show that it was then that weapons began to emerge in addition to the pots and pans of the earlier period. One could maybe say that it was during this transition period that evil in the form of violence, killing and warfare became part and parcel of everyday human life. To some extent this agrees with the opinion of Erich Fromm, a well-known psychoanalyst and social philosopher. He sees the origin of human evil as a developmental process and believes that we were not created evil or forced to be evil, but we slowly became evil over time through a long process of making wrong choices.

Maybe the emergence of evil by this process can be illustrated by what happened to an irrigation scheme I once visited in South America. The project as built was perfect: a large dam stored enormous quantities of water; large irrigation canals conveyed the water to a well-designed distribution system; and new roads and new villages had been built in what used to be a desert. The scheme was perfect, that is, until the farmers arrived and started irrigating the land. The first seasons were not too bad, the soil was good and they grew reasonable crops. But then disaster struck in the form of salt. By using the wrong method of irrigation, salt was leached out of the soil and deposited on the surface when the water evaporated. When I visited the scheme, the sun shone on a surface that looked as if it had snowed the night before, as everywhere the soil was covered with a fine layer of salt. The salt killed the young plants and the whole scheme was in fact almost useless. Here was this large, perfectly constructed project, but by repeatedly using it incorrectly, evil crept in, in this case in the form of salt. I believe something similar may have happened to humankind. God gave us the perfect world but by making repeatedly the wrong use of that creation, evil crept in and has been with us ever since.

To many people, the concept that because our forefathers did something wrong, we today have to suffer the consequences is unfair and not acceptable to them. Maybe the concept is somewhat easier to understand if we think of a modern equivalent. It is clear from the creation story that God has put us in charge of this world, and that it is our responsibility to look after it to the best of our ability. Today, as far as the world's resources are concerned, we live in a paradise. There is enough of everything to meet the demands for food, clothing and shelter for everyone. That not everyone receives an equal share of this abundance is one of our greatest collective sins. I will come back to this glaring failure of our modern society in Chapter 6.

God has given us a brain and it tells us very clearly that we cannot continue on the path of "exponentiality." Exponentiality is that process by which growth is added to growth, resulting in doubling values every 7, 10 or 20 years depending on the rate of growth. This is a fine concept for people with money in the bank, with money gathering interest upon interest. But, if this principle is applied to the unrestrained growth in population, to the unrestrained use of natural resources, to the amount of pollutants which destroy both the earth and the atmosphere, the end results will be disastrous. Maybe not so much for us today, but certainly for our children and grandchildren. For instance, with the present growth rate of the world population, it is estimated by the United Nations that the population will double to over 10 billion in the next 60 years. It is clear that the earth cannot sustain this growth. If unchecked it will, without a doubt, cause human suffering beyond imagination and on a scale never seen before on this earth.

So, here we are, we know that we should not be eating from this tree, but we are so programmed that we find it impossible to resist this call for exponential growth. The ultimate result we all know. We will be driven from this paradise, or maybe better stated, we are driving ourselves out of this paradise of abundance for all, to a world of starvation and impossible living conditions.

I believe that this is the modern equivalent of the disobedience of Adam and Eve, and the equivalent of losing a paradise. Without a doubt, the next generations will blame God for not having stopped this process in time. They will ask why they must suffer because their parents did not constrain their desire for continued, unrestrained growth. This analogy simply indicates that in a similar way early humans may have distanced themselves from God and gone against the rules God had given them, knowing full well what this disobedience was leading to. All these wrong turns, I believe, eventually ended up with human beings being unfit to live in the paradise God had made for them.

It is interesting to note that in the story of Genesis, when God asked Adam what had happened, he replied that it was the woman you gave me that tempted me. In other words, Adam does not only try to divert the blame for his mistake onto his wife, but he also puts part of the blame on God for having given him this woman as a companion. This tendency must be something that is ingrown in human nature, since we today want to blame everything that is wrong with this world on God for not having done a better job in creating the universe; just as our children will blame God, and not their parents for the collapse of the world's ecological system caused by our inability or unwillingness to act now.

The second reference to evil and sin in the Bible immediately follows the creation story. The first male children of Adam and Eve, Abel and Cain, are offering some of the products of their labour to the Lord. Somehow it is made clear to them that God accepted the offering from Abel and for some reason rejected the offering of his brother Cain. The story relates how Cain was very angry and his face fell. Then the Lord said to Cain:

> *Why are you so angry and cast down? If you do well, you are accepted; if not, sin is a demon crouching at the door. It shall be eager for you, and you will be mastered by it.*
>
> — *Genesis 4, The New English Bible*

Obviously Cain did not listen to the warning the Lord was giving him and went out and killed his brother: thus committing the first murder and proving that we cannot ignore the warning God gives us about falling in the clutches of evil and sin.

Somewhat further along in Genesis, it is recorded how evil, once having started, spread to the extent that God regretted that s/he had ever created humans, as shown in the following passage:

> *When the Lord saw that man had done much evil on earth and that his thoughts and inclinations were always evil, he was sorry that he had made man on earth, and he was grieved at heart. He said, "This race of men whom I have created, I will wipe them off the face of the earth, man and beast, reptiles and birds. I am sorry that I ever made them." But Noah had won the Lord's favour.*
>
> — *Genesis 6, The New English Bible*

The story then goes on to tell what happened to the earth and how Noah and his family were saved by building the ark. That this story is not a plain myth or legend is clear from the fact that several other sources from that general era contain similar accounts of a great flood having covered a large part of the known world at that time. Again, whether this story is historically correct or not isn't important. What is important is to note that God's patience with humankind eventually ran out and that God was ready to undo what s/he had created. To draw out our analogy with the way we are misusing the earth's resources, we do not need a great flood to destroy the earth. In our case it is not God directly, who runs out of patience, but it is this earth and atmosphere that will run out of ways and means to protect itself from the onslaught of humankind.

It is interesting to note that one of the consequences of our mistreatment of the atmosphere will be the heating of the earth's crust. This will result in the melting of the polar icecap which will raise the water level in the oceans to such an extent that it will cause flooding of a large part of the arable lands on the earth. Thus, if we do not stop this global warming in time, we will be creating our own flood. But who is building the ark?

The New Testament's References To Evil

Since we believe that Jesus is the Son of God and since God personifies love and goodness, it was inevitable that Jesus, during his time on earth, should frequently clash with the Devil as the personification of evil.

The New Testament tells us that, wherever Jesus met evil and suffering, he counteracted it by healing those who were suffering and by casting out the evil spirits from those possessed. But not only did he encounter evil in a general way, he also came face to face with the personification of evil in the form of Satan or the devil in his own personal life.

The New Testament records that at the beginning of his ministry, just after his baptism by John the Baptist, the devil came to him in the desert where he had gone to meditate and exposed him to a number of temptations. The most insidious of these was probably the one in which Satan showed him all the countries of this world and then told him, "I will give you all this power and splendour ... just do homage to me and it shall all be yours." In other words, Satan is tempting Jesus to take a short cut and gain the world without having to complete his mission, including the cross, by simply kneeling before Satan. Jesus' answer is a simple, "Away with you Satan. The scripture says, you shall do homage only to the Lord your God." (Matthew 4)

Later in his ministry, Jesus used two parables to show how evil operates and how it gains entry into our lives. It is interesting to note that in both cases, after telling the parables, he explained the meaning of the parables in detail, something he rarely did, or at least, it is recorded in only a very few instances.

The parable that is reproduced below, is often called the parable of the tares or the darnel. (Darnel or tares is a weed that looks very much like normal wheat and is mildly poisonous.)

He put another parable before them. The kingdom of Heaven may be compared to a man who sowed good seed in his fields. While everyone was asleep his enemy came and sowed darnel among the wheat, and made off. When the new wheat sprouted and ripened, then the darnel appeared as well. The owner's labourers went to him and said, "Sir, was it not good seed that you sowed in your field? If so, where does this darnel come from?" He said to them, "Some enemy has done this." And the labourers said, "Do you want us to go and weed it out?" But he said, "No, because when you weed out the darnel you might pull up the wheat with it. Let them both grow till the harvest; and at harvest time I shall say to the reapers, 'First collect the darnel and tie it in bundles to be burnt, then gather the wheat in my barn.' "

Later his disciples asked him what this parable meant and he replied as follows:

> *The sower of the good seed is the Son of Man.*
> *The good seed is the subjects of the kingdom;*
> *The darnel is the subjects of the Evil One;*
> *The enemy who sowed it, the devil;*
> *The harvest is the end of the world;*
> *The reapers are the angels.*
> *Well then, just as the darnel is gathered up and burned*
> *in the fire, so it will be at the end of time.*
>
> — *Matthew 13, The New Jerusalem Bible*

In the other parable, that of the sower, Jesus again compares the Kingdom of Heaven to a man who sowed seed in a field. This time, some of the seed fell on the edge of the path and birds came and picked it up. This, Jesus says later in the explanation of the parable, is like someone who hears the word of the kingdom without understanding it and the Evil One comes and carries off what was sown in his heart.

It is clear from these parables and from the account of the temptations Jesus himself endured that Satan, as the personification of evil, was very real to him. So real, in fact, that he included in the prayer he taught his disciples the following petition:

> *And lead us not into temptation,*
> *but deliver us from evil:*
>
> – *Matthew 6, The King James Bible*

Thus, for Jesus, evil and the personification of evil (the Devil, Satan or the Evil One) posed a real and continuing threat to his followers. As a consequence, he repeatedly warned his disciples, as he is warning us today, to be alert and not underestimate the power that the forces of evil can exert in this world.

Does Satan Exist?

While everyone will readily agree that there is much evil in this world, not everyone will agree that the personification of evil, that is Satan or the Devil, exists and can take control of individuals and even whole nations. In the Old Testament, Satan or the Devil is mentioned only four times as a distinct personality. In only one, the story of King David and the census, does the Devil use his power of temptation to make a person oppose the will of God. In the others, the Devil is only briefly mentioned as a subordinate to God. As we have seen, this is different in the New Testament where Jesus repeatedly refers to Satan by name. For instance, when Jesus explains to his disciples how he must suffer and die, Peter the fiery, impulsive disciple immediately jumps in with both feet and exclaims, "Heaven preserve you Lord, this must not happen to you." But after this perfectly understandable expression of concern, Jesus tells him, "Get thee behind me Satan, You are an obstacle in my path." (Mark 8)

Looking back at the history of our civilization over the last half century, it is not difficult to point to instances where the Devil took complete control, not only of individuals but of whole nations. How otherwise can we explain the massacre of 6 million Jews by one of the most "civilized nations" of the world, or the massacre of a million people by the Khmer Rouge in Cambodia, or for that matter the Mai Lai massacre by the U.S. troops of mostly women and children in Vietnam. Unfortunately, these are not just isolated instances of an evil spirit gaining the upper hand and causing human beings to behave in barbaric ways, thereby causing unbearable pain and suffering to women, men and children.

The world history is filled with similar incidents, to name just a few: the Spanish Inquisition; the indiscriminate extermination of the native population in the Americas; the slave trade; the extermination of millions of Russians by the Stalinist regime; and the atrocities that are being committed daily, as I write this, in the former Yugoslavia. The suffering humans have heaped on other humans seems to have gone on forever and, as the first three examples show, Satan does not seem to find it particularly difficult to exercise his evil sway over the minds of humans, even in these enlightened times. I believe that the greatest mistake modern humans can possibly make is to assume that, in this age of microchips and space travel, a notion such as the existence of an evil spirit can safely be done away with and is irrelevant to these times. This, I believe, would play straight into the hand of Satan. It would leave evil free to invade the minds of unsuspecting people and nations, thereby allowing evil to continue and, in particular, to continue its never-ending attempt to separate humankind further from its Creator.

In his book, *The People of the Lie*, Dr. Scott Peck, a psychoanalyst, describes how he continually encounters evil in his practice. In particular, he describes how he in fact physically struggled with Satan in an attempt to exorcise an evil spirit from the body of a person who was possessed by such a spirit. In his book he makes the following comments on the existence of Satan:

> *The experience of two exorcisms is hardly sufficient for one to unravel all the mysteries of the spiritual realm. But I think I now know a few things about it and also have the basis for making a few speculations.*
> * *While my experience is insufficient to prove the Judeo-Christian myth and doctrine about Satan, I have learned nothing that fails to support it.*
> * *The spirit I witnessed at each exorcism was clearly and utterly and totally dedicated to opposing human life and growth.*
> * *Satan has no power except in a human body.*
> * *The only power that Satan has is through human belief in its lies.*
> * *Satan can use any human sin or weakness, greed and pride for instance. It will use any available tactic, seduction, cajolerie, flattery and intellectual argument. But its principal weapon is fear.*
> * *Possession appears to be a gradual process in which the possessed person sells out repeatedly for one reason or another.*[4]

Reading Dr. Peck's description of the exorcisms of evil spirits reminds one of the fact that Jesus repeatedly cast out evil spirits during his ministry on earth. In one occurrence, that at Gadara or Gerasene, Jesus meets two men possessed of the devil, who obviously caused great fear among the people that lived in their vicinity. When the two meet Jesus, this is what happened:

> *Suddenly they shouted, "What do you want with us Son of God? Have you come to torture us before the time?" Now some distance away a large herd of pigs was feeding and the devils pleaded with Jesus, "If you drive us out, send us into the herd of pigs." And he said to them, "Go then" and they came out and made for the pigs; and at that the whole herd charged down the cliff into the water. The herdsmen ran off and made for the city, where they told the whole story, including what had happened to the demoniacs. Suddenly the whole city set out to meet Jesus, and as soon as they saw him they implored him to leave their neighbourhood.*
>
> *— Matthew 8, The New Jerusalem Bible*

It is clear from these and other accounts that the evil spirits immediately recognized Jesus for what he was, even addressing him as the Son of God. One other point that seems to emerge from these encounters of Jesus with Satan, or with demonic spirits, is the fact that these evil spirits obeyed him without putting up the struggle Dr. Peck records.

In many people's minds Satan is associated with an angel who rebelled against God. In the book of Revelation, which is very difficult to understand because of the many allegories, an account is given of Satan's expulsion from heaven. Whether we should take this account literally is difficult to say:

> *And now war broke out in heaven, when Michael and his angels attacked the dragon. The dragon fought back with his angels, but they were defeated and driven out of heaven. The great dragon, the primeval serpent, known*

> *as the devil or Satan, who had led the world astray, was*
> *hurled down to earth and his angels were hurled with him*
> *... and went away to make war on the rest of the chil-*
> *dren who obey God's commandments and have in them-*
> *selves the witness of Jesus ... but for you earth and sea,*
> *disaster is coming, because the devil has gone down in*
> *a rage, knowing that he has very little time left.*

— *Revelations 12, The New Jerusalem Bible*

It is interesting to note that in the Koran, the holy book of Islam, Satan is described as an angel who disobeyed God's command to pay homage to the newly created human being. As a result of that disobedience this angel was banished from heaven. Thus, in the Koran we encounter the interesting proposition that Satan was banished from heaven because he would not accept human beings as being superior to him.

In summary I believe we can say that:

a) There is an evil spirit in this world which opposes God's plans;

b) This evil spirit can in a real sense invade humankind, individually and collectively;

c) We can think of Satan as the personification of evil in this world;

d) The worst thing we can probably do is to deny or ignore the existence of this evil spirit and thus not be prepared to recognize it when we encounter it;

e) This is especially true in this modern age when many people believe that we have outgrown such simplistic ideas; unfortunately recent history has shown that evil can and does invade the soul of individuals as well as that of entire nations;

f) The best we can do is to live in such a way that evil has no chance to dominate our lives, and at the same time pray to God "to deliver us from evil" as Jesus taught us to do;

g) Satan is probably best visualized as a fallen angel who disobeyed God;

h) The reason God did not destroy the fallen angels immediately after they rebelled is probably the same reason why God did not do this to humans when they rebelled against God. That is, God gave us both the freedom of choice, and when we then made the wrong choice, God would not and could not destroy us because that would have negated the principle of free will God had established at the beginning of creation.

To close this section on the existence of evil, it may be well to remember that, as Thomas Keating put it in his book, *Invitation To Love*: "The devil and his influence can exist and thrive only on our refusal to love and our unwillingness to forgive."[5] So, the influence of evil in this world is not something that we can accept passively: on the contrary, it is something we must fight and neutralize, which can only be done by prayer, and the exercise, on our part, of love, compassion and forgiveness.

The good news for today is that no matter how strong the forces of evil may appear to be at any given time, they have in principle been defeated through the death and resurrection of our Lord Jesus Christ.

5

Jesus — Our Direct Link With God

The Promise Of His Coming

As was pointed out in the previous chapters, God promised Israel very early in its history that God would send them a special messenger, someone like a king or leader. This leader was visualized as someone especially anointed by God, like the kings of Israel who were anointed with oil by the High Priest at their installation as rulers over the country. This special messenger was given the name of the Messiah (the Anointed One), or the Christ in Greek.

So, all through Jewish history, whenever things did not go well for them, the Jews would remind themselves of the better days ahead when the "Anointed of God" would take charge and would lead them to freedom and national greatness. Of course, they did a lot of wishful thinking since the promise they had received did not refer to an earthly kingdom at all but to a heavenly one. It was this misconception that Jesus encountered time and time again all through his ministry and which, in the end, contributed to his death on the cross. For most Jews, it was the disappointment that Jesus was not going to lead them to expel the hated Romans that, in many ways, sealed Jesus' earthly fate. The following quote from the prophet Isaiah makes it very clear, though, that what they should have been expecting was not a conquering king but a suffering servant. The prophet Isaiah wrote some 700 years before Jesus' birth:

> *Who could have believed what we have heard, and to*
> *whom has the power of the Lord been revealed?*
> *He grew up before the Lord like a young plant*
> *whose roots are in parched ground;*
> *he had no beauty, no majesty to draw our eyes,*
> *no grace to delight in him;*
> *his form, disfigured, lost all likeness of a man,*
> *his beauty changed beyond human semblance.*
>
> *He was despised, he shrank from the sight of men,*
> *tormented and humbled by suffering;*
> *we despised him, we held him of no account,*
> *a thing from which men turn away their eyes.*
>
> *Yet on himself he bore our sufferings;*
> *our torments he endured,*
> *while we counted him smitten by God*
> *struck down by disease and misery;*
> *but he was pierced for our transgressions,*
> *tortured for our iniquities;*
> *the chastisement he bore is health for us*
> *and by his scourging we are healed.*
>
> *We all strayed like sheep,*
> *each one of us has gone his own way;*
> *but the Lord laid upon him*
> *the guilt of us all.*
>
> — *Isaiah 53, The New English Bible*

It does not require a great deal of interpretive power to understand that this does not refer to an earthly conquering hero.

It is interesting to note that this expectation of a world leader coming from Israel had spread far beyond the boundaries of the country itself and was common knowledge in the Greek and Roman world of that day. The Roman writer Suetonius wrote in his *Life of Vespasian*: "There spread over all the Orient an old and established belief, that it was fated at that time for men coming from Judea to rule the world."

The Political Situation During Jesus' Life

Before proceeding with the life of Jesus and his teaching, it may be useful to review briefly the political situation which prevailed during his life and at the time of his death.

Some 300 years before Jesus' birth, Alexander the Great established a Greek empire that stretched all the way from Greece in the West to the present day Pakistan and India in the East. In the South his empire included Egypt which he conquered in 334 B.C. In order to reach Egypt with his armies, he had to conquer first the land of Palestine which lay across the land route from Turkey to Egypt (see Fig. No 1) and which at that time was occupied by the Persians. Thus, Palestine briefly became part of the great Greek empire. This was the golden age of Greek culture: literature, architecture, sculpture and philosophy flourished as never before and probably have never done so since. Even before the arrival of Alexander's armies, this Greek civilization had already deeply penetrated the Palestinian way of life.

With the arrival of the new Greek rulers however, all Palestinians were forced to adopt the Greek way of life whether they liked it or not. Especially the forced identification of the Greek god Zeus with the God of Israel was greatly resented. And as happened so often before, the country split into two groups: those who accepted the new way and those who held on to their original beliefs and would have nothing to do with the new culture. The result was a period of great internal

FIGURE NO. 1

The Location of Palestine on the Land Route
From Europe and Asia to Egypt

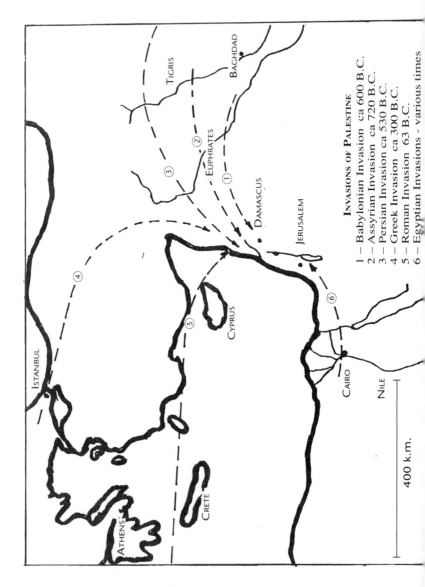

INVASIONS OF PALESTINE

1 — Babylonian Invasion ca 600 B.C.
2 — Assyrian Invasion ca 720 B.C.
3 — Persian Invasion ca 530 B.C.
4 — Greek Invasion ca 300 B.C.
5 — Roman Invasion 63 B.C.
6 — Egyptian Invasions - various times

TIGRIS

BAGHDAD

EUPHRATES

DAMASCUS

JERUSALEM

ISTANBUL

CYPRUS

CAIRO

NILE

CRETE

ATHENS

400 k.m.

instability especially after the Greek empire was divided among competing factions.

Some sort of stability returned when in 64 B.C. the Roman legions finally occupied Palestine. However, this peace and stability was short-lived when the country was overrun in the year 40 B.C. by the Parthians, the archenemies of Rome in the East. On the scene now arrived one of the main players in the Christmas story, Herod the Great. Herod, whose father had been a governor of Galilee, went to Rome and persuaded the Roman emperor to give him the troops to recover the lost territory from the Parthians. When he succeeded he was made king over Judea, but he remained subject to the central authority of Rome.

So this was the political situation at the time of Jesus' *birth* (see also Table No. 1 & Fig. No. 2): The Roman empire was ruled by Caesar Augustus and, under him, Palestine was governed by King Herod the Great. By all accounts Herod was an extremely capable administrator who did much to develop the country's agriculture and trade. However, at the same time, he was insanely suspicious of everyone around him and was unbelievably cruel. For instance, he had several of his sons put to death for fear that they would overthrow him. Similarly, anyone who opposed him was sure to be exterminated. When Herod died in 4 B.C., the Emperor Augustus divided the territory that Herod had ruled into three parts. Emperor Augustus himself died in 12 A.D. and was succeeded by the emperor Tiberius.

At the time of Jesus' *death*, the political situation was as follows (see Table No. 1 & Fig. No. 2): The Roman empire was ruled by Emperor Tiberius. In Palestine, the provinces of Judea and Samaria, which included Jerusalem and Bethlehem, were governed by the Roman Consul Pontius Pilate. The province of Galilee, which included the town of Nazareth where Jesus grew up and where Jesus did most of his teaching, was governed by Herod Antipas, one of Herod's sons who had survived his father's suspicious mind.

TABLE NO. 1

Rulers Over Israel During Jesus' Lifetime

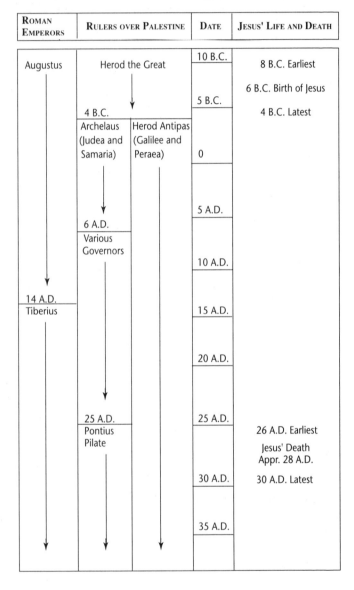

ROMAN EMPERORS	RULERS OVER PALESTINE		DATE	JESUS' LIFE AND DEATH
Augustus	Herod the Great		10 B.C.	8 B.C. Earliest
				6 B.C. Birth of Jesus
		↓	5 B.C.	
	4 B.C.			4 B.C. Latest
	Archelaus (Judea and Samaria)	Herod Antipas (Galilee and Peraea)	0	
			5 A.D.	
	↓			
	6 A.D.			
	Various Governors		10 A.D.	
			15 A.D.	
14 A.D. Tiberius				
			20 A.D.	
			25 A.D.	
	25 A.D. Pontius Pilate			26 A.D. Earliest
				Jesus' Death Appr. 28 A.D.
			30 A.D.	30 A.D. Latest
			35 A.D.	

FIGURE NO. 2

THE DIVISION OF PALESTINE AFTER THE DEATH
OF HEROD THE GREAT

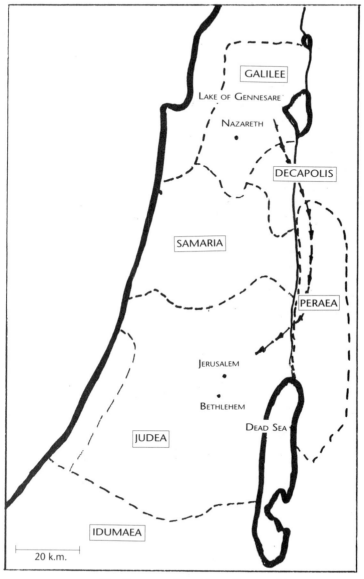

GALILEE

Lake of Gennesare

Nazareth

DECAPOLIS

SAMARIA

PERAEA

JERUSALEM

BETHLEHEM

DEAD SEA

JUDEA

IDUMAEA

20 k.m.

→ → THE ROUTE OF JESUS' LAST JOURNEY FROM
GALILEE TO JERUSALEM

As was mentioned before, Palestine itself was not of any great significance in the scheme of things, but it did happen to lie on the main land route from Greece to Egypt and from Persia to Egypt. This gave it some strategic value, but otherwise it had very little importance. Even today, the State of Israel is only important because of the people who are living there, and because of the threats to their continued existence by their surrounding Arab neighbours. Without that, it would be a country with very little economic or political significance. Certainly the Romans did not think very much of the country. To them Palestine was a place of banishment. For a Roman official to be assigned to Palestine was a sure sign of the emperor's displeasure.

The fact that Jesus' ministry took place during the time of the Roman empire, which lasted for more than 400 years after his death and which covered almost all of what was then known as the civilized world, greatly helped eventually to extend his message across the Roman world. While it is true that the empire was either under attack from outsiders or it was waging war to extend it's territory, the fact remains that the civilized center was safe and under firm control by a central government, something that had not happened before and has not happened since. For one thing, this meant that people could travel safely from one end of the empire to the other. At the same time, the never-ending warfare meant that the Roman legions were continually moving from one end of the empire to the other. This greatly helped to spread the Christian message through the soldiers and the slaves who had become Christians during their stay in Palestine. As a matter of fact, it is difficult to find a time in humankind's ancient history that better suited the rapid dissemination of the Christian message across the world than this mid-period in the life of the Roman Empire.

The Writers Of The Gospels

Jesus did not leave behind him any written text that could have been used by his followers to teach the next generations.

Neither did any of his immediate disciples write down what Jesus had taught them during the years they accompanied him on his travels around Palestine. So, we must depend on later writers, most of whom had not known Jesus personally and who, therefore, had to rely on the teachings of early followers of Jesus and on the personal testimony of those few who were still alive and had met the Christ in person. As could be expected this late recording of Jesus' teaching, by a number of different authors at different times after Jesus' death and resurrection, resulted in the texts not always agreeing about times, places and even names. This has bothered some Christians, especially those who believe in the infallibility of the Bible and who simply cannot accept that there could be mistakes of any type in the "Word of God."

I have often thought to compare the situation with what would happen if I were to record an event now that took place almost 50 years ago, about the same lapse of time between Jesus' death and the writing of the first gospels. The event in question was the airborne landing of Allied forces near Arnhem in Holland in September of 1944. The Allied armies were hundreds of kilometers away when suddenly on a Sunday morning there appeared in the sky the most amazing armada of fighter planes, cargo planes and gliders. When they landed near where I lived, there was instant liberation. Something completely unexpected and something I will never forget. But, if I were to write the story today about what happened during those days, without reference to official records, I am sure I would get some of the facts and the sequences of events wrong. Also, my story would probably differ widely from that of other witnesses who experienced the same events but from a different location and maybe from a different perspective. Worse, if the story were to be told by my children based on what they remember from what I have told them about these events, the story would have many errors about places and circumstances. Despite all that, however, the main facts would come through loud and clear in all versions: The wonderful elation at the sudden liberation and the terrible dejection when the operation did not succeed. The opposite happened to Jesus' disciples as they went from dejection at his death to the elation of his resurrection.

Much the same, I believe, is the case with the discrepancies between the various gospels. It would be an absolute miracle if all the four gospels were in exact agreement about the events and locations, especially considering the fact that some of the gospel writers never knew the places where the main events occurred. Despite these discrepancies, all gospels agree on the essentials of Jesus' teachings and all carry the same basic message.

There are four different accounts of Jesus' life and teachings which were singled out by the early church fathers, around the beginning of the second century, for inclusion in what came to be called ''The New Testament.'' The gospels were written in Greek, the common language at that time, but Jesus himself probably used Aramaic, the language spoken by the people of Palestine.

It is generally agreed that the Gospel according to Mark was written before the others, probably just before the destruction of Jerusalem in 70 A.D. It is thought that Mark was associated with the apostle Peter and, in fact, may have acted as his interpreter and biographer. Modern research also seems to indicate that Mark had the benefit of an earlier document, written by one of Jesus' contemporaries, which contained some of his sayings and teachings. Unfortunately this document has been lost to us.

The next two writers, Matthew and Luke, probably knew the Gospel of Mark and had other sources to draw from as well. Each one has its own special emphasis. The gospel of Matthew seems to have been directed more to the Jewish Christians, while Luke's gospel is more aimed at an audience of gentile Christians and others who wanted to know more about the principal teachings of this new movement. Both were probably written shortly after the destruction of Jerusalem, in other words 40 years after the death of Jesus.

The last gospel, that according to John, was written much later, probably somewhere around the year 90 A.D. It is very different in style from the other gospels; it gives little information about the life of Jesus and his disciples, instead it contains a number of lengthy prayers and discourses by Jesus which are not found in the other gospels. Also, it tends to reinterpret the Christian message for believers who, since this gospel was written some 60 years after Jesus' death, had not experienced or been witness to that first messianic outpouring which occurred immediately after Jesus' resurrection.

The gospels were written with only one thing in mind and that was to convey the essence of Jesus' teaching. The result is that there is very little biographical information about Jesus' early life in these gospels. Mark simply begins his account with these words: "Here begins the gospel of Jesus Christ, the son of God." He then continues with the story of John the Baptist and with the calling of the disciples of Jesus, without giving any details of Jesus' life before that time.

Matthew, on the other hand, starts his account with the sentence, "A table of the descent of Jesus Christ, son of David, son of Abraham." He then gives all the names of Jesus' forefathers, starting with Abraham and ending with Joseph, the husband of Mary, who gave birth to Jesus. Matthew then continues with an account of the birth of Jesus, followed by the baptism of Jesus by John the Baptist which occurred some 30 years later.

Luke, who was a physician, appears to have written his gospel for a Roman official, who may or may not have been a Christian. He starts his narrative as follows:

> *The author to Theophilus. Several biographies of Christ have been written already using as source material the reports circulating among us from the early disciples and other eye witnesses. However, it occurred to me that it would be well to recheck all these accounts from first to last and after thorough investigation to pass this summary*

> *on to you, to reassure you of the truth of all you were*
> *taught.*
>
> — *Luke 1, The New Jerusalem Bible*

After this introduction, Luke gives a detailed description of all the events that led up to the birth of both John the Baptist and Jesus. Luke also includes a list of the forefathers of Jesus, starting with Joseph, "who was thought to be Jesus' father," and tracing back to Adam. Needless to say, the genealogy of Matthew and Luke do not agree at all well. Considering that probably neither had access to detailed records, this is not very surprising. Luke also includes in his gospel the only story we have about Jesus' younger years — the story of Jesus' visit to the temple when he was about 12 years old. After that, Luke proceeds directly with an account of the activities of John the Baptist and Jesus' baptism by him some 18 years later.

The last gospel, that written by John, starts with one of the most memorable and profound passages in the Bible. John writes:

> *In the beginning was the Word:*
> *the Word was with God*
> *and the Word was God.*
> *He was with God in the beginning.*
>
> *Through him all things came into being,*
> *not one thing came into being except through him.*
> *What has come into being in him was life,*
> *life that was the light of men;*
> *and light shines in the darkness,*
> *and darkness could not overpower it.*
>
> *He came to his own*
> *and his own people did not accept him.*
> *But to those who did accept him*
> *he gave power to become children of God.*

The word became flesh,
he lived among us,
and we saw his glory,
the glory he has from the Father as only Son of the
Father, full of grace and truth.

No one has ever seen God,
it is the only Son, who is close to the Father's heart,
who has made him known.

— John 1, The New Jerusalem Bible

After this introduction, John also starts directly with the story of John the Baptist and Jesus' baptism.

Long before these gospels were written, some of the sayings and teachings of Jesus had been put in writing in the letters the apostles had written to the early churches in Asia. The first of these letters were probably written around the years 47 to 50 A.D., in other words 14 to 17 years after Jesus' resurrection.

In closing our story about the gospel writers, it may be well to stress once more that they were not written to record history but to pass on the message that Jesus had taught his disciples during his life on earth. In the words of M. Avi-Yonah and E. G. Kraeling, the writers of *Our Living Bible*:

> *However inadequate the gospels may be as source material for the biographer, they are deeply satisfying to a Christendom that worships Jesus as its Lord and finds this reporting of what he said and did a source of inspiration and instruction in the conduct of life.*[1]

The Forerunner, John The Baptist

As indicated in the previous section, all four gospels start with the ministry of John the Baptist before they begin to record the teachings of Jesus. So, who was this man who obviously had such a great influence on the people of that time, and on Jesus as well, even to the extent that Jesus himself asked to be baptized by him? Luke, who says that he has thoroughly investigated the beginning of the life of Jesus, also relates in considerable detail the story of John the Baptist's birth. According to Luke, John's parents had been unable to have children and Elizabeth, John's mother, was well beyond her normal child-bearing years when an angel from the Lord visited John's father, Zechariah, announcing the future birth of a son whom they were to call John. Zechariah, who was a priest, was actually serving in the temple at the time of this announcement. But he found it difficult to believe the angel when he was told:

> *Do not be afraid; your prayers have been heard; your wife will bear a son, and you shall name him John. Your heart will thrill with joy and many will be glad that he was born; for he will be great in the eyes of the Lord. He shall never touch wine or strong drink. From his very birth he will bring back many Israelites to the Lord their God. He will go before him as a forerunner, possessed by the spirit and the power of Elijah, to reconcile father and child, to convert the rebellious to the ways of the righteous, to prepare a people that shall be fit for the Lord.*
>
> *— Luke 1, The New English Bible*

As can be seen, this announcement includes the description of the mission John had to fulfill, that is to prepare the people for the arrival of the Messiah. Luke also refers later to a prophesy of Isaiah concerning this forerunner:

> *A voice crying aloud in the wilderness,*
> *Prepare a way for the Lord;*
> *clear a straight path for him.*
>
> *— Luke 3, The New English Bible*

John, when he was in his late twenties or early thirties, disappeared in the wilderness where he lived on honey and wild fruits and dressed in animal skins. He began his mission by calling people to repentance, for as he said, "The Kingdom of God is at hand." John certainly did not mince words. For instance, he told the Jews who set great store by the fact that they were direct descendants from Abraham, "Bring forth fruits worthy of repentance and don't begin to say to yourself, we have Abraham for a father, for I say onto you that God is able to raise up children for Abraham from these stones." (Luke 3)

His message must have hit home, because many of his hearers began to ask him what they should be doing and John told them to repent and mend their ways. If they did, he would then baptize them in the River Jordan, indicating by this act that the sins of their old life were washed away and that a new life was beginning. He obviously made a great impression on the Jews, to the extent that people began to wonder whether he was the long expected Messiah. But when asked outright, he answered, "I baptize you with water, the one that comes after me shall baptize you with the Holy Spirit and with fire." And indeed Jesus started his ministry after he himself was baptized by John.

During his ministry, John had attracted a group of followers, or disciples, around him, but after Jesus' baptism he told them to follow Jesus instead, and most apparently did. John himself must have continued his ministry after that because he continued to speak his mind about things that were wrong with Israel and its rulers. This naturally brought him into direct conflict with Herod Antipas, the ruler of Galilee and one of the few surviving sons of Herod the Great. This Herod was, if anything, even more paranoid than his father and when John started to rebuke him publicly about his personal life, he threw him in jail.

We next encounter John in Chapter 11 of Matthew. John had obviously become despondent in his prison cell and sent a messenger to Jesus to ask him, "Are you the one who is to come or do we expect another?" Jesus answered by saying to the messenger, "Go and tell John what you hear and see," referring to the many miracles Jesus was performing and to the large crowds that were following him.

The last time we encounter John is in Matthew 14. There in the middle of the gospel we run into a vignette, that has very little to do with Jesus' message, but because it has been the subject of countless paintings and writings, it is repeated here in full:

> *Now Herod had arrested John, put him in chains, and had thrown him into prison, on account of Herodias, his brother Philip's wife; for John had told him, "You have no right to her." Herod would have liked to put him to death, but he was afraid of the people, in whose eyes John was a prophet. But at his birthday celebrations, the daughter of Herodias danced before the guests, and Herod was so delighted that he took an oath to give her anything she cared to ask. Prompted by her mother, she said, "Give me here on a dish the head of John the Baptist." The king was distressed when he heard this; but out of regard for his guests and his oath, he ordered the request be granted, and had John beheaded in prison. The head was then brought on a dish and given to the girl; and she carried it to her mother. Then John's disciples came and took away the body, and buried it and they went and told Jesus.*
>
> — *Matthew 14, The New English Bible*

Later when Herod heard about Jesus' teaching he said, "This John the Baptist has been raised to life, and that is why these miraculous powers are at work in him." (Matthew 14)

Thus disappeared from the world scene one of the more interesting and in some ways, eccentric, prophets. One of whom Jesus said, "I tell you this; never has there appeared on earth a mother's son greater than John the Baptist," but then he adds, "and yet the least in the Kingdom of Heaven is greater than he." (Luke 7)

For us, today, it is encouraging to read that this John the Baptist who, according to Jesus, was the greatest of all men,

112

had such doubts about the person of Jesus occasionally that he sent messengers to Jesus asking him, "Are you the one we are expecting or are we to wait for another?" So, if you and I, who have never met Jesus personally sometimes have questions about the person of Jesus, we find ourselves in very good company.

In closing this account of the life of John the Baptist, it is interesting to note that in answer to the question of John, Jesus does not point to the message he is delivering but to the things he is doing and the effect his message is having on the people who are hearing it. In many ways, this is good advice for us today as well. If asked, "Who is this Jesus?" our most effective answer may well be to point to the effect Jesus' message has on the people who accept him as their Lord and Saviour.

The Birth Of Jesus

Every year around the time of the winter solstice, or the shortest day in the northern hemisphere, a large part of the world celebrates the birth of Christ on Christmas Day. Whether we are professing Christians or not, Christmas is not just passed over as any other day of the year — there is something special about this day. No doubt this has something to do with advertising campaigns in newspapers and on television, or with the familiar carols we hear everywhere. Nevertheless Christmas is a special day for almost everyone. For some, Christmas is the day we give gifts to close relatives or friends — the family day when people travel from all over to meet at least once a year for a family dinner. For others, Christmas has a deeply religious meaning: for them it is the day they celebrate the birth of the Christ child, the Son of God, the Saviour of the world.

This celebration of Christmas does not seem to be the least bit influenced by the fact that fewer people declare themselves

113

to be Christians today than before. On the contrary, it would appear that more people, not only in the West but also in the East, set this day apart as a time to reflect on the Christian message proclaimed by the angels at Christ's birth, ''Peace on earth and goodwill to all men'' — a time to express the eternal hope for a brighter future.

In recent years, there has been a movement by official government institutions, including the schools, to take the person of Christ out of Christmas and rename Christmas, the Festival of Light. This is apparently done so that non-Christians are not exposed to the Christian message, the message of peace and hope. It is hard to imagine that this message could possibly upset anyone, but that seems to be the case. If they succeed in doing so, the world will be the poorer. From a Christian point of view, however, the hoopla surrounding Christmas has in many ways obscured the message and so the removal of Christ's name from this annual buying spree may not be a bad thing.

As was pointed out before, the evangelists who wrote the first gospels did not particularly concern themselves with the birth of Christ. They were more interested in telling about his death and about the good news of his resurrection. Later, of course, people wanted to know more about his birth and childhood, and so the later writers included in their accounts some of the information they had gathered from the contemporaries of Jesus. Both Matthew and Luke relate how Mary, the mother of Jesus, was visited by an angel to announce the birth of Jesus. Since the story as written by Luke has become a part of our Western literature, the story is repeated here verbatim from the familiar old King James translation:

> *In the sixth month the angel Gabriel was sent from God unto a city of Galilee, named Nazareth: To a virgin espoused to a man whose name was Joseph, of the house of David; and the virgin's name was Mary. And the angel came in unto her, and said, "Hail, thou art highly favoured, the Lord is with thee; blessed art thou among*

114

women." And when she saw him, she was troubled at his saying, and cast in her mind what manner of salutation this should be. And the angel said unto her, "Fear not, Mary: for thou hast found favour with God. And behold, thou shalt conceive in thy womb, and bring forth a son, and shalt call his name Jesus. He shall be great, and the Lord God shall give unto him the throne of his father David. And he shall reign over the house of Jacob for ever; and of his kingdom there shall be no end." Then said Mary unto the angel, "How shall this be, seeing I know not a man?" And the angel answered and said unto her, "The Holy Ghost shall come upon thee, and the power of the Highest shall overpower thee; therefore also that holy thing which shall be born of thee shall be called the Son of God. And behold, thy cousin Elisabeth, she has also conceived a son in her old age: and this is the sixth month with her, who was called barren. For with God nothing shall be impossible." And Mary said, "Behold the handmaid of the Lord; be it unto me according to thy word."

— Luke 1, The King James Bible

Matthew in his account of the birth of Jesus, also mentions that the angel told Mary that the child would be conceived by the Holy Spirit. Naturally, over the centuries, people have wondered what this meant. As some observers have pointed out, the above passage refers to Jesus' descendancy from King David, which comes through his father, Joseph. Furthermore the inclusion, in both Matthew and Luke, of the long list of forefathers of Joseph does not make much sense if Joseph himself was not somehow involved in Jesus' conception. Today, it does not seem to be very important to us whether Joseph contributed his chromosomes, or whether they were only Mary's, for all the world to see Joseph was the actual father and Mary was his mother. In any case, what is clear is that a human being was used as the vehicle for the birth of the Christ child and that the Son of God entered this world in the form

115

of a human baby. The meaning of this term 'Son of God' has been subject to much debate. Its meaning will be discussed at some length in chapter 8.

According to the apostle Luke, the birth of Jesus happened as follows (again using the familiar King James translation):

And it came to pass in those days, that there went out a decree from Caesar Augustus, that all the world should be taxed. And this taxing was first made when Cyrenius was governor of Syria. And all went up to be taxed, everyone into his own city.

And Joseph also went up from Galilee, out of the city of Nazareth, into Judea, unto the city of David, which is called Bethlehem; (because he was of the house and lineage of David:) To be taxed with Mary his espoused wife, being great with child.

And so it was, that, while they were there, the days were accomplished that she should be delivered. And she brought forth her firstborn son, and wrapped him in swaddling clothes, and laid him in a manger; because there was no room for them in the inn.

And there were in the same country shepherds abiding in the field, keeping watch over their flock by night. And, lo, the angel of the Lord came upon them, and they were sore afraid. And the angel said unto them, "Fear not: for behold, I bring you good tidings of great joy, which shall be to all people. For unto you is born this day in the city of David a Saviour, which is Christ the Lord. And this shall be a sign unto you; You shall find the babe wrapped in swaddling clothes, lying in a manger." And suddenly there was with the angel a multitude of the heavenly host praising God and saying, "Glory to God in the highest, and on earth peace, good will towards men."

And it came to pass, as the angels were gone away from them into heaven, the shepherds said one to another, "Let us now go, even unto Bethlehem, and see this thing which

> *is come to pass, which the Lord has made known unto*
> *us." And they came with haste, and found Mary, and*
> *Joseph, and the babe lying in a manger.*

> *— Luke 2, The King James Bible*

Luke does not include the appearance of the three magi, or wise men, in his account of the circumstances surrounding the birth of Jesus. However, this is so much part of the total Christmas story that a brief description is included below:

> *After his birth astrologers from the East arrived in Jerusalem, asking, "Where is the child who is born to be king of the Jews? We observed the rising of his star and we have come to pay him homage."*

> *— Matthew 2, The New English Bible*

As the story continues, we learn that King Herod was greatly perturbed by this news, and he went to the representatives of the official religious body at that time and asked them, "Where is it that the Messiah is to be born?" The officials looked up the books of the prophets and told him that according to the prophet Isaiah the place would be Bethlehem. So the Magi went to Bethlehem where they did find Jesus as predicted and presented his parents with gifts of gold, frankincense and myrrh.

So far, this story throws a nice sidelight on the story of Jesus' birth and reinforces the impression that at that time there was a general expectation that a mighty ruler would come out of Judea. But here the niceties end. King Herod, who had not stopped at killing his own sons for fear that they might overthrow him and take his place on the throne, was of course more than anxious to find and get rid of this possible, new pretender for his throne. So, not knowing how to find the Christ child, he gave orders that all children under two years of age in Bethlehem and the surrounding countryside should be killed.

Matthew relates that an angel warned Joseph in a dream to take Mary and Jesus away from under the jurisdiction of Herod and to flee to Egypt. The young family remained there until the death of Herod in the year 4 A.D. Even then Joseph was afraid of what might happen to them in Judea, and so he took his family back to Nazareth in Galilee where they had originally come from. It was here in Galilee that Jesus grew up. It is reported that his father, Joseph, was a carpenter by trade; it is therefore very likely that Jesus, as the oldest son, was trained by his father to follow in his footsteps and become a carpenter as well.

It does appear that Joseph and Mary had several other children: at least reference is made in several places in the gospels to the brothers and sisters of Jesus. Also, although not explicitly stated anywhere in the gospels, it would appear that Joseph died sometime before the beginning of Jesus' ministry and thus we can expect that Jesus, for some period of time, must have been the head of the household and the principal breadwinner of a fairly extensive family.

Jesus' Ministry

1. His Baptism

The four gospels all start their accounts of Jesus' ministry with his appearance at the river Jordan where John the Baptist was preaching and baptizing people. At that time, both John and Jesus must have been in their early thirties. So there is a period of about thirty years during which both must have led normal lives. Both must have received the customary religious training in their homes and in the Synagogue. They certainly would have been familiar with the history of the Jewish people and with the expectations about the Messiah. However, there is not the slightest indication in any of the gospels that they received any special training or that they stood out from their fellow men. On the contrary, when Jesus began his teaching the people around him were astonished to hear him speak so knowingly; as they expressed it, "Is not this the son of Joseph and Mary, and are not his brothers and sisters with us here today?"

All four gospels relate what happened when Jesus and John met at the river Jordan. The accounts differ somewhat in detail but the essential message is the same. It may safely be assumed that Jesus and John knew each other well since they were related on their mothers' side. It is also more than likely that the parents of both Jesus and John had told them about the extraordinary events which occurred just before and at their births. It is, however, also fairly clear that neither Jesus nor John were, up to the point when they met at the Jordan, fully aware of their respective identities and destinies.

By the time Jesus came to see John at the river Jordan, John must have been preaching for some time because he had already attracted a considerable following. It is at his baptism by John that, as far as we know, Jesus became for the first time fully aware of his special status and of the mission he had to carry out.

The account of Matthew of this event runs as follows:

> *Then Jesus arrived at the Jordan from Galilee, and came to John to be baptized by him. And John tried to dissuade him. "Do you come to me?" he said; "I need to be baptized by you." Jesus replied, "Let it be so for the present; we do well to conform in this way with all that God requires." John then allowed him to come. After baptism, Jesus came up out of the water at once, and at that moment heaven opened: he saw the Spirit of God descending like a dove to alight upon him; and a voice from heaven was heard saying, "This is my Son, my Beloved, on whom my favour rests."*
>
> *— Matthew 3, The New English Bible*

The words, "Thou art my beloved son," are identical to the words used by the Psalmist in Psalm 2 where it is written, "You

119

are my son, this day I became your father.'' Apparently, the Jews had always considered this passage as referring to the expected Messiah. Thus, the people who heard these words could not help but connect the two in their minds, thereby reinforcing the impact of the message they were receiving. In the gospel of John, the writer adds, ''I saw it myself and I have born witness. This is God's Chosen One.''

At this point in time, one can only speculate what actually happened to Jesus at that moment. Had he been aware of his special status before this happened? It seems that the people around him did not see anything special in him, that is, until he started his ministry. Or, did the awareness that he was in fact the Messiah dawn slowly on him while he was growing up and worked in his father's carpentry shop? In any case it is clear from all the accounts that he was not fully aware of his mission and status until that moment at the river Jordan, after he was baptized by John and the Spirit descended on him and he heard himself be called, ''My Son, my beloved.''

2. The Temptations In The Wilderness

Immediately after this high point in Jesus' life, the proclamation that he was the long awaited Messiah, the gospel of Matthew tells us that Jesus was led away by the Spirit into the wilderness. For forty days and nights he fasted there. What went on during those forty days we do not know, but we can speculate. First of all, it must have been a time of getting used to the new identity and the changed situation in which he found himself. If Jesus up to then had not been fully aware of his status and mission, the announcement after his baptism by John must have come as a great surprise. As said before, it can reasonably be assumed that Mary must have told Jesus something about the extraordinary happenings before and after his birth, but the full impact of what he was told by his mother must have descended in full force on him for the first time when he was publicly proclaimed to be God's son.

Also, this time of solitude in the wilderness must have been a time of close communication with God, who from then on he called "Father." No doubt, this was also a time of preparation for the mission he was to fulfill. So, the time in the desert, alone with his new found identity and the realization of what lay ahead of him, was probably a very necessary prelude to the beginning of his ministry.

Matthew relates how at the end of this period Jesus was tempted by the devil. According to the fourth chapter of Matthew, he was subjected to three specific temptations which Jesus must have related to his disciples sometime later. These temptations are all very human ones and all try to make Jesus misuse the new powers that were bestowed on him as the Son of God. It is as if the devil is saying to Jesus, "You think that you are the Son of God; let's see what you are able to do if this is true." So, the devil starts with his taunts, "If you are, who you think you are, you should be able to do this or that."

The first temptation came when Jesus was hungry after his long fast. "If you are God's son, tell these stones to become bread." The second temptation, if Jesus had given in to it, could have been very useful in establishing his new identity. "If you are God's son, throw yourself from the top of the temple, for it is written that angels will come down to help you so that no injury will befall you." The third one was even more devious. The devil showed him all the kingdoms of this world and said to him, "All these I will give you, if you kneel before me and pay me homage." Presumably the devil meant that he would withdraw evil from these kingdoms if Jesus would just acknowledge him as his superior. For the short term, this would not appear to be such a bad deal, but in the long run it would have led to utter disaster with the devil in charge.

These temptations are very much the type of temptations that you and I might encounter ourselves in our own lives. For instance, at some time in our lives most of us will have been tempted to take shortcuts to gain some material objective; or to show off to impress people with our power or capabilities;

or to make, as it were, a pact with the devil to obtain our goals and objectives the easy way without regard for others. Jesus overcame all these temptations, just as we should overcome ours by referring to the rules God gave us to live by.

3. The Disciples Of Jesus

Early in his ministry, Jesus assembled around him a group of twelve disciples who travelled with him wherever he went. Most of the people he attracted were ordinary working people with nothing to distinguish them from the people around them. The first ones he called were fishermen who lived around the Sea of Galilee. Matthew recounts how they received Jesus' call:

> *Jesus was walking by the Sea of Galilee when he saw two brothers, Simon called Peter and his brother Andrew, casting a net in the sea for they were fishermen. Jesus said, "Come with me, and I will make you fishers of men," and at once they left their nets and followed him. He went on, and saw another pair of brothers, James son of Zebedee and his brother John; they were in the boat with their father Zebedee, overhauling their nets. He called them, and at once they left the boat and their father, and followed him.*
>
> *— Matthew 4, The New English Bible*

Obviously, these people did not leave everything dear to them just because some unknown person called them. It can safely be assumed that they had known Jesus before or at least had heard him speak.

Jesus did not call all the disciples directly himself as is shown in the following passage in John:

> *Philip, one of the disciples Jesus had called before, went to find Nathaniel, and told him, "We have met the man spoken of by Moses in the Law, and by the prophets:*

*It is Jesus son of Joseph from Nazareth!" "Nazareth!"
exclaimed Nathaniel; "Can anything good come from
Nazareth?" Philip said, "Come and see." When Jesus
saw Nathaniel coming, he said, "Here is an Israelite worthy of the name; there is nothing false in him." Nathaniel
asked him, "How do you come to know me?" Jesus replied, "I saw you under the fig tree before Philip spoke
to you." "Rabbi," said Nathaniel, "you are the son of
God; you are the king of Israel." Jesus answered, "Is
this the ground of your faith, that I told you I saw you
under the fig tree? You shall see greater things than that."
Then he added, "In truth, in very truth I tell you all, you
shall see heaven wide open, and God's angels ascending
and descending upon the Son of Man."*

— John 1, The New English Bible

These two stories are of special significance and interest
for us today, in that they show that right from the beginning
there were two entirely different ways by which people came
to Jesus: Either they did so by direct contact with the living
Christ, or they got to know him through the testimony of one
of his followers. In the latter case, this story includes the most
common reaction of most people when they first hear about
Christ, "Who is he?" Today, the same question is still asked
but with the additional question, "Can a person who lived two
thousand years ago possibly have any relevance to my life
today?"

Most of these disciples are very much unknown quantities.
The only thing we know about most of them is their name and
very little else. By all accounts they were, what someone has
called, a motley crew. Some of them were fishermen like John
and Peter; one was a much hated tax collector for his Roman
masters; another one was a Zealot, a member of an extreme
nationalistic and revolutionary party. In addition, it included
Judas Iscariot who betrayed Jesus for thirty pieces of silver
and who also pilfered from the common purse. Another, Peter,
was a hothead who exploded at the slightest provocation and

who later, during Jesus' trial, denied knowing him. Yet another one, Thomas, would not believe in Jesus' resurrection until he had physically touched Jesus. The original doubting Thomas!

As far as we know, not one of these had any special religious training or any special gifts that would have prepared him for the task ahead. Yet it was this unlikely-to-succeed group whom Jesus selected to receive his message in the first place, and to spread that message first in Israel and later across the whole world. For instance, Peter who had denied Christ had no special training other than as a fisherman, yet he ended up eventually preaching the message of Christ in Rome, one of the most sophisticated cities of the world at that time. Legend has it that he was crucified himself there under the cruel and ruthless emperor Nero.

Since, at that point in time, it would have been unthinkable to have women teach in public, the group of twelve disciples was entirely made up of men. This is not to say that women did not play a vital role in Jesus' ministry. On the contrary, it would appear that a group of women did travel with Jesus from the very beginning of his ministry, and that they did more than just look after the household chores. There is a beautiful vignette in Matthew about two sisters, Mary and Martha. Jesus and probably some of his disciples were staying at their house and, while Mary was listening to Jesus' teaching, Martha was busy in the kitchen trying to cope with all the extra work. In frustration, she asked Jesus to tell her sister to help her prepare the meal. Jesus however rebuked her and said to her, "Martha, Martha, you are fretting and fussing about so many things, but one thing is necessary. The part that Mary has chosen is best, and it shall not be taken from her." (Luke 10) In other words, Jesus encouraged the female members of his group to listen to his message just like his male disciples, and not get caught up in household chores at the expense of hearing him teach.

There is some historical evidence to suggest that Jesus may have spoken in private to some of his female followers about his mission. In particular, Mary Magdalene, whom Jesus had cured from a mental illness, seems to have been particularly close to him.

In a very fragmentary manuscript called, The Gospel of Mary, which probably dates from the first or second century, there are some revealing passages about the role Mary may have played in the early church.

The first passage quoted below shows that Mary took a leading role in the assembly of the disciples when, immediately after Jesus' ascension, the disciples felt dejected and unsure of themselves:

> *Then Mary stood up. She greeted them all and addressed her brothers: "Do not weep and be distressed nor let your hearts be irresolute. For his grace will be with you all and will shelter you. Rather let us praise his greatness, for he joined us together and made us true human beings."*
>
> *— Mary 5, The Complete Gospels*

Later the apostle Peter asks Mary:

> *Sister, we know that the Saviour loved you more than any other woman. Tell us the words of the Saviour that you know, but which we haven't heard.*
>
> *— Mary 6, The Complete Gospels*

In the concluding passages, the disciples try to discredit Mary, but one man, named Levi, stands up and rebukes the disciples with these words:

> *If the Saviour considered her to be worthy, who are you to disregard her? For he knew her completely and loved her devoutly.*
>
> *— Mary 10, The Complete Gospels*

How much credence we should give to this Gospel of Mary is difficult to say. However, it is clear from this and other evidence that from the beginning the female followers of Jesus took a very active part in the proclamation of the gospel and in the early life of the church.

When Jesus' disciples had been with him long enough to absorb some of the message he was proclaiming, he sent them out on their own to the countryside to spread the Good News and he gave them these marching orders:

> *As you go, proclaim the message, "The Kingdom of Heaven is close at hand." Cure the sick, raise the dead, cleanse the lepers, drive out devils. You receive without charge, give without charge. Provide yourselves with no gold or silver, not even with coppers for your purses, no haversack for the journey or spare tunic or footwear or a staff, for the labourer deserves his keep ... Look, I am sending you out like sheep among wolves; so be cunning as snakes and yet innocent as doves ... Anyone who welcomes you welcomes me; and anyone who welcomes me welcomes the one who sent me.*
>
> *— Matthew 10, The New Jerusalem Bible*

Luke in his gospel refers to 72 disciples who were sent out. It is possible that this pertains to the same mission, or it may be that Jesus did send out a second mission after the successful return of the first one. In any case, Luke reports that they returned jubilant and told Jesus, "In your name, Lord, even the devils submit to us." (Luke 10)

An interesting aspect of these missions on which Jesus sent his disciples is that they were sent out at a time when they apparently were still very ill-prepared to go and proclaim that message. Not only that, they were even ill-prepared to deal with the success of these missions.

When Jesus sent his disciples out on their own, they became, in effect, his accredited representatives; they acted for him and proclaimed his message across the country. It is for this reason that the disciples were called apostles (people sent forth) by the early church. It was this group of apostles,

126

together with the other companions of Jesus who, after his resurrection, changed the course of history. The importance of this change in direction is recognized in the West by the fact that we divide the history of the world into two parts — that which occurred before Christ's birth, we identify by placing the letters B.C. (before Christ) behind the date; while that which happened after his birth, we identify by placing the letters A.D. (Anno Domini, the year of the Lord) behind the date.

We know very little about what eventually happened to the disciples. In the book, Acts of the Apostles, we get some glimpses of the activities of Peter, John and Philip, but that is all. It is clear that they all proclaimed Jesus' message and, as a consequence, all must have been persecuted for their faith and some, if not all, probably died for their faith at the hands of the Roman authorities who would not tolerate people who had an allegiance to a higher power than the Roman Emperor.

4. The Sermon On The Mount

No account of the life of Jesus can be complete without mentioning that most famous of his teaching, "The Sermon on the Mount." Both Luke and Matthew include a section which can generally be considered as falling under this heading. The account of Matthew is much longer than that of Luke, although many of the things not mentioned by Luke under that heading appear elsewhere in Luke's gospel. It is clear from this, and other considerations, that the Sermon on the Mount is in actual fact a compendium of all the things Jesus taught his disciples before he sent them out on their own on their first mission. Some have called the Sermon on the Mount, "The Manifesto of the King," since it contains in summary form the entire message of Jesus.

The introductory sentence in Matthew reads as follows: "When he saw the crowds he went up the hill. There he took his seat and when his disciples had gathered around him, he began to address them." (Matthew 5) According to William Barclay in *The Daily Study Bible* the fact that Jesus sat down to do his teaching was an indication that he was going to say something that was central and official. Apparently, a Jewish Rabbi (teacher) would give general instruction to his students and followers while he was walking about or standing. However, when he sat down to teach, he was speaking in an official way. Barclay refers to the fact that we still speak of a professor's chair, and that when the Pope makes an official pronouncement he speaks ex-cathedra (from the chair).[2] In any case, it is clear that the Sermon on the Mount was meant to be a summary of Jesus' teaching, to be used by his disciples on their mission to spread his message among the people of Galilee.

The Sermon on the Mount starts with one of the best known passages in the Bible, The Beatitudes. According to Barclay, the beginning of each Beatitude which is most often translated as "How blest are those who ...," may be better understood if it were translated to read: "O the bliss of those who ..." Others have suggested that it may be better translated in modern English by: "Congratulations to those ..." The Beatitudes in Matthew read as follows:

> *How blest are those who know their need of God;*
>   *the kingdom of Heaven is theirs.*
> *How blest are the sorrowful;*
>   *they shall find consolation.*
> *How blest are those of gentle spirit;*
>   *they have the earth for their possession.*
> *How blest are those who hunger and thirst to see right*
>   *prevail;*
>   *they shall be satisfied.*
> *How blest are those who show mercy;*
>   *mercy shall be shown to them.*
> *How blest are those whose heart is pure;*
>   *they shall see God.*
> *How blest are the peacemakers;*
>   *God shall call them his sons.*

How blest are those who have suffered persecution for
the cause of right;
the kingdom of Heaven is theirs.

— *Matthew 5, The New English Bible*

Although, we can readily accept most of these beatitudes, there are some that go pretty much against our understanding of what it is to be called blessed. For a more detailed analysis of what is meant by these sayings, I refer the reader to Barclay's *The Daily Study Bible.*

Immediately after the Beatitudes, Matthew follows with a number of sayings about the importance of the disciple's mission and about the message they must bring to the people:

You are salt to the world. And if salt becomes tasteless, how is its saltness to be restored? It is now good for nothing but to be thrown out and trodden under foot.

You are light for all the world. A town that stands on a hill cannot be hidden. When a lamp is lit, it is not put under a meal-tub but on the lampstand, where it gives light to everyone in the house. And you, like a lamp, must shed light among your fellows, so that, when they see the good you do, they may give praise to your Father in heaven.

— *Matthew 5, The New English Bible*

Luke follows the beatitudes with the instruction to love your enemies and pass no judgement:

•*Love your enemies.*
•*Do good to those who hate you.*
•*Bless those who curse you.*
•*Pray for those who treat you spitefully.*
•*When a man hits you on the cheek, offer him the other cheek too.*
•*When a man takes your coat, let him have your shirt as well.*
•*Give to everyone who asks you.*
•*When a man takes what is yours, do not demand it back.*

> •*Treat others as you would like them to treat you.*
> •*If you love only those who love you, what credit is that to you? Even sinners love those who love them.*
> •*Again, if you do good only to those who do good to you, what credit is that to you? Even sinners do as much.*
> •*If you lend only where you expect to be repaid, what credit is that to you? Even sinners lend to each other to be repaid in full.*
> •*But you must love your enemies and do good; and lend without expecting any return; and you will have a rich reward; you will be sons of the Most High, because he himself is kind to the ungrateful and wicked.*
> •*Be compassionate as your Father is compassionate.*
> •*Pass no judgement, and you will not be judged.*
> •*Do not condemn and you will not be condemned.*
> •*Give and gifts will be given to you.*
>
> — *Luke 6, The New English Bible*

Both Luke and Matthew end the Sermon on the Mount with the parable in which Jesus compares the listening to and acting upon his word to the laying of a foundation for a house.

> *Everyone who comes to me and hears what I say, and acts upon it, I will show you what he is like. He is like a man who in building his house, dug deep and laid the foundation on rock. When the flood came, the river burst upon that house, but could not shift it, because it had been soundly built. But he who hears and does not act is like a man who built his house on the soil, without foundations. As soon as the river burst upon it, the house collapsed, and fell with a great crash.*
>
> — *Luke 6, The New English Bible*

So, the Sermon on the Mount ends with some good engineering advice, advice that has proved to be very sound through the ages for the construction of both our material and our spiritual homes.

5. The Kingdom Of God

All the gospels repeatedly refer to a kingdom which is variously described as "The Kingdom of God" or "The Kingdom of Heaven." John the Baptist told the people who had come to hear him speak, "Repent, the Kingdom of God is at hand." It is clear that his audience understood what he meant by that. To them he was obviously referring to the kingdom God had promised them from the time of David and the prophets. The listeners to Jesus and John thought of that kingdom as an earthly kingdom, which would be established by the Messiah after the Roman legions had been defeated and thrown out of the country. However, when Jesus uses the term he refers to the fact that the kingdom was already there among them. So in some mysterious way, Jesus was not only the herald and the proclaimer of the kingdom, but in a real sense he also was the personification of the kingdom.

It was not only the Jews who misinterpreted the meaning of the phrase. Later, certain movements within Christianity tried to give it a more concrete form by thinking of it as an utopia, or as a social order for which the world should be striving. It is clear, however, from Jesus' words that that is entirely missing the point. Just as the kingdom was with the Jews at the time of Jesus' sojourn on earth, so the kingdom is with us today in the form of God's presence that surrounds us through the Holy Spirit.

As will be shown in the next section, Jesus used a set of parables to describe what the kingdom is like. From these it is clear that the coming of the kingdom depends on a person's response to his call, and that it should be a person's highest goal to attain it. Nowhere does Jesus intimate that it is easy to enter into the kingdom or to attain it. On the contrary, Jesus warns his would-be followers that, "If any man would come after me, let him deny himself and take up his cross and follow me." (Matthew 16)

6. The Parables

As I have said before it is difficult, if not impossible, to describe God in human terms which we can understand. God is simply too different, and operates and exists in a different dimension in which we cannot enter at present. This difficulty is probably one of the reasons that Jesus in his teaching makes such extensive use of parables. A parable is essentially a comparison with a situation people encounter in their daily lives. The way Jesus uses the parables, they usually convey only one point — the stories have only one punch line. It is important to note that they are not allegories where almost every word has a special meaning, nor should these stories be read as commentary on the then existing practices, customs and social conditions.

In his parables, Jesus uses the most common and simple everyday activities such as women making bread, or patching garments; farmers seeding and harvesting grain; shepherds looking for lost sheep, and so forth. In some cases, he uses more elaborate stories which throw some light on the existing habits and customs of that time, such as the hiring and paying of labourers for work in a vineyard. It is the remarkable freshness of these stories, and the way they speak to us today, which gives these parables their effectiveness in conveying the message Jesus tried to bring to his listeners. For us today, the great value of these parables is that they are easy to remember and are not likely to have lost the essence of the message in the retelling. Considering that no one seems to have been writing down what Jesus was saying and teaching, this method of conveying a message is probably the most accurate and the least likely to lead to distortions or misinterpretations in repeated retellings.

The parables are generally divided into three groups: the first group is used by Jesus to describe what the kingdom of God is like. The second group is more intended to warn the disciples and Jesus' followers to be wakeful, to be diligent and faithful in the tasks they undertake. The parables in the third group are intended to give examples on how we should conduct ourselves; how we should love our neighbour; and how we should forgive those we think have wronged us. A number of examples of parables in the first group follow below:

> *The kingdom of Heaven is like a mustard seed, which a man took and sowed in his field. As a seed, mustard is smaller than any other; but when it has grown it is bigger than any garden-plant; it becomes a tree, big enough for the birds to come and roost among its branches.*
>
> *The kingdom of Heaven is like yeast; which a woman took and mixed with half a hundredweight of flour till it was all leavened.*
>
> *Here is another picture of the kingdom of Heaven. A merchant looking for fine pearls found one of very special value; so he went and sold everything he had and bought it.*
>
> *— Matthew 13, The New English Bible*

Two examples of the second set of parables follow below. In the first one, Jesus urges us to go the second mile and not to give up if our objectives are not met immediately. In the second one, Jesus tells us, in a rather amusing way, how we should be careful in judging others:

> *A man had a fig tree growing in his vineyard; and he came looking for fruit on it, but found none. So he said to the vine dresser, "Look here, for the last three years I have come looking for fruit on this fig tree without finding any. Cut it down. Why should it go on using soil?" But he replied, "Leave it sir, this one year while I dig around it. And if it bears next season well and good; if not, you shall have it."*
>
> *— Luke 13, The New Jerusalem Bible*
>
> *Why do you observe the splinter in your brother's eye and never notice the great big log in your own? How can you say to your brother, "Brother, let me take out the splinter in your eye," when you cannot see the great log*

*in your own? Hypocrite! Take the log out of your own
eye first and then you will see clearly enough to take out
the splinter in your brother's eye.*

— *Luke 6, The New Jerusalem Bible*

An example of the third group of parables is found in what is generally called, "The Parable of the Good Samaritan." For it to be understood properly, it must be remembered that generally the Jews did not consider the Samaritans as real Jews and they would have nothing to do with them. A person asked Jesus, "Who is my neighbour?" in the context of the great commandment to love God and your neighbour as yourself. Jesus then told the following parable:

*A man was on his way from Jerusalem down to Jericho
when he fell among robbers who stripped him, beat him,
and went off leaving him half dead. It so happened that
a priest was going down by the same road; but when he
saw him, he went past on the other side. So too a Levite
(a person who did temple duty) came to the place, and
when he saw him went past on the other side. But a
Samaritan who was making the journey came upon him,
and when he saw him was moved to pity. He went up
and bandaged his wounds, bathing him in oil and wine.
Then he lifted him on his own beast, brought him to an
inn, and looked after him there. The next day he
produced two silver pieces and gave them to the innkeep-
er, and said, "Look after him and if you spend any more,
I will repay you on my way back." Jesus then asked the
man that was with him, "Who do you think was neighbour to the man who fell among the robbers?" The man
answered, "The one that showed him kindness." Jesus
said, "Go and do as he did."*

— *Luke 10, The New English Bible*

As said at the beginning of this section these parables are clear in their meaning and mostly do not need long explanations or interpretations; they speak for themselves and their meaning cannot possibly be misunderstood.

7. The Miracles

All the gospels record that Jesus during his ministry performed a great number of miracles. While the greatest majority of these consisted of healing the sick, the gospels also describe a number of events that are supernatural in nature, such as the calming of the sea, or the walking on water. These miracles have always been a source of uneasiness for some of the more scientifically oriented Christians, even to the extent that some have tried to find natural causes for these miraculous happenings. However, while the discovery of some possible natural explanations for these happenings may give certain people some comfort, the fact remains that once having embraced Christianity, one in effect has acknowledged and accepted the three greatest mysteries of them all: First, there is the miracle of God creating the whole universe out of nothing. Second, there is the miracle that someone as close to God as Jesus could come down to our level of a human existence. Third, there is the miracle that God having done this allows Jesus, whom he called his son, to be killed by humans. Compared to these miracles, the events described in the gospels as miracles fade away to utter insignificance.

The ministry of Jesus seems to have been accompanied from the very beginning by the casting out of devils and the healing of the physically sick. Of course, once this healing power of Jesus became known across the country, the people flocked to him from far and wide. Sometimes, they used extraordinary means to get their sick to the attention of Jesus. There is one delightful story of some friends of a sick man who, when they could not reach Jesus, climbed onto the roof of the house Jesus was staying in: They actually went so far as to make a hole in the roof through which they lowered their sick friend so that he landed right in front of Jesus.

Jesus, true to his very nature, was incapable of meeting suffering of any kind without doing something about it, and being moved by compassion he healed the sick, made the blind see and made the lame walk.

135

Of the thirty-five miracles, described in some detail in the gospels, three relate to the raising-to-life of a person who had died; another two refer to the miraculous feeding of large crowds. The one that is recounted below refers to the feeding of five thousand people. It apparently happened immediately after the death of John the Baptist. Matthew tells us that when Jesus heard about John's death, he was saddened and he withdrew to a lonely place by crossing the lake in a boat. When he returned he was moved to see such large groups of people waiting for him in such an isolated place.

> *When he came ashore, he saw a great crowd; his heart went out to them, and he cured those of them that were sick. When it grew late his disciples came to him and said, "This is a lonely place and the day has gone; send the people off to the villages to buy themselves food." He answered, "There is no need for them to go. Give them something to eat yourselves." "All we have here," they said, "is five loaves and two fishes." "Let me have them," he replied. So he told the people to sit down on the grass; then taking the five loaves and the two fishes, he looked up to heaven and said the blessing, broke the loaves and gave them to his disciples, and the disciples gave them to the people. They all ate to their hearts content; and the scraps when they were picked up, were enough to fill twelve bread baskets. Some five thousand men shared in this meal, to say nothing of the women and children.*

> — *Matthew 13, The New English Bible*

Today, as always, there are many people who claim to have healing powers, some of that healing is carried out within the Christian ministry, while other healing is done outside any religious affiliation. Also, today, there is a renewed interest in extrasensory perception. We can see people like Rudi Geller on television bending metal bars without touching them, simply by concentrating his psychic powers on the metal. While many of these demonstrations are hoaxes, the fact remains that there are many other well-documented and scientifically controlled experiments, which clearly demonstrate that we possess capabilities and powers which are so far only accessible to a few. But there is no reason to believe that every person does not have these powers to some extent. So, maybe we can say that we have not yet reached our full human potential. Perhaps, we should not be surprised by this at all, since Jesus told us that if we had a faith the size of a mustard seed, we would be able to literally move mountains.

It is clear, however, that Jesus was not just using more or less common psychic powers, but that he used special powers given to him by God, because that was the answer he gave to the people when they asked him from where he received the power to do these miracles. It is interesting to note that Jesus performed these miracles sometimes because people had faith in him before he cured them; and sometimes the situation was reversed when people believed in him because of the miracles they saw him perform.

Today, we are living in an age that appears to experience very few outright miracles. But over the ages, people have remembered Jesus' promise that whatever we ask of him in faith he will grant. So, people have believed in this, and the history books are full of miraculous cures and miraculous escapes of people who have taken this promise to heart. No doubt these are happening today, and they will no doubt happen in the future. In his book, *Love, Medicine and Miracles*, Dr. Bernie Siegel, a well-known American surgeon and cancer specialist, describes a large number of cures that can be called nothing less than miraculous. The amazing and heartening thing about all these cures is that they came about by the healing capacity of the patients themselves. In his book, he makes the statement that he considers his role as a surgeon to be to buy time during which the patients can heal themselves.[3]

So, the miracle stories in the Bible, far from being an embarrassment to us, should provide us with the firm knowledge that they are not aberrations but manifestations of the love and power of God. Perhaps, we can go even further and say that, to some extent, the capacity for making these miracles happen is an integral part of our own human psychic make-up. If this is so, then the occurrences we now call miracles may eventually become everyday events.

The Death Of Jesus

1. The Animosity Of The Religious Leaders Towards Jesus

During Jesus' life in Palestine, religious life was almost entirely controlled by two very different groups of people, the Pharisees and the Sadducees. The Pharisees, who were mostly laymen, were extremely pious and demanded the strictest adherence to the laws of Moses. In interpreting these laws they had gone to extremes that seem pretty outrageous to us now, but to them the strict adherence to these laws was literally a matter of life and death. In particular, they had the strictest rules about the observance of the Sabbath. For instance, they objected violently when they saw some of Jesus' disciples pluck some ears of wheat and roll them between their hands to extract the kernels. To the Pharisees, this was threshing wheat and was considered work which was forbidden on the Sabbath under their interpretation of the laws of Moses. They even objected when they saw Jesus healing a sick person on the Sabbath. Jesus then asked them, "Is it permitted to do good or to do evil on the Sabbath; to save life, or to destroy it?" (Luke 6) Even they appeared to have been somewhat embarrassed by that question, because the Bible reports that they had nothing to say in reply.

That they took these so-called offences against their self-imposed laws very seriously is clear from the comment that

Mark makes after this episode: "But the Pharisees on leaving the synagogue began plotting against him with the partisans of Herod, to see how they could do away with him." (Mark 3)

Of course, the other unforgivable sin Jesus committed in their eyes was that he claimed to be able to forgive sin. To the Pharisee, the only one who could forgive sin was God and no one else. So, to them, not recognizing in Jesus the Son of God, this action by Jesus was utter blasphemy.

The second group of religious leaders which took great exception to what Jesus did and taught were the Sadducees. They were the aristocracy of the Jewish priesthood; among them were the chief priests who controlled the operation of the temple. In outlook these aristocrats were poles apart from the Pharisees who were drawn from the ranks of the common people. The Sadducees had great political power which they derived partly by collaborating with the Roman authorities. The last thing they wanted to do was to rock the boat and have their status-quo upset. So, when they heard of Jesus' teaching, the miracles he was performing, and the large crowds that were following him, they naturally began to feel uneasy. This unease grew more acute when they heard Jesus' teachings about the Kingdom of God, and his demand that the people change their ways in order to enter into this Kingdom.

Maybe they could have let this pass as a temporary fad if Jesus had not touched them in the one place that really hurt them, namely their pocket-books. Over the centuries, it had become accepted practice to sell live animals in the forecourt of the temple, so that people who came from far away, and who wanted to offer a sacrifice, could buy one on the spot. Especially during the Passover feast, Jews came from all parts of the globe to the temple in Jerusalem to offer the mandatory sacrifices. Since these people had only the currency of their home country to pay for these sacrifices, a lucrative business had sprung up in the exchange of currencies with the priests receiving a substantial income from this enterprise. When Jesus

139

arrived at the temple and saw the din and confusion that this custom was creating, he drove out the dealers and the animals and upset the tables of the money exchangers. Mark, in his version of this episode, ends with this sentence, "The chief priests and the doctors of law heard of this and sought some means of making away with him, for they were afraid of him, because the whole crowd was spellbound by his teaching." (Mark 11)

So it was that the two groups of people, who should have received him as the long awaited Messiah, began to make plans to actually kill him and to do so without upsetting the people. It is interesting to note that the reasons the Pharisees and the Sadducees had for rejecting the Living Christ are very much the same that we use in rejecting him today. We would also be much more inclined to follow Jesus if we could just make our own rules about how to follow him, and if following him did not interfere too much with our own plans and our material well-being.

In any case, it was the official religious leaders of that time who rejected him and eventually killed him. It is a lesson the Christian church has had to learn time and time again: That is, not to get so involved with the rules and with the material concerns of the church institution, that it does not recognize the reforming spirit which wants to reform the church and lead it to a new understanding of its mission.

2. The Events Leading Up To Jesus' Trial

It was the custom of Jesus, like that of so many other Jews, to go up to Jerusalem for the Jewish festival of Passover. This festival commemorated the exodus of the Jews from Egypt and it is still today one of the main festivals of the Jewish year. So, we see Jesus with his disciples making his way slowly from Galilee, where he had done most of his teaching, to the area around Jerusalem. Jesus had by now been teaching for a period of three years and, during this period, he must have visited Jerusalem a number of times. It is therefore not surprising to learn that he had a number of followers and close friends in and around that city.

The disciples knew, just as well as Jesus did, that it was dangerous for Jesus to go to the center of power of the groups who were plotting against him. They tried to dissuade Jesus from going but Jesus, who knew what lay ahead of him, refused to listen to them. To make matters worse, he severely attacked and chastised the two groups who were out to destroy him. Hear what he has to say to them:

> *Alas for you Lawyers and Pharisees, hypocrites! You clean the outside of cup and dish, which you have filled inside by robbery and self-indulgence! Blind Pharisee! Clean the inside of the cup first; then the outside will be clean also.*

> *— Matthew 23, The New English Bible*

And he goes on in this vein for some time.

All four gospels make it abundantly clear that there was a definite purpose in going on with the journey despite the obvious dangers. Luke reports that he called the twelve disciples together before they set out on their journey to Jerusalem and spoke to them as follows:

> *We are now going up to Jerusalem and all that is written by the prophets will come true for the Son of Man. He will be handed over to the foreign power. He will be mocked and maltreated, and spat upon. They will flog him and kill him. And on the third day he will rise again. But they understood nothing of all this; they did not grasp what he was talking about; its meaning was concealed from them.*

> *— Luke 18, The New English Bible*

The crowds that were gathering in Jerusalem were expecting Jesus and, when he did not immediately appear on the

141

scene, they began to wonder if he had been scared away. Then Jesus appeared among them, not in secret as might have been expected under the circumstances, but as a king.

This is the only time we read in the gospels that Jesus was actually making preparations for an event. From the stories in the gospels it is clear that this was a well-prepared happening. The gospels relate how Jesus sent some of the disciples ahead to borrow a donkey that had not been ridden before. As Mark reports it:

> *So they brought the colt to Jesus and spread their coats on it, and he mounted. And people carpeted the road with their cloaks, while others spread brushwood which they had cut in the fields; and those who went ahead and the others who came behind shouted, "Hosanna! Blessings on him who comes in the name of the Lord! Blessings on the coming kingdom of our father David! Hosanna in the heavens!"*

> *— Mark 11, The New English Bible*

Luke, in his account of the triumphant entry, adds that some of the Pharisees who were in the crowd said to Jesus, "Master reprimand your disciples." He answered, "I tell you, if my disciples keep silence, the stones will shout aloud." Thus, Jesus entered the city of Jerusalem as a king, acknowledged by the crowd as God's special messenger and in full sight of all his enemies.

During the last days of his life, Jesus taught in the temple while the Pharisees and the Sadducees were busy devising a plan to arrest him without upsetting the crowds who were following him. Because of the congestion in the city, caused by the many pilgrims and visitors, Jesus and his disciples spent the nights in the surrounding countryside with friends and followers. Part of the reason for this may also have been that Jesus did not want to be arrested before he had accomplished his mission.

At some time during this week while Jesus was teaching in the temple, Judas Iscariot, one of his disciples, made contact with Jesus' enemies and offered, for a sum of thirty pieces of silver, to lead them to the place where Jesus would be staying during the night. The motivation for this betrayal by one of his disciples has been the subject of endless speculation. The most reasonable explanation is that Judas was bitterly disappointed in Jesus for not assuming that earthly kingship that so many expected of him. He may have reasoned that by forcing Jesus' arrest, Jesus would have to reveal his true identity and assume his worldly role. Whatever his reasoning may have been, he has gone down in history as the man who betrayed the Son of God for the price of thirty pieces of silver.

Before Jesus was arrested, he celebrated with his disciples the Passover meal which every Jew observed, and is still observing, in memory of their departure from Egypt some 1,300 years before. Jesus told his disciples during this last meal they had together, to hold similar meals in the future in memory of him. Ever since then, the Christian churches have celebrated this event, Holy Communion, at regular intervals during the church year.

It was at this meal that Jesus pointed to Judas as the man who would betray him, and it is from there that Judas went straight to the priests to tell them where Jesus planned to spend the night. From the height of the fellowship of this evening meal amongst his friends, Jesus goes to a depth of despair which is impossible for us to imagine, when he prepares himself for the ordeal that lies ahead. Nowhere is the humanity of Christ more evident than at this crucial point. Certainly the temptation was there to leave and abandon everything and return to the safety of the wilderness faraway from his enemies. As the gospels record it, Jesus fell down on his knees and prayed, "Father if it be thy will, take this cup away from me, Yet not my will but thy will be done." Luke adds to this, that an angel from heaven brought him strength, and in anguish of spirit he prayed even more urgently and "his sweat was like clots of blood falling to the ground." And while Jesus was struggling in despair, the disciples he had asked to stay awake while he prayed actually had fallen asleep, as Luke reports it, "worn out by grief." (Luke 22) From this it can be concluded that the disciples must have finally realized where the journey would end, something that up until then they had never been willing to acknowledge.

3. The Trial

It is immediately after this that Judas arrives with a band of temple police. Judas had told them, "The man I kiss is the one you want." (Matthew 26) So Jesus, the one who taught and lived love, was betrayed with a kiss. As Jesus said to Judas, "Do you betray the Son of Man with a kiss?" (Luke 22) The temple police then arrested Jesus and brought him before an assembly of chief priests and elders of the nation, who must have been hastily called together in the middle of the night.

The problem that the assembly had was to find a legal reason to put Jesus to death. So they tried to use false witnesses to accuse him of all sorts of things, but even in the prejudiced minds of Jesus' enemies this did not sound very convincing. So the High Priest finally came up with the perfect question. The same question that people have asked ever since:

Are you the Messiah, the Son of God?

Jesus' reply to that question was crucial then and is crucial today. The answer Jesus gave is reported differently in the four gospels, but in all cases his accusers understood the answer perfectly well. Probably the clearest answer is found in Mark where he records Jesus' answer as:

Yes, I am; and you will see the Son of Man seated at the right hand of God and coming with the clouds of heaven.

— Mark 14, The New English Bible

The first three gospels all mention that when the High Priest heard this, he said to those assembled there, we have heard from his own lips that he claims to be the Son of God. This was all he needed, because this was clearly blasphemy and as such punishable by death under Jewish law. However, having condemned Jesus to death on this testimony, the assembly had the problem that under the Roman occupation rules they needed the Roman governor to confirm the death sentence. So they had to wait until early morning before they could reasonably expect to get an audience with Pilate, who was the governor over Judea at that time.

Now follows one of those travesties of justice that is hard to comprehend, especially considering that the Romans were in full control of the country and prided themselves on the fairness of their judicial system. For the Jewish authorities, the fact that Jesus claimed to be the Son of God was such a severe crime that there is maybe some justification for what they did. However, the Roman authorities had no such justification. For them the question should have simply been: Has Jesus done anything criminal under our law, or is he a threat to the security of the Roman empire or to the Roman occupying forces? So, when the Jewish high priests came to Pilate that morning demanding the death of Jesus, Pilate could not find anything Jesus had done that could reasonably constitute a threat to the security of the Roman empire and, since Jesus obviously was not a criminal, he wanted to let Jesus go. But the Jews were not satisfied with that and insisted that Jesus must die. Then Pilate thought that he had found a way around his dilemma when he learned that Jesus actually came from Galilee, which fell under the jurisdiction of Herod. Since Pilate knew that Herod, who normally resided in Galilee, was actually in Jerusalem for the Passover celebrations, he sent Jesus with his accusers to Herod's palace for him to deal with, hoping that by doing so he would get himself out of an awkward situation.

However, Herod, after examining Jesus could not find anything wrong with him either. All he was interested in was to

145

have Jesus perform some miracles for the amusement of himself and his court. When Jesus refused to perform for him, he sent him back to Pilate. Then followed one of the darkest chapters in all of human history. The following is Luke's account of what happened that day:

> *Pilate now called together the chief priests, councillors, and people, and said to them, "You brought this man to me on a charge of subversion. But as you see, I have myself examined him in your presence and found nothing in him to support your charges. No more did Herod, for he referred him back to us. Clearly he has done nothing to deserve death. I propose therefore to let him off with a flogging." But there was a general outcry, "Away with him! give us Barabbas" (a convicted murderer). Then Pilate addressed them again, in his desire to release Jesus, but they shouted, "Crucify him, crucify him." For the third time he spoke to them, "Why, what wrong has he done? I have not found him guilty of any capital offense, I will therefore let him go with a flogging." But they insisted in their demand that he should be crucified. Their shouts prevailed and Pilate decided that they should have their way. He released the man they asked for, the man who had been put in prison for insurrection and murder, and gave Jesus up to their will.*
>
> *— Luke 23, The New English Bible*

Matthew, in his account of what happened that day at that so-called court of justice, reports that Pilate took a basin of water and in full view of all the people washed his hands saying, "My hands are clean of this man's blood, see to that yourself." This must surely be one of the most callous, most self-serving and, at the same time, most mistaken statements ever made in any court of law anywhere.

One of the reasons for Pilate, the representative from one of the most powerful empires the world has ever known, to cave in to the demands of the mob, may well be something that is reported by John in his account of what happened on this crucial day in the history of the Christian world. When at the end of the interrogation of Jesus, Pilate was more than ever convinced of Jesus' innocence and was, in fact, anxious to release him, the assembled Jews, under the leadership of the Chief Priests, started to play politics. They told Pilate, "If you set him free, you are no friend of Caesar's." Later they went even further when Pilate asked them, "Shall I crucify your king?"; they answered, "We have no king except Caesar." (John 19) For a Jew, at that point in their history, to openly state that they accepted Caesar as their legitimate king must have really gone against all their deeply felt nationalistic instincts. But apparently, they were even willing to swallow their national pride in order to get rid of the Son of God.

For Pilate, who knew well how the Caesars of that time viewed any threat to their power, no matter how unrealistic, apparently this threat was enough for him to give in to the mob and allow Jesus to be crucified.

4. The Execution Of Jesus

Apparently, after having condemned Jesus to death while convinced of his innocence, Pilate was not satisfied with that and had Jesus tortured and humiliated by his soldiers. After having scourged him and spat upon him, they finally crowned him with a crown of thorns. Then Jesus was taken to the place of crucifixion called Golgotha, a hill located outside the city gate.

According to the Roman custom of that time, the people condemned to be crucified were required to carry their own crosses to the place of execution. But Jesus, after having gone through so much turmoil, was unable to carry such a heavy load all the way to Golgotha. When the guards saw that Jesus was at the point of collapse, they grabbed someone out of the crowd which was following the procession to Golgotha and forced him to carry the cross to Golgotha. So entered on the world stage for just the briefest of moments the only person who was of any help to Jesus in his physical ordeal, a man named Simon, a visitor from Cyrene, a city in North Africa in what is now Libya.

When they finally arrived at the place of execution, Jesus was nailed to the cross and hung between two other men who were condemned to death for various crimes. This type of execution, by means of crucifixion, must be one of the most inhumane and cruel ways of carrying out a death penalty ever devised by human beings. In the end, a crucified man died from exhaustion and/or asphyxiation.

In some ways, the two criminals executed with Jesus were lucky that this happened on a Friday, the day before the Jewish Sabbath. For the Jews, it would have been a defilement of their Sabbath if there were people dying on a cross on that day, so they asked the soldiers to hasten their deaths by breaking the bones of the crucified men. The guards did so, but when they came to Jesus they found that he had already died: However, one soldier, just to make sure, pierced the side of Jesus with a spear. The time of the crucifixion was about 9 o'clock on Friday morning, and he died according to Matthew around 3 o'clock in the afternoon. During this entire time, his disciples were in hiding except for the apostle John who was at the site of the crucifixion together with some of the other followers of Jesus, among them Mary, the mother of Jesus.

The four gospels give somewhat differing accounts of what Jesus said, or more likely shouted, during this six-hour ordeal. First of all Jesus prayed for his executioners:

> *Father, forgive them; they do not know what they are doing.*
>
> — *Luke 23, The New Jerusalem Bible*

Later, one of the criminals beside him shouted, "If you are the Messiah, save yourself and us." But the other criminal shouted back at him, "Have you no fear of God? This man has done nothing wrong" and he then asked Jesus to remember him when he comes to his throne. Jesus then told him:

> *I tell you, today you will be with me in paradise.*
>
> — *Luke 23, The New Jerusalem Bible*

About midday, Jesus must have felt completely abandoned both by men and God when he cried out:

My God, My God, why have you forsaken me?

— Matthew 27, The New Jerusalem Bible

These are exactly the same words that appear in the opening sentence of Psalm 22, which reads as follows:

My God, my God, why hast thou forsaken me, and art so far from saving me, from heeding my groans? O my God, I cry in the daytime but thou dost not answer, In the night I cry but get no respite.

— Psalm 22, The New English Bible

Then at 3 o'clock in the afternoon, Jesus cries with a loud voice:

It is fulfilled.

— John 19, The New Jerusalem Bible

These are, without a doubt, the most significant and victorious words ever spoken on earth. It must be assumed that, up to that point in time, Jesus could have freed himself and saved his earthly life, but he would have failed to complete the mission for which he had come. When, after the six-hour ordeal he loudly proclaimed that his task was finished, the world turned a corner and the world would never be the same again.

Of course, this was not at all evident to those watching Jesus die; for them they saw only the person they had believed in die an inglorious death on a cross. But, in fact, the world changed irrevocably that Friday at 3 o'clock in the afternoon. The apostle John ends his account of what happened that day with the following statement:

This is vouched for by an eye witness, whose evidence is to be trusted. He knows he speaks the truth, so that you may believe: for it happened in fulfillment of the text of the scriptures, "No bone of his shall be broken and they shall look on him whom they pierced."

— John 19, The New English Bible

Some of the gospels relate that, at the time of Jesus' death, various natural and unnatural events happened. The first three gospel writers also mention that the Roman officer who was on duty at that time exclaimed, "Truly this was a Son of God."

After his death, Joseph, a wealthy follower of Jesus, asked Pilate for the body of Jesus for burial. When Pilate agreed, Joseph wrapped the body in a clean linen sheet and buried him in a tomb that he had prepared for himself and his family. This tomb was cut out of the rock in his own garden and, after the body was placed inside, a great stone was rolled in front of the opening. This was normal procedure for a tomb of a wealthy man to prevent robbers from opening the grave and taking the ornaments which were usually placed beside the body.

All this happened on Friday. The next day was Saturday, the Jewish Sabbath day, on which no work was to be done at all. This, however, did not prevent the chief priests and the Sadducees from going to Pilate again and asking him for yet another favour. They told Pilate that Jesus had said at one time that he would be raised again in three days. The chief priests had obviously listened better to Jesus than his own disciples, because the latter certainly did not expect anything of that kind to happen. In any case, Pilate went along with the request, and he provided a guard of Roman soldiers and even went so far as sealing the stone in front of the tomb. So it came to pass, that from Saturday morning onward, the sealed tomb of Jesus was guarded by a detachment of Roman soldiers.

The Resurrection

Up to this point in Jesus' life, as far as the world could see, nothing earth-shattering had happened. There had been lots of teachers before Jesus who had gathered a following around them. If their message had unwanted political overtones, they were disposed of by the authorities in much the same way as they thought they had disposed of Jesus. After the death of these teachers, their followers might continue to preach the message of their master for some time, but sooner or later the movement would run out of steam and fade away. No doubt, the Jewish leaders expected much the same to happen this time and so, after having posted the guards at Jesus' tomb, they were ready to forget the whole episode as a distasteful but necessary operation.

Now in Jesus' case an event happened that shattered their complacency, an event that became a turning point in human history. As Jesus had promised, he became the first man to defeat death when he rose from his grave on that Sunday morning, on the third day after his death. From the standpoint of historical importance, it is this event that should be used to divide history into two parts and not his birth some thirty years earlier. It was at this point in time that history changed and that the world moved from one era into another. The thousands of years of human evolution and development that had gone on before culminated in this first and final victory over death and evil. Everything humankind had hoped for and prayed for finally came to pass on that Sunday morning in Jerusalem. What happened on that morning makes all that ever happened afterwards appear to be insignificant: finally death and evil were overcome. No wonder that people in the early church used to greet each other with the proclamation, "Jesus is risen," which was answered by the phrase, "He is risen indeed."

By overcoming death, Jesus established and confirmed his own identity once and for all. It is of course possible to argue that, if Jesus was really the Son of the creator of the universe, then humanly speaking it is not his resurrection that is astonishing, but the fact that his death by human hands was not accompanied by an universal upheaval.

What exactly happened on that Sunday morning will forever remain a mystery, something we will never fully understand. The one fact we know for certain is that the tomb was empty on that Sunday morning, even though guards had been placed there for the express purpose of preventing the removal of the body.

151

The first ones to find the tomb empty were the women who arrived at the tomb early on Sunday morning to embalm the body. They could not have done this earlier because they were forbidden to do so on the Saturday because of the Sabbath restrictions against working on that day. As Matthew reports it, when the women came to the tomb they found an angel of the Lord there who said to them:

> *You have nothing to fear. I know that you are looking for Jesus who was crucified. He is not here. He has been raised again as he said he would be. Come and see the place where he was laid, and then go quickly and tell his disciples. He has been raised from the dead and is going before you to Galilee; there you will see him.*

> *They hurried away from the tomb in awe and great joy, and ran to the disciples. Suddenly Jesus was there in their path. He gave them his greetings, and they came up and clasped his feet, falling prostrate before him. Then Jesus said to them, "Do not be afraid. Go and take word to my brothers that they are to leave for Galilee. They will see me there."*

> — *Matthew 28, The New English Bible*

For a period of forty days after that Jesus met with his disciples: sometimes he met them individually, other times in groups and mostly in Galilee. During this time, he once again explained to them the reasons for his coming, for his death, and for his resurrection. Then he gave them their final instructions as reported in Matthew:

> *Full authority in heaven and on earth has been committed to me. Go forth therefore and make all nations my disciples; baptize men everywhere in the name of the Father, the Son and the Holy Spirit, and teach them to observe all that I have commanded you. And be assured, I am with you always, to the end of time.*

> — *Matthew 28, The New English Bible*

Sometime during those forty days, the disciples must have returned from Galilee to Jerusalem because it was from there that Jesus said his farewell and disappeared, and it was in Jerusalem that they remained waiting for that special gift that Jesus had promised them.

Over the ages people have speculated about the bodily form of Jesus after his resurrection. Obviously it was different from a normal human body. For instance, he moved freely like a spirit from one place to another, obviously not concerned with material obstacles. On the other hand, he made it perfectly clear that he was with them in a material form as well. People touched him, and he actually ate with them on several occasions. It is something that can be argued about endlessly, but in the end we have to say that we simply do not know in what form he reappeared. In final analysis, of course, it is not of the slightest importance what form his body assumed after the resurrection. What is important and beyond question is that the tomb was empty, and that he appeared to his disciples and followers not as a ghost or some vague spirit but as the living Christ.

The Outpouring Of The Spirit

All the gospel writers end their accounts of Jesus' life on earth with his resurrection and ascension. However, the account of Jesus' life would not be complete without mentioning what happened after his final disappearance. Towards the end of his ministry, Jesus repeatedly promised his disciples that they would receive a special gift from God that, "would clothe them with the power from on high." (Luke 24)

We owe most of the written account of what happened to the disciples and the early church to the same Luke who wrote one of the gospels. As he wrote in the foreword to his second book, The Acts of the Apostles, "This is a continuation of my attempt to write down all that happened after having scrupulously considered all the facts."

As we saw, on leaving his disciples, Jesus told them to remain together in Jerusalem to await the arrival of the special gift they were about to receive. In the first chapter of the Acts of the Apostles, Luke reports Jesus as instructing his disciples as follows:

> *Wait for the promise made by my Father, about which you have heard me speak: John, as you know, baptized with water, but you will be baptized with the Holy Spirit and that within the next few days.*
>
> — *Acts of the Apostles 1, The New English Bible*

When the Spirit of God did descend on them they were transformed men and women. It changed the apostles themselves from an inarticulate, mostly uneducated group of men, who had abandoned Jesus during his trial and execution, to a fearless and eloquent group of evangelists who transformed the world. Luke reports how they were suddenly able to speak in foreign languages, so that the many foreign visitors to Jerusalem were able to hear the apostles speak in their own tongues. As Luke reports the event, this is what happened on that very special day in the life of the church:

> *While the day of Pentecost was running its course they were all together in one place, when suddenly there came from the sky a noise like that of a strong driven wind, which filled the house in which they were sitting. And there appeared to them tongues like flames of fire, dispersed among them and resting on each one. And they were all filled with the Holy Spirit and began to talk in different tongues, as the Spirit gave them power of utterance ... we hear them telling in our own tongues of the great things God had done. And they were all amazed and perplexed, saying to one another, "What can this mean?" Others said contemptuously, "They have been drinking!" But Peter stood up with the eleven, raised his voice and addressed them: "Fellow Jews, these men are not drunk as you imagine; for it is only nine o'clock in the morning. No this is what the prophet spoke of: 'God*

*says, this will happen in the last days: I will pour out upon
everyone a portion of my spirit; and your sons and daughters will prophesy, your young men shall see visions . . . '
Men of Israel, listen to me: I speak of Jesus of Nazareth,
a man singled out by God and made known to you
through miracles, and portents, and signs . . . The Jesus
we speak of has been raised by God, as we can bear witness. Exalted thus with God's right hand, he received the
Holy Spirit from the Father as was promised, and all that
you now hear and see flows from him.''*

— *Acts 2, The New English Bible*

In the beginning, the apostles and the original followers
of Jesus were living in a commune sharing their possessions
while preaching daily in the temple. It is interesting to note
that the apostles, after the day of Pentecost, were given the
ability to heal the sick, just as Jesus had done.

Of course, all this could not be hidden from the chief priests
and the Pharisees, and they became very concerned about the
continuation of a sect they thought they had disposed of once
and for all. So they had the apostles arrested and asked them,
''By what power or by what name have men such as you done
this?'' It is interesting to note the phraseology used by the interrogators: ''men such as you'' would seem to imply that the
apostles in speech and in appearance were not of the educated elite like the interrogators themselves. They must, therefore, have been the more surprised when they heard Peter
answer them as follows:

*Rulers of the people and elders, if the question put to
us today is about help given to a sick man, and we are
asked by what means he was cured, here is the answer
for all of you and for all the people of Israel: It was by
the name of Jesus Christ of Nazareth, whom you crucified, whom God raised up from the dead; it is by this
name that this man stands here before you fit and well.
This Jesus is the stone rejected by the builders which has*

155

> *become the keystone — and you are the builders. There*
> *is no salvation in anyone else at all, for there is no other*
> *name under heaven granted to men, by which we may*
> *receive salvation.*

> — *Acts 4, The New English Bible*

It was in this fearless and, at the same time, eloquent way that the apostles went on to spread the Good News, first in Jerusalem, then in the rest of Palestine, and eventually throughout the entire Roman empire. While it is not reported in the Acts of the Apostles, it is generally believed that Peter finally ended up in the cultural and political center of the world at that time, Rome. Here he preached and taught his master's message for many years until he was imprisoned by the Roman Emperor Nero. It is reported that he asked his executioners to be crucified upside down, because he did not think it was appropriate that he should die in the same way as his master had. Whatever the truth may be about this story, it was the willingness of these early apostles to die for their cause, which impressed the people so much that it was said, "the blood of the martyrs is the seed of the church." It was in this way that this very small band of imperfect men was able to spread Jesus' message across the Roman world in such a short time: a message that is still the mainstay for hundreds of millions of people and is as pertinent to our lives today as it was to the apostles when they first heard it from Jesus himself.

The Proof And The Evidence

All the events described above occurred some 2,000 years ago when there were no newspapers and no reporters to record what was happening. Of course, even if they had been around, it would have been very unlikely that they would have reported the events which took place in Galilee and in Jerusalem at that time. It all happened in a small insignificant corner of the Roman empire far away from its center. At best, some of the events might have been reported in the local newspaper, if there had been such a thing, and then probably hidden away somewhere on the third page.

This lack of historical evidence has led some people to deny the fact that Jesus even existed, insisting that he was a figment of the imagination of the apostle Paul and of the gospel writers. But, while there is not a great deal of independent corroboration of the existence of Jesus, we are not without some outside substantiation. In addition to some chance remarks about the followers of Christ made during the first century by some Roman officials in their reports to Rome, we have the account of Flavius Josephus, a Jewish historian. Josephus was born in 37 A.D. in Galilee, the province in which Jesus spent most of his life. Josephus had been educated as a Pharisee but later became a prolific writer and historian. In his book, *The Antiquities of the Jews*, which he wrote around the year 93 A.D. some 60 years after Jesus' death, he makes the following statement:

> *About this time there arose Jesus, a wise man, if indeed it be lawful to call him a man. For he was a doer of wonderful deeds, and a teacher of men who gladly receive the truth. He drew to himself both of the Jews and the gentiles. He was the Christ; and when Pilate, on the indictment of the principal men among us, had condemned him to the cross, those who loved him at the first, did not cease to do so, for he appeared to them again alive on the third day, the divine prophets having foretold these and ten thousand wonderful things about him. And even to this day the race of Christians, who are named after him, has not died out.*[4]

The fact that Josephus was not a Christian gives this testimony added weight. Since he lived for the first 30 years or so of his life in the same place Jesus had taught, he must have had access to many people who had actually met Jesus and had listened to his teaching. I believe we can therefore safely assume that what he wrote is essentially correct and conclude that Jesus was indeed a historical figure.

Much more difficult to prove is the fact of Jesus' resurrection. After all, no one was present, other than the Roman soldiers who were supposed to be guarding the tomb. They, however, had left their post and fled, and they were for obvious reasons not inclined to draw attention to that fact by repeating what actually happened on that fateful Easter morning.

In the final analysis, the only proof we will ever have of what happened on that day can only come from examining the effects the event had on the lives of the people most immediately involved. In a book, *Verdict of the Shroud, Evidence for the Death and Resurrection of Jesus Christ*, the authors, Stevenson and Habermas, make the following comment:

> *Our argument for the historicity of the resurrection rests on three major points:*
> *1 — No one has advanced a plausible naturalistic explanation for the resurrection of Jesus which accounts for the known historical facts about it.*
> *2 — The literal resurrection of Jesus is corroborated by a number of historical facts:*
> > *a — the disciples, who did not expect it, saw and believed and they were changed men;*
> > *b — the behavior of the early church, they believed it;*
> > *c — the change from Saturday (the Jewish Sabbath) to Sunday (the day of the resurrection).*
> *3 — A few known and virtually undisputed historical facts alone are sufficient to build a probable case for this event:*
> > *a — Jesus' death by crucifixion;*
> > *b — the disciples' eyewitness experiences;*
> > *c — the corresponding transformation of the disciples;*
> > *d — Paul's conversion experience.*[5]

As can be seen, most of the arguments come back to the changes that the resurrection made to the people who were involved with Jesus. Some, like Peter changed, from a coward who denied even knowing Jesus at Jesus' trial, to a person who was not afraid to stand up in front of all the people to testify about Jesus and his message. He even managed to stand up to the highest authority in his religion, the High Priest, who, for a simple fisherman like Peter, must have been the most authoritarian figure in his life before he met Jesus.

It also changed a young Pharisee by the name of Saul, who had been persecuting the early Christians. The story is told in the Acts of the Apostles how Saul, when he was on his way from Jerusalem to Damascus to persecute the Christians in that city, met the living Christ in person and became an instant believer and follower of Jesus. After that encounter, he changed his name to Paul and began proclaiming the message of Christ all over the known world of that day. He became one of the most influential apostles, but he did so only after he had met Christ himself.

One of the more interesting arguments for the historical truth of the resurrection I have ever read comes from Dr. Principal Hill as quoted by D. James Kennedy in his book, *Why I Believe*. In this quotation, Dr. Hill enumerates what we are saying if we do *not* believe that the disciples were inspired by the resurrection and by the consequent outpouring of God's spirit on them. He writes:

> *But if not withstanding every appearance of truth, you suppose the testimony of the apostles to be false, then inexplicable circumstances of glaring absurdity crowd upon you.*
>
> *You must suppose that twelve men of mean birth, of no education (living in that humble station which places ambitious views out of their reach and far from their thoughts), without the aid from their state, formed the noblest scheme which ever entered the mind of man, adopted the most daring means of executing that scheme, and conducted it with such an address as to conceal the imposture under the semblance of simplicity and virtue.*

You must suppose:

- *that men guilty of blasphemy and falsehood, united in an attempt the best contrived, and which has in fact proved the most successful for making the world virtuous;*
- *that they formed this singular enterprise without seeking any advantage to themselves, with an avowed contempt of loss and profit, and with the certain expectation of scorn and persecution;*
- *that although conscious of one another's villainy, none of them ever thought of providing for his own security by disclosing the fraud, but that amid sufferings to the flesh and blood they persevered in their conspiracy to cheat the world into piety, honesty and benevolence.*

Truly they who can swallow such supposition have no title to object to miracles.[6]

This may be a negative proof, but it makes its point very forcefully. Indeed, if the disciples were not inspired by the resurrection and the outpouring of the spirit, what possibly could account for their changed attitude and their persistence in the face of such formidable opposition?

Taking all this evidence together, I believe we can safely say that:

1 — There is enough *historical* evidence to show that there was indeed a person named Jesus, who was a teacher and who was executed by the Roman authorities around the year 30 A.D.

2 — There is enough *circumstantial* evidence to show that the closest associates of Jesus were convinced that this teacher had risen from the dead on the third day, and that they considered him to be the Son of God.

3 — There is enough *factual* evidence to show that there were Christians spread throughout the Roman Empire even as early as the end of the first century. That they persisted in spreading the message of Jesus, despite the cruel persecution they suffered everywhere, can only be explained by their

absolute and firm belief in the validity and the importance of the message they were proclaiming.

Of course no one can prove that Jesus was indeed the Son of God, that will forever remain a matter of faith, trust, and personal encounter with the living Christ.

The good news for today is that Jesus, as the Mediator between God and humans, reconciled us with God forever.

6

The Things That Separate
Us From God — Sin And Suffering

Introduction

In Chapter 4, I briefly mentioned the forces that oppose God and God's plan for this world. These opposing forces have proven to be so strong that they were able to seduce humankind to rebel against God, and they thus caused a rift to develop between God and God's creation. This action by humans against God's will is what is called "sin" in Christian terminology.

In addition to sin however, there is another barrier which tends to keep humans separated from God and which is not caused by any wrongdoing on the part of humans. This barrier, human suffering, is the direct result of the conditions under which you and I are forced to exist. It is the belief that God is the author of this suffering which causes many people to turn away from God. They feel that the suffering humans undergo is not compatible with the idea of a benevolent Creator, nor with the concept of a loving Father/Mother.

This chapter is therefore divided into two sections:

Sin   — Human actions against God's commands which caused a rift to develop between God and humankind, and which could have resulted in a complete break between the two.

Suffering   — One of the conditions of human existence which tends to cause humans to reject God because they believe it to be incompatible with the idea of God as a benevolent Creator.

Sin

1. Humans' Rebellion Against God

Unfortunately, the word sin has become so loaded with misconceptions, mainly by the pronouncements of T.V. evangelists and fundamentalist Christians, that many do not have any idea what the word sin means and stands for within the context of Jesus' teaching. Most people will admit to making the occasional mistake, but they certainly do not want to be classified as sinners. After all they do not steal and, if they occasionally forget about their marriage vows, they rationalize this by saying that it is or was done in the name of love.

When the Bible talks about sin, however, it is as a result of measuring our actions against the standard set by Jesus' commandment: Love God and love your neighbour as yourself. With that sort of measuring stick we all fall short and there is no one who can honestly say that s/he is without sin. Yet, we all know that if we lived up to that standard, the world would be transformed. The great majority of the evil things that happen to us in this world would disappear, since most are the direct result of either ourselves, our country, or our society not living up to that standard. A non-Christian friend, on reading this, suggested that I could make the definition of sin more universal by redefining it as, "A selfish act which causes pain in others." This is certainly part of it, but for most Christians it probably does not go far enough because we believe we also sin if we do not actually love that other person.

Because it is very difficult to understand the Christian message without acknowledging that sin exists and is an almost integral part of everyone's daily life, I have listed in the following sections some of the things you and I do wrong both as individuals and collectively as a nation.

2. The Sins We Commit As Individuals

The sins we commit as individuals are a result of those actions or non-actions over which we ourselves have direct control. In essence, they are the acts of commission and of omission that violate the rules God has set for us.

In the Old Testament, which deals mainly with the history of the Jews and the special covenant the Jewish people had and have with God, the Lord gave them a set of rules that they had to follow. These rules, better known as the Ten Commandments, are still the basic rules by which the orthodox Jews live today. They are also, with some minor differences, the rules by which a Christian should live; for centuries they also have been the foundation on which the laws of the Western countries have been based.

Moses, the leader of the Israelites who led his people out of slavery in Egypt, was given these rules by God on Mount Horeb, and he inscribed them on stone tablets so that they would last indefinitely. The commandments start with God identifying himself, since the Jews at that time still believed that their God was one among many others. He says: "I am the Lord your God who brought you out of Egypt, out of the land of slavery." Then follow the Ten Commandments:

> *1 — You shall have no other gods to set against me.*
> *2 — You shall not make a carved image for yourself;*
>   *you shall not bow down to them or worship them.*

3 — *You shall not misuse the name of the Lord your God; the Lord will not leave unpunished the man who misuses his name.*

4 — *Keep the Sabbath day holy as the Lord commanded you. You have six days to do all your work, but the seventh day is the Sabbath of the Lord your God, that day you shall not do any work.*

5 — *Honour your father and mother.*

6 — *You shall not commit murder.*

7 — *You shall not commit adultery.*

8 — *You shall not steal.*

9 — *You shall not give false evidence.*

10 — *You shall not covet your neighbour's wife; you shall not set your heart on your neighbour's house, his land, or on anything that belongs to him.*

— *Exodus 20 and Deuteronomy 5, The New English Bible*

In examining these rules it can be seen that they are basically divided into two sections. The first four commandments give the basic rules that govern the relationship between God and God's people. The second section defines the rules that should govern the relationship between individual people.

During Jesus' ministry, he was asked what the most important commandment was. He answered by saying that you can compress all these rules into one:

You shall love God with all your heart and all your strength and you shall love your neighbour as yourself.

— *Matthew 22, The New English Bible*

As we have said before, that appears to be a simple rule and should be easy to follow. In practice, however, it has turned out to be very difficult indeed, if not impossible. When we speak in the following pages about sin, we mean this inability to live up to that simple command to love God and our neighbour as ourself. Not meeting that standard makes us all sinners, and we all sin repeatedly everyday of our lives, even the best of us. Measuring ourselves against that yardstick, it is obvious that anyone who believes that he is without sin is simply deluding himself.

In most cases our sins are caused by that all overpowering instinct of selfishness and self-interest which all of us are born with. If we honestly examine the motivations for most of our actions, we will find that it is almost always the gratification of our own desires and the placing of these above the needs of others. Maybe we can forget our egocentricity when we are dealing with our children, but Jesus' command is not only to love our family, but also to love our neighbours and even our enemies.

When Jesus gave this simple rule to his disciples, one of the bystanders asked him, "But who is my neighbour?" Jesus answered the man by telling him the parable of the Good Samaritan quoted in chapter 5. The message of this parable is clear and cannot possibly be misunderstood. Our neighbour is the person whom we encounter in our lives and who needs our help regardless of race, nationality, social status, or anything else. It is those people we are to love, regardless how difficult this may be some times.

There remains for us the question, "How can we love God who is so different from us and so infinitely greater than we are?" Clearly we can express our gratitude through prayer in which we give thanks for his/her blessings and for his/her love for us. But besides that, the only way we can express our love is to have love and compassion for the person God has placed next to us. So in some ways, the whole commandment of God can be compressed into the simple phrase, "Love your neighbour as yourself."

On the other hand, we must never forget that the worst sin we can possibly commit is not believing in God in the first place. If for a moment we accept that God created the world and sent his/her Son, Jesus Christ, who died for us so that we might live, then the denial of that must surely be the worst sin we can commit. On a worldly scale, it is something equivalent to

167

a father or mother who gives a kidney to one of their children who would otherwise die of kidney failure: Then, when the child has recovered, it turns to its parent and disclaims that it even knows this person and that it didn't need that kidney anyway. I wonder what our reaction would be if this happened to us. But that, I believe, is only a weak reflection of what we do when we reject Christ's sacrifice and in doing so reject God's gift to humankind.

One area where we sin as individuals, and often with the most disastrous consequences for others, is in the workplace, whether it be the craftman's shoddy work or the unnecessary triple by-pass operation by the surgeon. The newspapers abound with horrifying accounts of accidents with cars, planes, and trains that cause suffering beyond measure just because the machines were not made well enough in the first place, or were not maintained regularly, or were not operated properly.

When an earthquake hit Mexico City several years ago it killed thousands of people. Some were killed in highrise buildings that collapsed, while next to them stood equally high or even higher buildings which were hardly damaged at all. Some of these anomalies may have been caused by geological variations in the conditions of the soil on which the buildings were founded, but considering the close proximity of some of these buildings, one can only conclude that the major reason for the difference in behaviour of these buildings was the difference in workmanship.

There is no trade or profession which is excluded from the long list of evil things that have happened to people because other people did not live up to their own professional standards. The reason can only be one of two things, either greed or laziness or both. Dr. Peck, whom I have quoted before, believes that the original sin of man was laziness. While this may seem to be somewhat far fetched, the fact remains that a great deal of evil and suffering is the result of our laziness or reluctance to do the right thing at the right time. As people in the work place, we all have responsibilities for products or services that can do great harm to others if we do not perform our duties as well as we should, and it is our sin if greed and/or laziness make us do work that is not as good as it should or could be.

I believe that considering all this, we can safely say that at the level of the individual, we are not without sin: If we do not do anything wrong actively, we certainly do so passively by turning a blind eye to the problems of our neighbour.

3. Collective Sins

The things we do wrong as a nation or as a Western Society I have called "Collective Sins." Most of us, most of the time, find it very convenient to disclaim any personal responsibility for these because we feel we do not have a direct influence in the corridors of power where the issues are being decided. However, in our Western society, we live in a democracy and that makes us all collectively responsible for what our governments are doing in our name and on our behalf. In the following pages, I have listed some of these collective sins which have caused suffering beyond imagination and for which I believe we, together, must assume responsibility.

War

Surely, there is no other action of humankind that could possibly be more fundamentally the opposite of God's law to love your neighbour as yourself, including your enemy, than the act of warfare. Most people will probably go along with that statement. Nevertheless, in the 2,000 years since Jesus taught this simple rule, history has been nothing but a long series of wars. There have been wars of aggression, wars of independence, economic wars, preventive wars, civil wars, and even religious wars. Some of these were fought for the highest motives of combating evil, but all caused people to be killed often in the most atrocious manner. All were the result of humankind collectively not living up to Jesus' command.

Take for instance the Second World War. Surely you will say that never was a war fought for a better reason from the Allied point of view. There could not possibly be a better reason for conducting a war than to destroy the utterly evil regime in Nazi Germany. Yet, even that war, I believe, must still be considered as one of the worst sins humankind has ever committed. Something like 55,000,000 people were killed and today, 50 years later, there are still millions of people who were scarred for life both physically and emotionally by that war. Maybe the sin was not the actual fighting to get rid of the evil regime, but more in the things we did wrong that caused this situation to arise in the first place. Most historians today agree that the roots of the Second World War can be traced to the conditions that were imposed on Germany at the end of the First World War in 1918. These conditions were certainly not governed by such considerations as loving your enemy but far more by feelings of hating your enemy. If, during this period between the two wars, all the world's thinking had been dominated by the simple rule of loving your enemies, there is very little doubt that all the suffering of the Second War could have been avoided. For that matter, the spirit of evil that took possession of Germany might never have found a foothold in the fertile ground of anger, hatred and bitterness that resulted from the conditions imposed on Germany after the armistice in 1918.

Today, fortunately, the possibility of a major war erupting has considerably decreased in the last few years. But, for forty years or more, we have lived with the distinct possibility that an atomic war between the U.S.S.R., and the Western countries would wipe out a large part of the earth's population. For what noble cause would we have exposed the world to this calamity, you may ask? The answer most likely would have been to prevent the Communists from overrunning Western Europe and maybe eventually North America. But would that have been worth all the suffering that would have resulted from such a war? Some will say in defense of risking such a war that a Communist regime would have banned the Christian church. That may be true, but the Christian church

170

did all right in Poland during all the years they were under Communist rule. Surely we would not have put the continued existence of God's creation at risk for that reason. If the Christian church could not have survived a Communist regime, or have modified the excesses of that regime, it would have had no business of being there in the first place. A church that could not have survived under those conditions would have been a dead church to start off with.

However, whatever the consideration or whatever the motives, I cannot believe that God's purpose for this world could possibly have been served by a nuclear holocaust. Nothing I can think of is further removed from the command God gave us to love our neighbours as ourselves.

Sister Chittister, a Benedictine nun, in a recent television interview put it most succinctly when she asked, "Can you possibly imagine Jesus pushing the button on a nuclear warhead in an underground bunker?"

Hunger And Starvation

The second collective sin for which we all must take responsibility is that of allowing half a billion people to go hungry everyday of their lives. The hungry live in every country and every continent; they are of every race and religion, but mostly they live in the underdeveloped countries of this world. A recent publication of the United Nations Children's Fund states that most of the 100,000,000 children who are expected to die in the 1990s could be saved for the amount of money American companies will spend on cigarette advertising during that same time. The report includes the following statement that surely we can all agree on: "It is impossible to accept for one moment the notion that the world cannot afford to prevent the death and malnutrition of so many of its young children." One may find it difficult to precisely pinpoint the responsibility for these conditions, but no one can dispute that they exist or that we have enough resources to remedy these ills.

The world at large has made tremendous progress in agricultural production, in transportation, and distribution techniques. So large, in effect, that it is entirely possible to feed, clothe and house the whole population of the world and to do so without upsetting the world economy. Yet it is not done. Why not? The only reason for the lack of decisive action on our part to remedy this situation can be human greed and/or laziness which prevents us from taking effective action and living up to that high standard God has set for us. The truth of the matter is that if we lived up to that standard, these conditions would not exist.

Poverty

The World Bank in Washington produces every year a map of the world showing the gross national product (GNP) of each country. It is recognized that the gross national product may not be the most accurate indicator to measure the economic well-being of people in a country: nevertheless, the fact that in some countries the GNP per person is $80 a year, while in others it is in excess of $25,000 a year, tells of a situation that no Christian can accept. The people in the countries with an average gross product of $80 a year per person are living in such dire poverty that their existence cannot even be called human. In the Western countries a small-sized cat consumes more than that annually. Surely we, as the privileged people of the developed countries, have our priorities wrong if we accept this situation without taking effective steps to remedy it. I believe it is one of the major sins of the developed world, that instead of this situation getting better it actually is getting worse.

Today, most industrialized countries have overseas development programs which have made large amounts of money available to assist the less developed countries. No doubt this assistance has helped and without it the situation in some countries would be much worse. But, what most developing countries need is not aid but trade; that, however, is something we do not readily allow. The fact is that most underdeveloped countries are producing, or could be producing, a wide variety of agricultural products and manufactured articles much cheaper than we can. To import them without restrictions though would cause additional hardships to our own industries which are already hard hit by imports from many developed countries. Additional low-cost imports from the less developed countries would therefore inevitably result in further lay-offs and unemployment which is something no politician can support. Let us admit, it is also not something that we ourselves would readily support if it were to involve our own industry. But this is exactly what is needed to make life bearable for a large part of the world's growing population.

Somehow we must find a solution that will rectify the situation. For decades now, there has been an attempt to reduce the trade barriers between all countries, but this General Agreement on Tariffs and Trade (GATT) always seems to run into some sort of obstacle before it can go into effect. Even if and when it goes into effect, it remains to be seen how much this will actually help the worst of the underdeveloped countries. So, until we can find a permanent solution to these problems, we do not effectively love our neighbour and we live therefore in sin. As Dorothy Soelle puts it in her book, *Suffering*:

> *This toleration of exploitation, oppression, and injustice points to a condition lying like a pall over the whole of society; it is apathy and unconcern that is incapable of suffering.*[1]

4. Summary

Any action we take only becomes an illegal act if we measure that action against a certain norm and fail to measure up to that norm. Wrongdoing against the state, or against society, is measured against the yardstick to which we have all agreed, the laws of the land. Wrongdoing against God, in other words sin, was originally measured by a fairly simple set of straight forward rules, the Ten Commandments. With a bit of effort a person could have followed these rules, except maybe the last one which tells us not to covet our neighbours' possessions.

When Jesus came, he changed these ten simple rules to one rule only. However, by simplifying it, he made it much more difficult for a person to live in accordance with that rule, because he left it up to us to interpret that rule in any given situation. For instance, Jesus said in one of his discourses, "You were told of old, an eye for an eye and a tooth for a tooth, but I tell you love your enemies and do good unto those who hate you." Later when he was asked to summarize the law he said, "Love God and love your neighbour as yourself." By that standard we all fall short:

we do so as individuals;

we do so as a society.

Looking at the ways we fail, it is fairly obvious that our collective failings do more harm and cause more suffering than anything we can possibly do wrong as individuals. Yet it is probably these sins that we feel least responsible for. But, if we are not responsible, who is?

With the fantastic strides we have made in the field of communications, the whole world has become our neighbourhood and therefore our responsibility. Gone forever are the old days of only having to live up to a set of straightforward rules. Gone are the days when our neighbourhood was restricted to the limits of our village. Today, our neighbourhood is the whole world, and therefore our sins of commission and omission are being measured on a global basis.

To prove to ourselves that we are not effectively practicing what we believe (and therefore sin), just consider for a moment what the world would be like if we all lived up to that simple rule of loving our neighbour as ourselves:

> *There would be no more war;*
> *There would be no more hunger and poverty;*
> *There would be no more crime;*
> *There would be no more discrimination for any reason;*
> *There would be no more drug and alcohol abuse;*

174

There would be no more lonely and forgotten people;
There would be no more family violence and abuse;
and so on.

Suffering

1. Our Perception Of An Uncaring God

According to the Bible, when God created the world, God looked upon it and said it was good. There was no pain. There was no suffering. There were no beasts killing beasts, and there were no humans killing humans. The world lived in perfect harmony with God and with its fellow creatures. Into this ideal world entered evil and with it, suffering and death. Beast killed beast for food, and humankind's ego began to assert itself with all its evil consequences. This is how suffering and evil entered the world according to the creation story in Genesis.

As stated before, we believe this account to be one which tells us who we are rather than how we came to be. So, if we do not accept the Genesis story as historical fact, the question then arises whether in our long evolutionary history there ever was such a state of paradise in which humankind lived in perfect harmony with its Creator. As we pointed out in chapter 4, with all we know today about the evolution of humans, it is difficult to identify a time period in which such an ideal state might have existed, although there seems to be convincing evidence that up to about 10,000 years ago humankind basically lived a peaceful existence on fruits and plants.

In this context, it also is interesting to note that our most immediate animal predecessors were not, and are not today, hunters of other animals: they do not appear to kill each other, nor do the various family groups fight with each other except when their territory is threatened, and even then they apparently do not cause serious injury to one another. In short, they appear to live in perfect harmony with all of God's nature that surrounds them. Of course, they are subject to illness and death. Nevertheless, it would appear that they live much closer to the ideal life that we associate with living in paradise than we humans do.

In any case, regardless of the way we think we came to be, as Christians we believe that we were created in God's image and that evil and suffering were not part of God's plan for this world. We affirm that the God we know is a God of love and hates suffering which is contrary to God's will and nature. This affirmation is a statement of what we believe to be true, but it does not provide answers to the many questions posed by the existence of pain and suffering in this world which is, after all, God's own creation. We will only know the final answers to these questions when we can see the whole picture of God and creation. But that will not likely happen in this life.

The questions people have been asking throughout the ages concerning suffering are many, but I believe they can be summarized in the following eight:

1 — Why does God allow humankind to suffer?

2 — Is God impotent to stop the suffering?

3 — Is there any meaning or value to suffering?

4 — Is a guarantee against suffering worth acquiring at any cost?

5 — Should we wish for a life without any pain or suffering?

6 — Should we wish for a life without death?

7 — Should we wish for a life without justice, that is without punishment for things done wrong?

8 — How should we respond to pain and suffering?

When people suffer, they often perceive God as uncaring. The reason suffering often has this effect on people is that subconsciously we often believe that God is the cause of our suffering, and God is therefore perceived as part of the problem and not part of the solution. In his book, *How Can I Believe When I Live In A World Like This*, Dr. Reginald Stackhouse asks the question: What would we do if we were God for one day?[2] Would we take away human freedom and prevent people from doing wrong? Would we suspend the laws of nature for that day so that a fall from a tree would not cause broken bones?

Would we suspend death, and so forth. When in the following sections we examine the eight questions we posed above, it may be helpful if we were to ask ourselves once in a while that same question: What would I change if I were God for a day?

2. Causes Of Suffering

Suffering can come in many forms, it can be physical, psychological, social or spiritual. The direct and indirect causes are legion: physical pain, grief, loneliness, ostracism, racism, poverty, unemployment, abuse, abandonment, etc. Each one of us may not encounter all of them, but we are sure to experience some of them at one time or another in our lives.

In order to try to make some sense out of the various causes behind human suffering, and to help in formulating some reasonable answers to the questions posed in the introduction, I have listed below what I believe are some of the main causes behind suffering:

a) suffering resulting directly from our sins and mistakes and those of our forefathers;

b) suffering resulting from the chances we take and the choices we make;

c) suffering from disease and the fact that we all must die;

d) suffering that results from applying justice;

e) suffering that is the direct result of our love for others which makes us suffer with them.

At the same time, if we look at suffering and try to find a possible meaning behind it, we can look at suffering from the following perspectives:

suffering that has some meaning or value;

suffering that can possibly have some meaning or value;

suffering that has no meaning and appears to be completely senseless and meaningless.

177

Before continuing, it may be well to briefly mention what other religions teach about suffering, since they, like Christianity, are confronted with the same problem; that is, to explain the existence of suffering in this world and to find an explanation for the fact that suffering seems to be so unevenly distributed among people.

For the Hindus, the explanation is rather simple: suffering in this world is attributed to bad works carried out in a previous incarnation. To get rid of suffering, one must simply live a good life in this existence; later in the next incarnation, one will then be promoted to a better or higher order of life.

For the Buddhists, suffering is one of the keys to their religion. They believe suffering is the result of craving and wanting things. Buddha taught that to get rid of suffering one had to get rid of craving, and to get rid of craving one must follow the Eight Fold Path of right views: right intent, right speech, right conduct, right means of livelihood, right endeavor, right mindfulness and right meditation. (See also Appendix 1)

In short, both religions present a rather simple, in principle, explanation of both the origin of suffering and the elimination of suffering. This, however, is not possible for a Christian; s/he must always live with the contradiction of the existence of suffering in a world created by a God whom they believe to be the personification of love.

3. Suffering Resulting Directly From Our Sins And Mistakes And Those Of Our Ancestors

This, the first one of the causes behind human suffering listed above, begs the question: Why does God allow this; why does God let us make mistakes that cause pain and suffering not only to ourselves but to others as well? I believe that the only answer we can give is that God created us with a free will. God gave us freedom to love each other but also to hurt each other: God gave us freedom to do the right thing but also to do the wrong thing. If God interferes with that, God simply takes away our basic freedom and thereby the basis of our true humanity. If God were to intervene every time we did something wrong, we would in effect be reduced to a race of puppets dangling on a set of strings.

If we want to put it in more current terms, God is standing by helplessly when we condemn millions of people to die of malnutrition and starvation while there is an abundance of food, enough to meet everyone's need. God stands by, literally helpless, watching humanity make mistake upon mistake, because by interfering God would take away our responsibility and our ability to choose — to choose between love and hate, between good and evil.

In a recent book, *Before The Beginning, Cosmology Explained*, George Ellis poses the question whether the features of evil and pain are implied in any universe that allows free will. His answer is Yes, because any restrictions on the free will would simultaneously destroy the possibility of free response and loving action.[3] In effect, he is saying that the existence of free will automatically implies the existence of suffering and evil.

Today, if humankind decides to ignore all the warnings we have been given about the state of our environment, or if we do not take any action to prevent unrestrained growth of the human population, God will not interfere and the result will be immense suffering in the future. When this happens, people will no doubt ask again: Why did God not prevent this from happening? The answer to this question must always be that God cannot interfere without taking away our free will, and thereby the essential element of our humanity. If God took that away it would destroy the purpose of creation, which was to create a freely responding human being, created in God's own image and who has the unrestricted freedom to choose between following or rejecting God.

179

4. Suffering Caused By The Chances We Take
And The Choices We Make

Everyday of our lives we make deliberate choices and take chances: In most cases we are well aware that we are taking these chances and, in fact, we are so well aware of them that we insure ourselves against the financial consequences of these acts. The insurance companies calculate to the last decimal point what our chances of survival are. Everytime we step into a car, we take a chance our forefathers never had to take. Everytime we board an airplane we make a choice and accept a risk. If you want to know how much of a risk, you can go to a dispensing machine and take out an insurance policy against the possibility that the plane will have a major accident. The premium you have to pay is a very accurate indicator of the risk you are taking. Obviously we know we are taking a risk and, equally as obviously, we are quite willing to accept that risk.

However, if the plane did crash and we did get killed, it would be very natural for the people who were nearest to us to ask, How could God have allowed this? The answer of course is that it was not God who took the chance, it was us; it was not God who caused the plane to crash, it was the pilot or the air traffic controller or the manufacturer of the plane or inadequate maintenance. Regardless of who or what actually was at fault, it was the imperfection of other human beings which caused the crash. I know, in our anger and despair we will probably blame God everytime a disaster of this type strikes us, but in our hearts we know that we cannot reasonably ask God to temporarily suspend the laws of nature to prevent these tragedies, or in this specific case, to suspend the laws of gravity so that the plane can safely land without engines or wings.

An example of social suffering, which is a direct result of the choices we make, is the effect a downturn in the economy has on our lives. The basic reason for the depression may be difficult to pinpoint, but by its nature it is a result of a human type of activity for which we must accept full responsibility. Not only do economic recessions and depressions cause financial losses to many people who can ill afford them, but they are also the main reason for lay-offs in the workplace. These lay-offs and the long periods of unemployment, which often follow these economic downturns, cause great hardship to the people involved. However, the selection of who will be laid off is made by another human being.

Take the case of a company that gets into financial difficulties. The company, in order to survive, must either reduce salaries or layoff staff. Whatever solution is selected, someone will suffer and the lives of a lot of people will be adversely affected. So, here is suffering. Who is to blame? The person who does the firing? He may be laid off himself in the next round of staff reductions. The company's management? They may have done everything possible to survive the recession. In the end, we can only blame society for having created an imperfect economic system in which this type of thing happens regularly. The society we live in is created by us, so if that society does not perform as well as we had hoped we can only blame ourselves. God gives us the freedom to create any society or social system we want, be it communist, capitalistic or whatever. However, one thing is clear, so far we have not been able to develop a social-economic system which does not cause great harm at regular intervals to the people that are part of that system.

5. Suffering Caused By Natural Disasters

In insurance policies, these are called "Acts of God." This phrase seems to have stuck, but it is certainly a most improper way of describing events that are beyond the control of humans. There is no doubt that much suffering is caused by natural disasters such as earthquakes, volcanic eruptions, typhoons, hurricanes, floods, tidal waves, droughts, etc. As human beings, we have little or no control over these events; but, at the same time, we must acknowledge that some of the resultant suffering might have been prevented by timely human intervention. I have already mentioned the differences in the effects earthquakes have had on buildings: while some collapsed, others remained standing and received little or no damage at all. The difference in the behaviour of these buildings was caused by such human factors as the adequacy of design or soundness of construction.

In engineering, structures are designed for a certain probability of failure: In other words, they are designed only to withstand forces that will occur with a certain frequency. If these design conditions are exceeded the structure will fail. For rich countries, it is possible to design most structures to withstand the worst set of adverse conditions that can possibly be imagined to occur during the lifetime of the structure. But for poorer countries this is impossible. For instance, in Bangladesh it is completely impracticable to build dykes high enough to prevent flooding under all possible combinations of high tides and adverse winds. Nevertheless, people live in these low lying areas; they, their government, and the international aid agencies, know full well that at regular intervals these dykes will be overtopped and hundreds of thousands of people will die, and this is precisely what happens on a regular basis. But in that country there is nowhere else to go, and unless the whole world community takes action, the people in that country will have to live and die with that situation. We can say that this is completely senseless suffering, but the fact is that it could be prevented by people of good will.

While there is obviously a great deal humanity could do to prevent the suffering from natural causes, the fact remains that there is much suffering caused by natural phenomena which we cannot prevent even with the best of intentions. What are we to make of that?

I believe that we should begin by accepting the fact that we live in a natural environment. An environment that is shaped and moulded by the forces of nature which are all subject to some fairly simple, easy to understand, laws of nature. As long as these laws of nature govern the behaviour of this planet, there will be pain and suffering. Take the laws that govern our weather. As long as they are valid, there will be atmospheric conditions that cause floods and droughts. Or take the law that governs the effects of gravity. As long as it is valid, planes will fall from the sky if the engines fail and busses will go over precipices when their brakes fail. Or take the case of our own central nervous system. As long as it is there, we will feel pain when we hurt ourselves. Or take the laws that govern the wear and tear on our bodies. As long as they exist, our bodies will wear out and eventually they will cease to function and we will die. The fact is, that as long as we have physical bodies, and as long as they are subject to the laws of nature, we will hurt ourselves when we fall and we will feel pain when we burn ourselves.

The question we must ask ourselves is: Do we want to change these laws and live in a world that has no cause and effect? We certainly cannot mean that we want to suspend these laws just for the moment our family or our friends are being threatened by them and that, once that threat has passed, the natural laws can become effective again and cause harm when they impact on other people. The logical question we must ask ourselves is: Could God not have created a world that did not operate on the basis of laws which cause these natural disasters? In the past, this question was often countered by reminding us that we are mortal people for whom it would be very presumptuous to question God about the adequacy of creation. Today, we are more likely to respond that God purposely created us with a capacity to reason, which implies that we are invited to ask questions even if we cannot find reasonable answers. At this point in our development we can only say, that as long as we live on a planet that is governed by the existing laws of nature, there will always be earthquakes, floods, droughts, etc.; and as long as they occur there will always be people who suffer. It is only when we lose our physical bodies, in other words when we become spirits, that physical suffering will cease.

6. Suffering Caused By Sickness And Death

We all have a one hundred percent chance that we will die. Some will die young; some will die old. Some will die without ever having been sick; others will die as the result of a long and painful illness. While still others will suffer from almost the day they are born.

A number of books have been written recently that try to address the problem of human pain and suffering, and the fact that pain and suffering seem to be so unevenly distributed amongst people.

The first book, by Harold S. Kushner, *When Bad Things Happen To Good People*, was written as the direct result of the author's son being diagnosed at the age of three with a disease which caused him to age prematurely and to die within ten years. The author does not ask, Why do bad things happen to good people? He asks, What happens when bad things happen to good people? and, What should be our response to that when it happens to us? In the book, the author poses the question, "Would anyone want to live without any pain?"[4] Maybe this sounds like a strange question. But in fact, life as we know it without some pain would be impossible. It is pain and our central nervous system that make it possible for us to feel things, and to warn us when something is wrong with our body. Pain warns us that the stove is hot, that we have appendicitis or that we have cancer. It is only as the result of this pain that we seek medical help, and that we can take full advantage of the medical services that are available to us today. So, in some ways, pain is a necessary condition for living and therefore indispensable.

Of course, this takes nothing away from the fact that there is bodily pain and suffering that goes far beyond the "warning" function of pain. Pain, that seems to serve no useful function and which appears to us to be completely meaningless. Pain, which leaves us numb; especially so, since we cannot and will not accept that this pain is a punishment for some personal sin.

So in answer to the question, Would anyone want to live without pain? we must answer that some pain, given the physical body we are created with, is essential to the continued well-being of that physical body. Beyond that, however, there is pain and suffering that seems to serve no purpose and is therefore an evil which we must combat with all the resources God has given us.

Similarly, we might ask ourselves the question: Do you want to live forever? In the first instance, we are almost automatically tempted to answer, Yes, of course, provided I would be in good health. But after thinking it over for a few moments, we might change our minds even if that condition were to be accepted. Without death, the world would become hopelessly overcrowded in just a few decades. Alternatively, the no-death condition would have to be accompanied by the no-growth and no-birth-either condition. Just imagine a world with no parenthood, a world without children, without growth and with all people remaining at the same stage of development. Always the same people around you and no prospect for real growth or improvement. For most of us, the fact, that we have a limited time to do the things we want to do, gives us the zest for life that makes us create things and strive to meet certain goals. In the end, I believe, most of us would rather opt for an earthly life that comes to an end at sometime, than for a life that goes on and on, a life without children and without growth.

However, we must ask ourselves the same question we asked before: Could God not have created the world without the pain and suffering which so often accompanies death? The answer, I believe, must be the same answer we gave to the question regarding the existence of evil and the occurrences of natural disasters. We do not know. What we can say is that we trust God implicitly to have created us with a potential to overcome all these evil things that may occur to us in our lives. As far as we can see today, with the central nervous system an integral part of human bodies, pain and therefore suffering are an essential part of life. At the same time, we must accept the fact that as long as we have physical bodies, they will deteriorate with time, and the life of that physical body will eventually come to an end.

7. Suffering Caused By The Application Of Justice

There is no doubt that one of the causes of human suffering is the application of justice to people who have acted against the laws of the land. Sometimes the application of justice for a minor misdemeanor causes more suffering and pain to the offender and his family than the offense warrants. But, even in the case of severe crimes, our justice system often causes inhuman suffering. In some of the states of the U.S.A. the death sentence is still being applied but, in most cases, the sentence is carried out only after years of legal wrangling; the convicted person spends these years in continuous suspension, waiting literally for the axe to fall. Also, our jails are often badly overcrowded resulting in conditions that can hardly be called human.

In the Bible we read that God is a just God. The evildoers will eventually be punished and the righteous will eventually be rewarded. But we know from what we have said before that there is no such thing as a righteous person. We all make mistakes and no one lives up to God's commandment of love. So in the end, punishment in some form or another should come to all of us.

For many people the application of justice is a prerequisite for life in a just society. Before, I quoted the French writer, Albert Camus, who found it absolutely intolerable to think that there would be no final justice done. He despaired about that because he could not believe in a Christian God or in a life after death, and therefore could not see that justice would ever be done and that evil doers would ever be punished.

J. C. Beker in his book, *Suffering and Hope*, points out that the notion of retributive justice is deeply ingrained in human nature. He goes on to say that we seem to have an innate sense that, unless retributive justice is honored, our world will collapse in chaos.[5]

186

In today's society we probably place less emphasis on the retribution aspects of justice and punishment, and more on the rehabilitation and deterrence aspects of the punishment in order to hopefully reduce the incidence of similar crimes in the future. Nevertheless, in most cases, the sentence that is passed often includes punishment for the sake of pacifying the call for revenge by society. This, in effect, assumes that society can restore a balance by causing more pain and suffering to offset the pain and suffering caused by the perpetrator of the crime. Maybe this is not senseless suffering as we encountered it when we discussed suffering caused by sickness and natural disasters, but it gets very close to it, and this time it is directly and purposely caused by other humans.

8. Suffering As A Result Of Love

Probably some of the most intensive pain and hurt any person can undergo is caused by the pain, hurt and suffering of someone close to him or her, and the closer we are to that person the worse our pain. It is the suffering no one who has a family or has close friends is immune to. This suffering is especially intense and strongly felt when adversity of any kind strikes our children. In fact, it is often the parent who suffers more than the child itself when the child is hit by illness or any other adversity, because the parent may better understand the full implications of what is happening to the child. This suffering becomes even worse when the parents feel, rightly or wrongly, that they are responsible for what is happening to the child.

This suffering, as a result of love, is probably the one cause of suffering that we potentially can do something about: Love no one, do not get close to anyone. This is, of course, the exact opposite of what we, as Christians, are taught to do. The Christian message is one of loving your neighbour and suffering with him/her in adversity. Dorothy Soelle in her book, *Suffering*, makes the case that we may be able to abolish some suffering in this world by improving social conditions. But, as she states, we always come up to barriers we cannot cross such as death. She goes on to say:

187

> *Death is not the only barrier. There are also brutaliza-*
> *tion, mutilation and injury that no longer can be reversed.*
> *The only way these boundaries can be crossed is by shar-*
> *ing the pain of the sufferers with them, not leaving them*
> *alone and making their cry louder.*[6]

In other words we must deliberately share in the pain and suffering of our neighbour. Especially when that neighbour suffers from something that cannot be reversed or undone.

Maybe we can call this type of suffering, "God's suffering." It is the suffering God undergoes when the people God loves make such terrible mistakes as going to war or polluting the earth beyond recall. When God sees humans make these mistakes God can only suffer with them, because if God were to prevent them from doing so God would take away their freedom to choose and thereby take away their humanity.

It is the suffering that we undergo when we stand by helplessly while a loved one suffers. Fortunately there is always one thing we can do and that is to ask God to take the suffering away and if, that is not possible, to give the person the strength to bear the suffering and even to make something positive out of it.

So, love, in addition to all the good things it gives us, by its very nature also makes us suffer. Maybe this was best put by Agatha Christie, the famous English writer of detective novels, in her biography when she wrote:

> "If you love, you will suffer, and if you don't love
> you do not know the meaning of a Christian life."

9. Can Suffering Possibly Have A Meaning Or Be Beneficial?

In thinking about this subject, we should start by reaffirming that it is our firm belief that suffering and tragedies

a) are not part and never were part of God's plan, and

b) are not punishments for our own sins and mistakes.

We do not and cannot believe in a God who daily parcels out a certain number of tumors and strokes, and so forth, on the basis of our shortcomings or as part of a grand design for this world.

We can learn from life around us, however, that a certain amount of pain can, in some cases, be necessary and beneficial for us. As a demonstration of that we might use, what I have called, the evil and good of friction. Almost everything that moves in this world has to overcome friction, and a lot of energy is used by all forms of transport to overcome that friction. In that sense, friction could be called an evil thing. However, consider what would happen if there were no friction. The best way to find that out is by walking or driving on a smooth ice surface. You cannot walk because there is no friction between your shoe and the surface beneath it to allow you to step forward; if you ever get going, you cannot stop because there is no friction which will allow you or your car to slow down. So friction can be both evil and beneficial; so it is with many things we encounter in life. Things that may be harmful and evil in one situation, may be helpful and beneficial in another.

A good example of how pain may be beneficial is the case of my granddaughter. She is a lovely girl, a doll, a great pleasure and a constant source of love for all who know her. But she has Down Syndrome. When she was very young she had a bad habit of banging toys, and anything else she could find, on windows to make a noise. Unfortunately, in addition to being one of the loveliest persons I know, she is also one of the most stubborn. There was simply no way to discourage her from doing this potentially very dangerous thing. Talking did not help, shouting did not help, a pat on the hand did not help — she would just smile. In order to get the message through you had to give her a real hard whack on the hand, something she could really feel. Everyone hated it, but in the end that was the only way we could stop her. Maybe someone else could have found a better way, maybe slapping her hand taught her how to hit others, but in the end the only way I could find to stop her from hurting herself was by hurting her, but hurting her in love.

In his book, *Peace, Love and Healing*, the author Dr. Bernie Siegel, whom we have already quoted in the section on miracles, describes his experience with self-healing and the positive effects some severe illnesses can have on people. The book contains some startling and surprising examples of cancers and illnesses that were cured by people concentrating their minds and prayers on the part of the body that was sick. Towards the end of this book he has two surprising chapters called "Disease as a Gift" and "Disease as an Agent for Transformation." There is probably no better way to illustrate what he means by these statements than to quote from the book itself:

> *Now when I tell an audience of five hundred people with AIDS that they have a gift, they do not throw shoes at me or get up and run out yelling, "What are you telling us?" — because they know. They understand that illness can help heal their lives, that it can bring new meaning to relationships with lovers, family and friends. In some cases, it has enabled critically ill young men to find love in a home from which they had been rejected because they were gay. It has brought a community together to love and support each other. And so they say, "My disease is a gift." That does not mean they do not wish to be well, but that they would not give up what they have achieved because of their illness.*

> *Does it take courage to be open to this kind of healing? Do I have the right to tell you your disease is a gift? No, I do not. The gift is yours only when you choose to create it — as I have seen thousands of others do. Listen to the people who have lived the experience and realize you are the source of your healing.[7]*

He goes on to tell stories of many people who have found that living through a serious illness was an enriching experience that they would not have wanted to miss.

Harold Kushner in his book, *When Bad Things Happen to Good People*, comes to the same type of conclusion when he writes:

And finally, to the person who asks, "What good is God? Who needs religion, if these things happen to good and bad people alike?" I would say that God may not prevent the calamity, but he gives us the strength and perseverance to overcome it. Where else do we get these qualities which we did not have before? The heart attack that slows down a forty-six year old businessman does not come from God, but the determination to change his lifestyle, to stop smoking, to care less for his business and care more about spending time with his family, because his eyes have been opened to what is truly important to him — those things come from God. God does not stand for heart attacks; those are nature's responses to the body being overstressed. But God does stand for self-discipline and for being part of a family.

The flood that devastates a town is not an act of God, even if the insurance companies find it useful to call it that. But the efforts people make to save lives, risking their own lives for a person who might be a total stranger to them, and the determination to rebuild the community after the flood waters have receded, do qualify as acts of God.[8]

In answer to our question, Can suffering possibly have a meaning or in any way be beneficial to us? The answer must be, Yes it can. But for us to derive the maximum benefit from it we must be open to God and the inner resources we have to both cure ourselves or, if that is not possible, to overcome the adversity to the advantage of both ourselves and others.

Reading the history of the world and noting the achievements of humankind, it is obvious that humans raised themselves to the highest level of dedication and achievements when they were battling adversities. In combating tyranny, slavery, prejudice and disease, individuals and nations have reached peaks of achievement. For instance, Dr. Stackhouse asks who would have ever heard of Mother Teresa if she had spent her ministry in a fashionable girls' school instead of in the slums of Calcutta? I am sure that most of us can quote similar occurrences where the fight against disease, injustice and suffering have brought out the best in ordinary people. This is certainly not a reason for proclaiming that suffering is a necessity of life, but maybe we can say that our response to these adversities can sometimes have a positive side effect.

Hans Küng in his book, *Christianity and the World Religions*, makes the following statement when he discusses the meaning of suffering:

> *To be sure, even faith in Jesus cannot reverse the fact of suffering and it will always be possible to doubt. But there is something vital we can say as a result of the life and pain of this one person, to people living and suffering for no apparent reason: Even patently absurd human life and pain can have a meaning, can take on a meaning. This meaning is a hidden one, not an automatic gift, but a permanently open offer of meaning that challenges me to choose it. Obviously I can reject this hidden meaning out of defiance, cynicism, or despair. But I can also accept it out of faith and trust in the One who has given meaning to the meaningless suffering and death of Jesus.* [9]

So in the end, we conclude that finding meaning in meaningless pain and senseless suffering is a matter of faith and trust in Jesus Christ who himself appeared to undergo meaningless and senseless suffering, but in doing so reconciled us with God our Maker.

10. How Do We Respond To Pain And Suffering?

In the previous chapters we have seen that suffering can have meaning, and that sometimes it can have a beneficial effect. However, this leaves us still with a residue of suffering either caused by ourselves, or by the forces of nature, or by chance, that leaves us numb and leads us to despair and makes us question the goodness and power of our Creator. When that happens to us we can only do one thing, and that is turn to

God for help in the knowledge that God is just as outraged at suffering as we are, and in fact suffers with us. It was Jesus' death on the cross that was the most outrageous and most undeserved example of senseless suffering. It only loses that senselessness when we consider it in this wider context of God's plan for reconciliation with humans.

In his book, *Suffering and Hope*, J. P. Beker writes that he believes that the death and resurrection of Christ are the most important considerations in dealing with our experience of suffering and hope. He points to the seemingly tragic suffering of Jesus on the cross followed by his resurrection which has given hope to all humankind as being the ultimate victory of good over evil. So our own suffering, we may believe, will be followed by our resurrection to a new existence. This is the hope and trust that must and will sustain us when suffering and pain strikes us, as it surely will, all of us, at some time in our lives. Hans Küng, whom we have quoted before, puts it this way in his book, *Does God Exist?*:

> *Suffering, doubting, despairing man finds an ultimate support only in the forthright admission of his incapacity to solve the riddle of suffering and evil ... Positively, in that certainty unsecured and yet liberating venture, in doubt, suffering and sin, in all inward distress and all outward pain, in all fear, anxiety, weakness and temptation, in all emptiness, desolation and anger, simply and straightforwardly to show **an absolute and unreserved trust** in the incomprehensible God. Yet, to cling to him even in absolutely desperate situations, simply empty and burnt out, when all prayer dies out and not a word can be spoken: **a fundamental trust of the most radical kind,** which does not externally appease anger and indignation but encompasses and embraces them, and which also puts up with God's permanent incomprehensibility.*[10]

To put it slightly differently and shorter, there is only one way by which we can conquer despair and that is through faith and trust. Only a person who believes and trusts in God can overcome despair and accept pain and suffering in the certainty that God has overcome evil, and that in the end all things will return to God's original plan before evil entered this world. That requires faith and trust.

One of the best examples of such faith and trust, I believe, can be found in the writing of Dietrich Bonhoeffer, a well-known German theologian, who died at the age of 39 on the gallows in a German concentration camp. In one of his letters from prison he wrote: "I believe that in any trial and tribulation God will give us all the power we need to withstand it. But he does not give it in advance, lest we rely on ourselves alone. If we trust in him we can overcome all anxiety for the future."[11]

As indicated before, suffering has given some people unexpected inner resources to endure and overcome adversity, even to the extent that Harold Kushner finds in that a source for belief in the existence of God. He writes in his book, *When Bad Things Happen to Good People*:

> *One of the things that constantly reassures me that God is real, and not just an idea that religious leaders made up, is the fact that people who pray for strength, hope and courage, so often find resources of strength, hope and courage that they did not have before. Some people see life's unfairness and decide that there is no God, the world is nothing but chaos. Others see the same unfairness and ask themselves, Where did I get this sense of fairness? Where did I get this sense of outrage and indignation, my instinctive response of sympathy when I read about a total stranger who has been hurt by life. Don't I get these things from God?*[12]

One of the most touching and inspiring responses to human suffering I have heard of concerns a Jewish girl living in occupied Holland during World War II. Etty Hillesum was 23 years old in 1941 and was studying at the University of Amsterdam. In 1941 she began to jot down her thoughts and feelings in a diary. It was not until 1981, forty years later, that some of her surviving friends assembled her writings in a book entitled, *The Interrupted Life, Diary of Etty Hillesum*. When this book became a best seller, two more books were published about her life in the concentration camps. Most of the information contained in these other books came from the letters she wrote her friends during this period. (See also the note at the end of this chapter.)

Although Jewish by race and upbringing, she was a profound student of the New Testament. All her letters and notes are comments about her life and her loves, but most of all they are about her inner thoughts. To me, these books are a revelation and an example of the heights the spirit can soar to even under the most adverse and cruel conditions. In July 1942, when she still lived in Amsterdam, but knowing full well what lay in store for her and her family, she wrote:

> *I have experienced so many great events my God. I thank you that I can bear it all and that you let so little of life pass me by.*

The next day she added:

> *My God, this life is too hard for fragile people like me. I would like so much to continue to live. But somewhere within me I feel so light and so without any bitterness and I have so much strength and love within me. Yes my God, I am very true to you through thick and thin and I will not go under and I still believe in the most profoundest meaning of this life and I know how I must continue to live and there are so many certainties within me; you will find it unbelievable, but I find life so beautiful and I feel so happy. Isn't that fantastic? I don't even dare to express this feeling to others.*

Later, in August of 1943, when she was in a transit camp where she was surrounded by utter misery, and everyone lived in continuous fear that they would be put on transport to an extermination camp, she wrote:

> *You have made me so rich, my God. Give me the ability to distribute it with full hands to others. In the evening when I rest in bed, I am sometimes so grateful that tears stream down my face.*

In the transit camp she was a constant help and inspiration to people who were sick, and to those whose names were on the most recent lists for people to be put on transport to the final extermination camp. Then on 15 September 1943, she and her family were pushed into an overcrowded cattle car on their way to the extermination camp in Auschwitz. Somewhere along the road she found a place to write a postcard to one of her friends and managed to push it through an opening in the wall of the cattle car. A farmer, who lived near the railway tracks, found the card and sent it on to the friend to whom it was addressed. On the card she wrote:

> *I am sitting on my rucksack in the middle of the cattle car. I have opened my little Bible at random and found these words, "The Lord is my high place."*[13]

On the 30th of November 1943, she was reported to have died in Auschwitz. So ended the life of a most remarkable young woman. To have such faith, such love, such trust and such zest for life under those awful conditions, is most inspiring and certainly proves the point made by Harold Kushner.

This example, to what height a human being can reach under adversity of the worst kind, goes a long way to show that the most important thing for us to possess in times of adversity is a positive attitude and to know that, with God's help, we are indeed able to meet suffering and pain head on, and even make something positive out of it. J. P. Beker concludes his book, *Suffering and Hope*, with the following affirmations:

> *1 — Hope despite its inherent problems still provides the most adequate response of a Christian to the problem of suffering.*
> *2 — Without thinking about suffering in terms of hope, God's purpose for his creation will have been defeated.*

3 — *Hope incorporates individual suffering into a final solidarity of all humans.*

4 — *Hope allows us to be realistic and honest about the poisonous reality of death and dying in our world.*[14]

So it is hope, and the firm belief in the world to come, that makes it possible for us to respond in a positive way; to live with those things for which we know do not have any rational explanation, including the suffering and pain which appears to us to be completely senseless. It is that hope and that belief that makes it possible for someone on the way to an extermination camp to say, "The Lord is my high place."

Note:
Holland was overrun by the Nazis in May 1940. Almost immediately after that they started, with the help of some Dutch collaborators, to harass the Dutch Jews. First they were obliged to wear at all times a yellow star with the word Jew stitched on it. Later on they were systematically rounded up and sent to transit camps in Holland from where they were transferred by train to the final extermination camps in Germany and Poland. Auschwitz was one of the most infamous of these.

11. Concluding Remarks

After examining the question of evil, sin and suffering, we, with the Christians of all ages, acknowledge that much of this is incomprehensible to us, and it will no doubt remain so until we are reborn in a new age. Nevertheless, there are a number of things we can say that, while not explaining the existence of evil, sin and suffering, do throw some light on these baffling problems.

1 — Evil, sin and suffering are against God's will and are contrary to God's purpose for this world.

It is very clear from reading the Bible that these three things separate us from God. God's plan on the other hand was that we should live in close proximity to, and in close union with, God in a world without evil, sin or suffering.

2 — God wants to be loved by humans of their own free will and not because they have no other choice.

It is clear, and obvious, from all accounts that God created humans to be companions to live with him/her in the paradise that God created especially for this purpose. But, in order to be a meaningful companion to God, we must choose to do so with our free will, otherwise God's companion would be a mere puppet.

3 — God, having given humans the freedom to make choices, does not interfere when they use that freedom to make the wrong choices.

Humankind would obviously not be free if, every time it made the wrong choice, God stepped in and reversed its decisions. Thus, God does not interfere when we choose to go to war or when we decide to ignore all the warning signals and pollute the world beyond recovery.

4 — God's yardstick for measuring human behavior is the rule: to love God with all your heart, mind and strength and love your neighbour as yourself.

This simple rule, if obeyed by all, would transform the world. It is obvious, judging from the state of the world today, that after having received this rule some 2,000 years ago, we are no nearer to meeting this command than we were when Jesus first gave it to his disciples.

5 — The direct result of human freedom is an avalanche of pain and suffering caused by the evil things we do to ourselves and to our neighbors.

The world is full of pain and suffering resulting from the mistakes we are making today and the mistakes our ancestors made before us, just as the future world will be full of suffering resulting from the mistakes we are making now and the mistakes we are sure to make in the future. The great tragedy is that we are fully aware of what we are doing to the next generations, but we seem to be unable or unwilling to reverse the process.

6 — God, having created the world and the laws by which the universe operates, does not interfere with nature even when it affects us adversely.

The natural phenomena that occur in this world only become disasters when they adversely affect human lives. Humans can do much to alleviate the suffering and pain caused by these events by using their God-given intellect. In many cases we know the chances we are taking by living in certain places that are subject to natural disasters. In fact, we take out insurance against the possibility that these events will occur and affect us.

7 — Suffering and pain can, under certain circumstances, be beneficial to humans.

Pain in particular warns us that there is something wrong with us physically. In many cases, timely action can prevent major illnesses and further pain and suffering. Sometimes suffering can enrich our lives by giving us greater insight into ourselves and into that of our friends and relatives.

8 — There is a great deal of suffering that is not caused by humankind and appears to be completely senseless. We believe that God is not the author of that suffering, but instead suffers with us.

There is a force opposed to God in this world that causes us to sin and not to live according to the simple law of God, even though we may fully intend to live according to that law. Similarly, this force of evil causes suffering that makes no sense and does not appear to have any positive value. The greatest and most senseless suffering appeared to be that of Jesus when he died on the cross. Nevertheless, that suffering took on a most significant meaning when he arose from death. Maybe, one day, our seemingly senseless suffering will also take on such a hidden significance.

9 — God gives people inner resources that make it possible for them to overcome even the most senseless suffering and to turn that suffering into something positive.

When suffering strikes us, we are most likely to turn to God and ask God to take away the cause of that suffering. There is no doubt that sometimes God hears our prayers and does what we have prayed for. In most cases however, God does not respond the way we would like, but instead gives us the strength and fortitude to live with our pain and suffering. The perfect example of this was Christ's own suffering. He prayed three times that God would free him from the suffering to come. God did not answer Christ's prayer, but instead gave him the strength to turn that suffering into the final victory over evil.

10 — For a Christian, all suffering, and especially senseless suffering, can only be borne if it is considered in the light of hope for a better world to come, and in trust that God will not fail to live up to his/her promises.

No matter how dark things may seem to be, and no matter how hopeless things may appear to be, we can trust that God has not abandoned us. Sometimes, God may appear to be completely absent and hidden from us. Sometimes, God may not appear to be listening to our prayers and the heavens may be silent. But, if there is one promise that God has made, it is that we are not alone in this world, and that God is with us always both in this life and in the life to come.

In closing this chapter on sin and suffering, it may be well to remind ourselves of Dr. Stackhouse's words:

> *Evil and innocent suffering are part of this world and as in a mystery, they motivate some people to scale heights of greatness while they beat others to the ground. At the same time no amount of believing will take it away or even explain it.*[15]

The good news for today is that we are assured that suffering eventually will disappear in the age to come, and that the meaningless suffering we presently experience is not now, and never was, part of God's plan for this world.

7

Humankind's Reconciliation With God

Introduction

In the previous chapters I have described and discussed some of the things we do that separate us from God such as:
- our lack of faith and trust in God as our Creator and Sustainer;
- our rejection of Jesus as the mediator between God and ourselves;
- our selfishness which makes us always put ourselves first, thereby preventing us from loving our neighbours as God commanded us.

It is clear from the Bible that this was not always so, or at least that it was not God's intention that it be so. God's plan was for people to live in perfect harmony and in close communion with their Creator. However once humankind rebelled against God, the direct link could not be maintained since God's nature of perfection made that impossible. But God did not give up on creation and sought ways and means to re-establish that relationship. A pale comparison might be the all too human situation of teenagers rebelling against their parents and the rules they have set. As a result of this rebellion, the teenager may leave home and break with the parents. But no matter how much that direct link is broken, real parents will never give up loving him or her and will try to find ways and means to forge a reconciliation.

This chapter is about the way we believe God re-established that relationship with humankind after it had been broken. I have tried to show this pictorially in Fig. 2.

- In the first stage, humankind is surrounded by God's love and has a direct relationship with God.
- In the second stage, evil arrives and drives a wedge between God and humankind and causes that direct link with God to be broken. Nevertheless, God's love has not changed and continues to surround us still.
- In the third stage, evil is driven back by the grace of God which came to us through the life, suffering, death and resurrection of Jesus Christ. Thus the link with God is re-established through Christ. However, evil is still there and is continuing to exert a ruinous influence on humankind, and will continue to try to break that newly forged link with God. We are assured, however, that it will be to no avail, because God's grace is strong enough to overcome all the forces that evil can muster and our link with God will remain unbroken and secure.
- In the fourth stage, in the fullness of time, the original relationship we had with our Creator will be re-established and evil will have completely disappeared. This is the future God has promised us and to which we look forward with great anticipation.

This is a visual presentation of what I believe to be the message and the significance of Jesus' life, death and resurrection:

- he reconciled us with God;
- he re-established our direct link with God; and
- he assured us that God's grace is strong enough to overcome all forces of evil forever.

202

Figure No. 3
The Four Stages In Our Relationship
With God

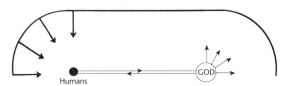

Stage 1 - The Original Situation

1. We have a direct two-way line of communication with God.
2. God emanates love.
3. God's love surrounds humankind.

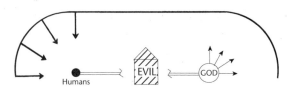

Stage 2 - The Situation Before Jesus' Birth

4. Evil has broken our direct link with God.
5. God's love continues to surround us.

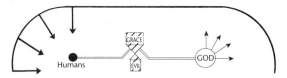

Stage 3 - The Situation After Jesus' Resurrection

6. God's grace through Jesus' sacrifice overcomes evil.
7. Our link with God is reestablished through grace.
8. Evil is still there but it cannot separate us from God any longer.

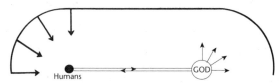

Stage 4 - The Final Situation At The End Of Time

9. Evil has disappeared completely.
10. Our original relationship with God has been reestablished.

The question then is, How did this happen? How sure are we that this is true? and, Who participates in that reconciliation? For an answer to these questions we have basically two sources:

•the Bible, through the testimonies of Jesus; his disciples and the apostles who spread his message across the world after his ascension, and

•the evidence of our own experience and that of other Christians over the last two thousand years.

Jesus' Own Testimony And That Of His Disciples About His Mission

The first testimony in the New Testament about Jesus' mission was given even before his own birth by Zechariah, the father of John the Baptist, who prophesied:

And you little child, (John)
you shall be called "Prophet of the Most High."
For you will go before the Lord
to prepare a way for him,
to give people knowledge of salvation
through the forgiveness of sins.

— Luke 1, The New Jerusalem Bible

At Jesus' own baptism an old and devout man, Simeon, who had received a promise through the Holy Spirit that he would not die until he had seen the Messiah, testified as follows:

Now, Master, you are letting your servant go in peace
as you promised;
for my eyes have seen the salvation
which you have made ready in the sight of the nations;
a light of revelation for the gentiles
and glory for Israel.

— Luke 2, The New Jerusalem Bible

Two of the best known testimonies of Jesus about his mission are two passages in the Gospel according to John:

For God so loved the world, that he gave his only begotten Son, that whosoever believes in him should not perish, but have everlasting life.

— *John 3, The King James Bible*

I am the good shepherd;
I know my own and my own know me,
just as the Father knows me and I know the Father;
and I lay down my life for my sheep ...
I lay it down of my own free will.

— *John 10, The New Jerusalem Bible*

All four testimonies point to Jesus as the Saviour or the one who brings salvation to humankind. Probably one of the clearest statements about his mission was given by Jesus himself to his disciples after his resurrection and, just before his ascension, when he gave his disciples their final instructions with these words:

He then opened their minds to understand the scriptures and he said to them:
"So it is written that the Christ would suffer, and on the third day rise from the dead, and that in his name repentance for the forgiveness of sins would be preached to all nations, beginning from Jerusalem.
You are witnesses to this."

Luke 24, The New Jerusalem Bible

Throughout the gospels and the letters of the apostles to the newly formed churches, the forgiveness of our sins and the consequent reconciliation with God is always connected with the requirement to have faith, that is, to believe in Jesus. Sometimes the need for repentance and the requirement for deeds that show the effect of this repentance are mentioned as well. Because this faith is so crucial for our reconciliation with God, we must find a clear understanding of what Jesus means when he says, "Believe in me," or "Believe in me and him who sent me."

From what Jesus taught it is clear that this belief must include:

1 — Belief that Jesus is the Son of God;

2 — Belief that Jesus has come to show us what God is like;

3 — Belief that Jesus has come to reconcile us with God;

4 — Belief that reconciliation could only happen by Jesus assuming the role of a mediator between God and humankind;

5 — Belief that for Jesus to become a true mediator, he had to assume the essence of a human being, who suffered pain like ordinary humans do and who died like ordinary humans do;

6 — Belief that for reconciliation to become real, Jesus had to be raised from the dead and be re-united with God.

These six statements give in capsule form what I believe Jesus meant when he said, "Believe in me and him who sent me." Later in this chapter, I will broaden this description to include not only what we mean when we say we believe in Jesus the Son of God, but also what we mean when we confess our faith in God.

For some people the word faith has lost much of its original meaning. As Sam Keen, the author of *Fire in the Belly*, said recently in a television appearance, "Faith is believing in something you know ain't so." For him, and for many others, the word trust has a much deeper meaning. We trust that God exists and knows us personally. For the remainder of the book, I will therefore use the words faith and trust together.

How Can Suffering And Death Of An Innocent Man Possibly Cause Reconciliation?

The Bible, in both the Old and the New Testaments, lays great stress and emphasis on the fact that if God is perfect, God must also be just. In other words, perfect goodness demands that there is also some form of final justice which rewards people who have lived a good life and punishes people who have lived evil lives.

206

This theme of justice is worked out in great detail by the more fundamentalist churches, which insist that Jesus' suffering was God's price for our reconciliation and the price for our sins being forgiven. God is thus understood to be such a stern judge that nothing less than the suffering of an innocent person would satisfy his/her sense of justice. This point of view seems to be supported by some of the teachings of the apostle Paul when he writes:

> *... it is to be counted in the same way to us who have faith in the God who raised Jesus our Lord from the dead; he was given up to death for our misdeeds, and raised to life to justify us.*
>
> — *Romans 4, The New English Bible*

There are similar passages in other places in Paul's writings. At the same time, however, nowhere in the gospels is it reported that Jesus himself indicated that his suffering and death were in direct payment for the sins of the world or that he endured them to satisfy God's sense of justice. The only time Jesus came close to mentioning anything like this was at the last supper he had with his disciples when he asked them to have a communal meal once in awhile to remember him. As reported by Matthew, these were the words he used when he instituted this meal of remembrance, which later became known as The Lord's Supper or Holy Communion:

> *Now as they were eating, Jesus took the bread, and when he had said the blessing he broke it and gave it to the disciples. "Take it and eat," he said, "this is my body." Then he took a cup, and when he had given thanks he handed it to them saying, "Drink from this, all of you, for this is my blood, the blood of the covenant, poured out for many for the forgiveness of sins."*
>
> — *Matthew 26, The New Jerusalem Bible*

It is important to realize in reading this saying of Jesus that, in Jewish thought at that time, blood represented the essence of life. So, Jesus said in effect that the very essence of his life was the source of forgiveness of sins and not just the pain and suffering.

I believe that a God who demands suffering to equalize human sin is not the God revealed in the New Testament, because it is in direct contradiction with what Jesus taught us about the nature of God, which is love. I believe that when we talk about reconciliation with God through Jesus Christ, we must consider the saving grace of Jesus' entire life on earth, and not just his death.

In both the Old and the New Testament, Jesus is described as the one who will reconcile us with God and as the mediator between God and humanity. In his letter to Timothy, the apostle Paul expresses it as follows:

> *For there is only one God, and there is only one mediator between God and humanity, himself a human being, who offered himself as a ransom for all.*
>
> — *1 Timothy 2:5, The New Jerusalem Bible*

According to the dictionary, a mediator is someone who acts as an intermediary or conciliator between two parties, a person who settles differences and who acts as a go-between for two sides of a dispute. In human affairs, a mediator is normally a person who is familiar with both sides of the dispute because he can only effectively mediate when he can understand both positions.

So, I believe that for Jesus to become a true mediator between God and us, he had to experience for himself what it was to be a human being in the world. It is for this reason that he came down to live among us and assumed all the attributes of a human being and experienced the full range of human feelings. He experienced not only joy but also pain and suffering, since both of these are an integral part of the human existence. Dr. Victor E. Frankl, a world famous psychiatrist who survived three years of life in Nazi concentration camps, wrote in his book, *Man's Search for Meaning*:

> *If there is a meaning in life at all, then there must be a meaning in suffering. Suffering is an ineradicable part of life, even as fate and death. Without suffering and death, human life cannot be complete.*[1]

Thus, for Jesus to become truly human, he had to experience not only joy, friendship and peace, but also pain, suffering and death; only then could he be considered to have assumed the full identity of a human being. It certainly shows how seriously God takes human sin and evil, that he did not spare Jesus the dark side of our human existence, that of suffering and death. And his death was not an easy death as we might wish for ourselves, but instead he experienced a horrible death on a cross.

We believe, therefore, that reconciliation with God was effected not by God wanting to inflict more pain and suffering on an innocent being, but by sending a mediator who came down to our level and placed himself beside us and experienced for himself the entire range of emotions and conditions that form part of our human existence. God did this, not in some token form, but by using as the Mediator, the Son, Jesus Christ, who assumed a human form in all things, except that he did not sin. I believe that it is only in this way that we can say that Jesus' suffering and death was part of our reconciliation with God, and it is only as the Mediator between God and humanity that Jesus became the Saviour of the world. It was not because God wanted to equalize a wrong that Jesus suffered, but in order to become an effective mediator he had to come down to our level of existence; and because suffering and death are an integral part of our human existence, Jesus also underwent the same human experiences.

How this reconciliation through the intermediary of God's Messenger actually was accomplished will forever, at least in this world, remain a mystery. But I believe far less of a mystery than assuming that God's love included sentencing the person closest to him/her to suffering and death to equalize an account. Maybe we can sum up the history of God's involvement with humankind in this way:

- At the beginning of time, God created humans to be his/her companions, and for a time there existed a perfect relationship between humankind and its Creator.
- After some time, evil arrived and seduced humans to rebel against their Creator.
- As a consequence of this rebellion, humans lost their direct link with God and eventually lost their first-hand knowledge of God.
- As a further consequence of that loss of innocence (goodness and perfection), pain, suffering and death entered into God's once perfect creation.
- When God saw how humans were developing, God's love for creation caused God to seek a way to re-establish that link with humankind. God did this by sending the Son, Jesus Christ, as a Mediator.
- The specific objectives of this Mediator were:
    - to re-establish a closer contact with humans and also to show them what they had lost by their rebellion against God;
    - to show humans how they should live by giving them his life on earth as an example to follow;
    - to experience for himself what human life was like in an imperfect world: a world, as it were, under occupation by a foreign power — the devil.
- All his time on earth, Jesus was subject to the same temptations as humans are, but he rejected them all, some with considerable difficulty: for instance, in the Garden of Gethsemane he asked three times to be relieved of the suffering on the cross he saw lying ahead of him.
- It was only after having experienced all of the human temptations, emotions, and pain including death that Jesus could act as our true Mediator, because it was only after experiencing the full life of a human being that he knew the two sides of the dispute intimately enough to assume the role of an effective mediator.
- As the Mediator, he then pleaded our case with God, and because of this plea and because of God's love for creation,

God accepted that plea and restored us back to our former position of God's eternal companions.
•To make that possible, God literally took away our mistakes and sins so that we would appear before God again pure and unblemished as we were before our separation.
•The only condition God put on that reconciliation was that we must believe in him/her and continue to try to live according to the laws and the examples set by Jesus Christ.
•The end result is that, although death and suffering are still here, in the new life to come we will be restored to a life that is in perfect harmony with that of our Creator.

I believe that if we look in this way at Jesus' death and suffering, we can continue our belief in a God who is truly love. God loved us so much that he/she sent a personal mediator who, in order to gain full knowledge of our side of the dispute he was to mediate, assumed a human existence. Only in this way could he experience what human life was like and what it was to experience the whole range of human conditions, including mental and physical suffering and even death. I believe that it was on the basis of this experience of the Mediator that God forgave humans their sins and that we were reconciled with our Maker.

It is Jesus' claim, and that of the gospel writers and the apostles, that if we believe in God and in Jesus' mission in this way, our sins are forgiven and we are in fact reconciled with God, as it is written:

> *I mean God was in Christ reconciling the world to himself, not holding anyone's faults against him, but entrusting to us the message of reconciliation.*
>
> *— 2 Corinthians 5:19 — The New Jerusalem Bible*

> *You have been washed clean, you have been sanctified, and you have been justified in the name of the Lord Jesus Christ and through the Spirit of God.*
>
> *— 1 Corinthians 6:11 — The New Jerusalem Bible*

> *My brothers, I want you to realize that it is through him,*
> *Jesus Christ, that forgiveness of sins is being proclaimed*
> *to you.*
>
> — *Acts 13:38* — *The New Jerusalem Bible*

> *Grace and peace from God the Father and our Lord Jesus*
> *Christ who gave himself for our sins to liberate us from*
> *this present wicked world, in accordance with the will of*
> *our God and Father, to whom be glory for ever and ever.*
>
> *Galatians 1:3* — *The New Jerusalem Bible*

The Roman Catholic Church has a sacrament of Confession and Absolution by which a believer confesses to a priest the things he has done wrong since his last confession. The priest hears the confession, in a confessional box which is constructed in such a way that the priest cannot see the person making the confession, thereby assuring his or her anonymity and privacy. At the end of the confession, the priest asks the person making the confession if they regret their sins and, if they do, he gives them a token task to do as a penance and then gives them absolution by declaring that their sins are forgiven.

In many ways, this process is probably of great psychological benefit to people who are excessively preoccupied with the mistakes and errors they have made in their lives. Most of the other Christian churches, however, do not follow this practice because they believe that we do not need a priest as an intermediary to obtain absolution of our sins and mistakes. In fact, they believe that all true believers are priests. The following may illustrate what I mean by that.

Some years ago, my son, who lives in Western Canada, had a serious car accident. Because of flight connections, I did not arrive in the hospital until late at night. Since I had left directly from the office, I was dressed in a dark suit and a dark overcoat. After visiting my son in the intensive care unit, I was approached by an elderly patient who, mistaking me for a priest, asked me to hear her confession. I told her that I was not a priest and that she should ask one of the nurses to phone her parish priest in the morning. However, she persisted; so, I sat down with her and heard her confession. When she was finished she said, "And now I want absolution." I told her that only a priest could do this, but that did not make the slightest impression on her and she kept insisting that after making her confession she now needed absolution. I hesitated a moment; then asked her if she regretted what she had done and when she said, "Yes," I said, "In the name of Jesus Christ I declare that your sins are forgiven." At that, she was satisfied and she went to sleep. My son told me later that she died several days after that. I have wondered once in awhile since then if I did the right thing that evening. But, on reflecting on it, I am sure that I was right. If we truly believe that Jesus' life and death have reconciled us with God and, that as a result, our sins are forgiven, then we can and must declare to all believers who truly repent of their wrongdoing that they are forgiven and are again reconciled with God. This is our firm belief and the ground for our hope in a glorious future relationship with God, the Maker of all things.

What Is Faith And Trust In God?

It is clear from Jesus' teaching and the writings of the apostles that in order to be part of that reconciliation we must have, in the first place, faith in God. At some places in the New Testament the need for faith is coupled with the need for repentance; in other places the need for good deeds is added as well. While this appears to indicate that there are three requirements, in practice it boils down to one, because faith, unless it is accompanied by repentance and good works, is as dead as the proverbial doornail. Repentance for things done wrong in the past, and determination to live a new life in which we share our talents and gifts with our neighbors are the natural results of having faith; without them, the faith we think we have is an illusion. As the apostle James put it when he wrote about

213

the fact that faith without deeds is dead, "You believe in the one God — that is creditable enough, but demons also believe and they tremble with fear."

In the previous section we mentioned some of the things we understand to be part of the profession of faith in Jesus Christ, the Son of God. If we extend that profession to also include faith in God, we must add the following:

- a belief that God is the Creator of this world;
- a belief that we are God's children and that we can approach God as our Father or Mother;
- a belief that we cannot be separated from God;
- a belief that we will enter a new life after death;
- a belief that God has a plan for this world and that we are an integral part of that plan.

So, if we say that we believe and that we have faith in God, we at the same time reconfirm that we trust God to fulfill the promises listed above, which he made to us in the past through the prophets and later through the Son, Jesus Christ.

Faith and trust in God also means that we believe that eventually we will find answers to a number of questions that are a complete mystery to us now, such as:

- Where does evil come from?
- Why is suffering such an integral part of life?
- Why does God not interfere when human beings perpetrate such terrible things as war or let millions of people die of starvation?
- Why does God not reveal himself/herself more openly today, or why is it so difficult for us to perceive God's revelation in the world of today?

For the present, we have no final answers; the best we can do is to speculate and to trust in God's final plan. Maybe the reason is that, in our present state of existence, we might not be able to comprehend the answers if they were given to us.

In any case, we believe that this faith and trust in God has reconciled us with God, and that this faith and trust in God gives our lives direction and meaning. As an illustration of how faith and trust in God are an essential ingredient to a Christian's life, I have used the following scene out of everyday life. I have called it, "The parable of the snow covered car."

> Sometime during winter you must have left your car outside overnight to find it the next morning covered with snow and ice. Have you ever looked at that cold piece of steel and wondered how that contraption could possibly ever generate any heat and ever move again to take you someplace?

> That is how most of us look at this world. Without faith and trust in a living God, the world is a cold and mechanical place without any warmth and unable to take us anywhere.

> But that car has an engine and fuel that together can generate heat and can make it move.

> In the same way, I believe God gives meaning and purpose to this world and gives it direction.

> However, knowing that there is an engine does not help us very much unless we have a key to the ignition to make it work.

> So it is with God: Knowing that God is there is not much use to us unless we have the key. God is there but we receive no warmth and no direction. The key we need to make the engine work is our faith and trust in God which makes us God's children and even co-creators. Without that key the world, our lives, and God's entire creation make no sense, just as a car without a key to the ignition can do nothing for us and can not take us anywhere. But we must turn the key ourselves. God in his mercy and compassion approaches us, seeks us out and even gives us the key, but we ourselves must turn it on in order to make it work. It is we who must approach God in faith and trust to become fully reconciled with our Creator.

In the chancel of the church in which I worship, there is a splendid stained glass window, similar, I believe, to one in St. Paul's Cathedral in London. The window shows a picture of Jesus standing in front of a house knocking on the door. The interesting thing about this picture is that the door does not have an outside handle, so that it can only be opened from the inside. In other words, Jesus comes to us and calls us, but we ourselves must open the door to him, just as in the parable of the snow covered car, we ourselves must turn the key before the engine will come to life.

I am convinced that Jesus knocks on our doors, on everyone's door. The question is, are you and I there to hear it; even if we are there, do we have a sufficiently open mind to hear it above the noise and confusion of our everyday concerns? It is only when we open the door to him and let him in that faith and trust in God can come into our lives, and provide us with that sure footing that we need to meet the challenges and disappointments that we are sure to encounter on our journey through life.

Who Is Reconciled With God?

For the last 2,000 years, people have argued back and forth about this question. Who is reconciled with God through the life and death of Jesus? Is it only the believers, the people who have faith in God and repent of the things they have done wrong?

For many people in the past, and even for some people today, the answer to this question is quite clear. They are convinced that only the people with faith are reconciled, or as some say, are saved and will go to heaven, while the rest of humankind remains condemned and will go to hell. This hell was envisioned and, in some people's minds even today, remains a place of eternal torment as is so vividly portrayed in some medieval paintings. However, this idea of eternal torment for things done wrong during a very short sojourn here on earth has mostly disappeared. I believe that such an image of God is completely contrary to God's nature, as revealed to us by Jesus Christ, which is love.

Today, if and when we think about hell, it is thought of as a place without God, a place where people are still separated from God, while heaven is thought of as a place where we live in God's presence.

Are we then justified to make even that distinction between the two groups? What about:

- the children who died before they could know God?
- the mentally handicapped?
- the people who have never heard about God?
- the people who were brought up with other concepts of God?

Do we truly believe that God has condemned these people, who are by far the greatest majority in this world, to an eternal existence without God? I don't think so for the following reasons:

1 — Jesus said that he had come to earth for *all* people, not for just a few. He said: "God so loved the *world* that he sent his only son." He did not say that God had sent Jesus for the benefit of only a few chosen ones.

2 — Jesus made it clear that we are all God's children. He said, "that through him the *world* may be saved."

3 — As said before, we believe that God is the personification of love. No matter how love is defined it cannot possibly include the condemnation of the majority of the people in this world to a permanent judgement, no matter what that judgement might be.

The apostle Paul, who was very strong on the final judgement by God, and felt that reconciliation could only be achieved through faith and repentance, nevertheless wrote in a letter to Timothy the following:

> *I mean that the point of all our toiling and battling is*
> *that we have put our trust in God and he is the Saviour*
> *of the whole human race but particularly of the believers.*
> *This is what you are to instruct and teach.*
>
> *— 1 Timothy 4, The New Jerusalem Bible*

Also, in another personal letter, this one addressed to Titus, he wrote:

> *You see God's grace has been revealed to save the whole*
> *human race.*
>
> *— Titus 2, The New Jerusalem Bible*

It is clear from these quotations that the apostle Paul was convinced that the whole human race would participate in the grace of God and in the reconciliation between humans and their Creator.

At the same time, there is no doubt that we will all be judged for the things we have done wrong. Since all of us are far from perfect, we will all be found guilty. But before sentence is passed on us we can all claim that:

•we are God's children;

•we all fall under God's grace and are all reconciled with God, through the life and death of Jesus Christ.

So we believe that in God's mercy and love there is an ultimate plan and destination for all of us, Christians and non-Christians alike. What these plans are we do not know, and whether they are the same for both groups we also do not know. One thing we do know is that God's plans for the future does not include eternal damnation for any group of people.

We affirm that we serve a God of love and compassion, a God who has created humans to be his/her companions and who has great plans for us. We should never think of God as being too small with human limits and limitations. We believe God's love and compassion is large enough to encompass all of creation without exception.

The good news for today is that through Jesus the old link with God, the Creator, has been re-established.

8

The Essence Of Jesus' Teaching

Introduction — The Creeds

As I have commented before, Jesus did not leave anything behind in the form of the written word. He left no book such as the Koran, written by Mohammed's followers almost immediately after his death, and believed to be an exact copy of the original which they believe is preserved in heaven. This makes the Koran inviolate and not to be questioned in any way. In contrast, what Jesus left behind was his teaching, and his message for humankind etched in the memories of his disciples.

After his death, his disciples and early followers spread his message by word of mouth, first in Palestine and later throughout the entire Roman empire. But it was not until some forty years after his death that the first written account appeared about what Jesus had taught, and what had happened during the last three momentous years of Jesus' life on earth.

However, before the first gospels were written, the early missionaries, or apostles as they were called, had started to travel across the Roman world telling people the Good News. Also, they had begun to write letters to the small communities of believers they had established in Asia and Europe. Some of these letters were eventually included in the New Testament as the "Letters of the Apostles." These letters are an interesting mixture of instruction, encouragement and criticism about the community's behavior during the absence of the apostles.

Since the gospels and the letters of the apostles were written by people who differed widely in temperament, education and experience, it is no wonder that they do not always agree on the details of what Jesus' message had been. Also, it is fairly certain that none of the writers of these gospels had actually been with Jesus during his life on earth, and they therefore had received the message second-hand. Some of them had probably never been in Palestine with the results that some gospels contain geographical errors.

In addition to all of this, the nationality and the previous religious allegiances of the people, who came to accept the message of Christ and formed the early churches, differed widely. Some of the early believers came from areas that are now called Lebanon and Turkey; others were citizens of Greece and Italy. Some were brought up in the old Jewish tradition, while yet others came from the Greek and Roman practice of worshipping a multiplicity of gods. Partly because of this great diversity in background, the various churches started to stress some parts of Jesus' message to the detriment of other parts.

These different interpretations eventually led to some very heated arguments and discussions among the early church members. In response to this, the church started to write down in an abbreviated form what they considered to be the essence of the Christian faith. In doing so, they hoped that these formal statements, or creeds as they were called, would settle all disputes once and for all. As could be expected their hopes did not come true. Disputes about the correct interpretation of Jesus' teaching continued, and other statements were written periodically to reflect the changes in attitudes and the changes in external circumstances. For instance, a creed written in a time of severe persecution obviously tended to stress other aspects of Jesus' message than one written after the Christian religion had become the state religion.

Eventually a creed emerged that is still extensively used in many churches today — The Apostolic Creed. It states in a very condensed form the basic things Christians believe in, and it is as relevant today as it was when it was first formulated some 1,700 years ago. It reads as follows:

> *I believe in:*
>> *God, the Father Almighty, maker of heaven and earth;*
> *I believe in:*
>> *Jesus Christ, his only son, our Lord,*
>>> *who was conceived by the Holy Spirit,*
>>> *born of the virgin Mary,*
>>> *suffered under Pontius Pilate,*
>>> *was crucified, dead and buried;*
>>> *He descended into hell;*
>>> *the third day he rose again from the dead;*
>>> *He ascended into heaven and sitteth on the right*
>>> *hand of God the Father Almighty;*
>>> *From whence he shall come to judge the quick and*
>>> *the dead.*
> *I believe in:*
>> *the Holy Ghost;*
>> *the holy catholic church;*
>> *the communion of saints;*
>> *the forgiveness of sins;*
>> *the resurrection of the body; and*
>> *the life everlasting.*

While this ancient creed is still widely used, it is neverthe-less a fact that most Christians today would state their faith in somewhat different terms. I believe it is important to real-ize that our faith, and therefore the creeds, can never be a static thing but must be alive and change with new insights and new understanding of Christ's message. That message needs re-interpretation with the changing conditions and circumstances of life. For instance, slavery was a long established fact of life during Jesus' time, and neither Jesus nor his apostles ever made it a point to condemn that practice which is so alien to us today. What they did do was to state clearly that the slave was no different from his master, and that they were in fact brothers in Christ and should treat each other as such. Later generations of Christians saw in the practice of slavery something evil and contrary to the most elemental rights of humankind and, in accordance with that belief, they acted and placed themselves in the forefront of those fighting to abolish slavery.

Similarly, the Church must continually rethink the implications of Christ's message for the changed conditions and circumstances of every age. At this point in time, great shifts are occurring in our understanding of the position of women in the church, in our attitude towards homosexuality, and towards our responsibility for the earth God has entrusted to our care. Future creeds no doubt will include references to these aspects of our evolving faith.

A creed that is presently in use in the United Church of Canada not only states what we believe in but also outlines what we should be doing as Christians in today's world. It stresses the belief that we are not alone in this world, not now and not after death. It reads as follows:

> *We are not alone, we live in God's world.*
> *We believe in God:*
>   *who has created and is creating,*
>   *who has come in Jesus, the Word made flesh,*
>   *to reconcile and make new,*
>   *who works in us and others by the Spirit.*
> *We trust in God.*
> *We are called to be the Church:*
>   *to celebrate God's presence,*
>   *to love and serve others,*
>   *to seek justice and resist evil,*
>   *to proclaim Jesus, crucified and risen,*
>   *our judge and our hope.*
> *In life, in death, in life beyond death, God is with us.*
> *We are not alone.*
> *Thanks be to God.*

Even this very new creed was changed recently to allow the use of inclusive language which is now generally accepted as reflecting our concept of God as being a spirit and therefore neither male nor female. As a consequence, the sentence that used to read: "He calls us to be his Church," now reads, "We are called to be the Church."

Comparing this creed with the Apostolic Creed shows that they are not different in any essential way, both stress that:
- God is the creator of the universe;
- Jesus has come to reconcile us with God;
- The Holy Spirit is God's presence with us here and now;
- There is a life beyond death.

As pointed out before, the second creed also includes a section on what God expects humans to do. This was missing in almost all the other creeds, and its inclusion in this creed is a very necessary and welcome addition. I will return to this in the next chapter.

With this background we will now examine and summarize what Jesus taught us about:
- God, the Father/Mother;
- Himself, the Son;
- The Holy Spirit;
- The importance of humans;
- The meaning of life;
- Eternal life and life after death;
- Prayer, the open line of communication we have with God the Creator.

In the previous pages we have touched upon all these subjects so some duplication is unavoidable, but I believe that it is important to summarize in one chapter all that Jesus taught so that we have a complete picture of his message in a logical sequence.

The Personal God

During his ministry, Jesus indicated repeatedly that we could only know God through him. Matthew reports him as saying:

> *Everything has been entrusted to me by my Father; and*
> *no one knows the Son except the Father, just as no one*
> *knows the Father except the Son and those to whom the*
> *Son chooses to reveal him.*

— *Matthew 11, The New Jerusalem Bible*

Later on in the gospel, Jesus states very clearly that if you know
him, the Son, then you also know God, the Father. So, in many
ways, it is difficult to separate Jesus' teachings about himself
from his teaching about God.

If we concentrate on what Jesus said about God, we are
struck immediately by the fact that Jesus speaks of God, the
Father, as a personal God — a God who wants to have a personal relationship with us, the children. As shown in Appendix 1, it is this aspect of the Christian religion that distinguishes
it more than anything else from the other major faiths. Even
in Islam, the individual, while responsible for his actions to
God, does not have that same relationship with God which
is characterized by the relationship between a father or mother
with his or her children. In Islam, although God is felt to be
close to humans, God is nevertheless thought to be too great
and too far removed from humankind to have any direct relationship with human beings on an individual basis.

It is only in Christianity and Judaism that we are taught
and encouraged to approach the Creator of the universe as
we approach our own father or mother. We are God's children known by name, and we are not nameless specks in a total population of 6 billion people. Instead Jesus tells us that
we are known to God personally and that he/she cares for us
on an individual basis. Both Luke and Matthew report Jesus
as saying:

> *Can you not buy five sparrows for two pennies?*
> *And yet no one is forgotten in God's sight.*
> *Why, every hair on your head is counted.*
> *There is no need to be afraid,*
> *You are worth more than many sparrows.*

Think of the flowers growing in the fields; they never have to work or to spin; yet I assure you that not even Solomon in all his royal robes was clothed like one of these. Now if that is how God clothes the wild flowers in the field, which are here today and thrown in the furnace tomorrow, will he not much more look after you.

— *Matthew 6, The New Jerusalem Bible*

Elsewhere, Jesus compares our situation with that of a shepherd who, when he loses one sheep out of a hundred, goes out to look for it until he finds it. Following this, Jesus uses the example of a woman who has lost a coin and looks for it until she finds it. In each case Jesus finishes by saying that, as these people rejoiced about finding that one thing they had lost, so is there great rejoicing in heaven over *one* sinner who repents. I will come back to this personal relationship we can enjoy with God in later sections on prayer and on the importance we have in God's eyes as his companions and co-creators.

The point I want to stress here is that Jesus taught his disciples that we are known individually to God, just as a child is known individually by its father and mother no matter how many brothers and sisters there are in the family. This certain knowledge, which is expressed in the last creed as "We are not alone, God is with us," is one of the fundamental and essential parts of Christianity. This assurance puts us on an entirely different footing: we have a parent to whom we can turn — a parent who will listen to us and who will never abandon us, not now, not in death, and not in life after death. This assurance of God's continuing presence with us is especially important today when technological breakthroughs threaten even the continued existence of the earth as we know it, and when we often have the uncomfortable feeling that things are completely out of control.

Sometimes it appears to be utterly unrealistic to believe that the God, who created the universe and is so utterly beyond our comprehension, actually is involved with each individual person. Nevertheless, that is what Jesus kept repeating and is part of the Good News which Jesus brought to us. For instance, when Jesus is talking about prayer, he makes it very clear that God hears our individual prayers. Just imagine millions of people praying at the same time, and God hearing each one and knowing the particular circumstances of each one as well. But, if we state that we believe in a personal God, that is exactly what we are saying. Today, this does not sound as far-fetched as it did even thirty years ago. Today, anyone can come close to doing something very similar. With the aid of super computers and the newest communication technologies we could, if we wanted to:

- •transmit millions of pieces of information from all over the world to one central location;
- •record the personal information of everyone in a data bank in this central place and have this information available for almost instant retrieval;
- •process millions of requests (prayers) almost simultaneously and, by using the built-in guidelines, provide appropriate answers.

If we can do this today with computers and radio waves, it should not be too difficult for us to imagine what God can do who does not need radio waves or computers to communicate with us. The basic difference between what we can do now, and what we might possibly be able to do in the future, is that we must depend on information provided to us by others which is then fed into the computers, while God can see into our hearts and take into account our entire human situation, our hopes and our fears, our strengths and our weaknesses.

Anyone who comes to believe in this incredible message of a personal God cannot help from changing. To begin with, we cannot help but change our opinion of ourselves because we now know that we are important to the most Powerful Entity in the whole universe. At the same time, it must change our attitude towards our particular situation in life because we know that our suffering, our failures and our triumphs are known to the Creator of the universe.

In some ways it is a little like you meeting a king, queen or president of a large country who calls you by your name and talks to you about your family and your job. You most certainly would feel elated and flattered that a person in such a high position would know all about you and seems to care about you. It would probably give you an entirely different outlook on life, and it would certainly give you an added feeling of importance. How much more then would your attitude change when you find out that the Maker of this entire universe knows about you and cares for you individually!

Also, this knowledge that you are known personally to God must change your attitude towards other people because you know that God knows them as well as God knows you. You are in fact their neighbour, their brother or sister, and eventually you will be living in the same house side by side. Jesus tells us that God knows us so well that we do not even have to ask for anything from him because as he said, "Your Father knows what you need before you ask him." (Matthew 6) It is this knowledge and this faith and trust in a personal God that has sustained Christians through the ages and will do so in the ages to come.

The God Who Is Love

During his three-year ministry here on earth, Jesus must have taught many things about the qualities and attributes of God other than his revelation that God is a personal God who knows and cares for people individually. It must be remembered at this point that Jesus was speaking to Jews who were, from the day they were born, steeped in the teachings about God as found in the Old Testament. Thus Jesus does not often speak, or at least the writers of the gospels did not find it necessary to repeat what Jesus had said, about these other qualities of God. He must have talked to his followers extensively about God, the Creator, the Infinitely Great, the Holy One and about God, the Judge and Just. Instead of these qualities, the gospels emphasize the quality of God that is most relevant to us today, which is that God is love. This was of course not new to the Jews: in fact, the Old Testament is full of references to the love God has for humans. Consider for instance what the psalmist says in what is probably the best known passage in the Bible, Psalm 23:

> *The Lord is my shepherd; I shall not be in want. He makes me lie down in green pastures, he leads me beside quiet waters, he restores my soul. He guides me in paths of righteousness for his name's sake. Even though I walk through the valley of the shadow of death I will fear no evil, for you are with me; your rod and your staff, they comfort me. You prepare a table before me in the presence of my enemies. You anoint my head with oil; my cup overflows. Surely goodness and love will follow me all the days of my life, and I will dwell in the house of the Lord forever.*
>
> — *Psalm 23, New International Version*

There are countless other references in the Old Testament to this love God has for humankind, and it is this quality of God that Jesus seems to have emphasized more than any other. The fact that God does not leave humans on their own, but actually goes out to seek them is stressed by Jesus time and time again. Such parables as the shepherd looking for a lost sheep, and the woman sweeping the house for a lost coin, all point to a God who is searching for us and asking us to come back to him/her. Probably the best known parable which illustrates God's concern for us better than any other is the parable of the "Prodigal Son" as it is recorded in chapter 15 of the gospel according to Luke.

In this parable, which Jesus told his disciples, a young man wants to get away from the confining environment of his home and taste life in the fast lane. So he asks his father for his share of his future inheritance and the father gives it to him. The young man goes to the city and leads a dissolute life, until his money runs out. When this happens, his new found friends melt away like snow before the sun, and the young man finds himself destitute in a foreign country. In order to survive, he takes on one of the lowest paid menial jobs, that of looking after a herd of swine, which, for a Jew, must have been especially repulsive since swine were considered to be unclean.

One day, when he remembers how well the servants at his father's house are treated, he decides that it would be far better for him to be a servant in his father's house than a starving stranger in a foreign land. So he goes home. His father, in the meantime, has never given up hope that the lost son would one day come to his senses and return home. So he never gives up looking down the road to see if his son will return. Eventually he sees him coming and he rushes into the house to tell the servants to prepare a great feast because his son, who was lost, has returned. He then goes out to meet his son and embraces him as a lost son who has returned to his father's home.

We may believe that in the same way God will welcome us when we return to him/her, since that is the extent of God's love and concern for us. No matter how much the son had hurt his father by leaving him, the father was there waiting for him to welcome him back.

It is above all the apostle John who, both in his gospel and in his letters, returns time and time again to this love of God for humankind. The following quotation comes from the beginning of the gospel according to John, but it says all there is to say on this subject in just two sentences:

> *For God so loved the world that he gave his one and only Son. So that whoever believes in him shall not perish but have eternal life.*
>
> — *John 3, New International Version*

Jesus, The Son Of God

When one reads any of the four gospels and compares them with the writings of the other founders of great religions, one is struck immediately by the seemingly fantastic claims Jesus is making about himself and his true identity. Claims that are

229

so far-fetched and so blasphemous in the eyes of the devout Jews that they repeatedly tried to stone him because that was the proper and approved punishment for blasphemy. When Mohammed founded Islam, he only claimed that he was a messenger, a prophet, who was told by God to recite what he perceived God was telling him. Nowhere did he claim that he was part of God or that he was close to God. Similarly, Buddha, the founder of the Buddhist religion, never claimed to be anything else but a normal human being who had achieved enlightenment.

The claims Jesus is making on the other hand are so incredible that they can only be regarded as the utterances of a deranged mind, of someone who should be in a mental institution, unless of course what he claims is true. The first and foremost claim he is making is that he is the Son of God and that he has a very special and close relationship with God whom he calls his Father. For instance, he is quoted as saying of himself:

> *I and the Father are one.*
> *I am in the Father and the Father is in me.*
> *Everything has been entrusted to me by the Father.*
> *I have my origin in God and have come from him.*
>
> — *John 10, 14, and 16:28, The New Jerusalem Bible*

To show that this claim is not only of his own making, the first three gospels report how on a number of occasions God called down, as it were from heaven, to confirm Jesus' close relationship with God. Matthew and Mark both report hearing a voice from heaven saying, "This is my beloved Son on whom my favour rests," while Luke reports that people heard a voice saying, "You are my Son; today I have fathered you." (Luke 3)

On occasion Jesus also calls himself the "Son of Man" which is interpreted to mean that he identified himself fully with the human race and that he was fully human. But the thing that most distinguishes Jesus from ordinary men is the fact that he claims to be so close to God that the relationship can only adequately be described by comparing it with the relationship and the bond that exists between parents and their children. To make it abundantly clear to his followers that this was not a mere figure of speech, and that he had come with a special mission from his Father, he used the following parable:

> *A landowner planted a vineyard, leased it to tenants and then went abroad. When the time came to collect the rent, he sent some of his servants to collect it, but the tenants refused to pay and even killed some of his servants. The landowner then sent more servants but they fared no better. Finally he sent his son to them, thinking: "They will respect my son." But when the tenants saw the son, they said to each other: "This is the heir, come let us kill him and take over the inheritance." So they seized him, threw him out of the vineyard and killed him.*

— *Mark 12, The New Jerusalem Bible*

There cannot be much doubt about the meaning and implication of this parable. Jesus was the Son of God sent by God on a special mission to straighten out the relationship between God and humans, but humankind did not take this opportunity and instead put the Son to death. In a book, *Basic Christianity*, John Stott makes the following observation: "So close was Jesus' identification with God, that it was natural for him to equate a man's attitude to himself with his attitude towards God." For instance he says:

> *To know him was to know God.*
> *To see him was to see God.*
> *To believe in him was to believe in God.*
> *To receive him was to receive God.*
> *To hate him was to hate God.*
> *To honour him was to honour God.*

John Stott further points out Jesus repeatedly makes claims that all start out with the personal pronoun. He says of himself:

> *I am the bread of life; he who comes to me shall not hunger, and he who believes in me shall never thirst.*

> *I am the light of the world; he who follows me will not walk in darkness, but will have the light of life.*
>
> *I am the resurrection and the life; he who believes in me though he die, yet shall he live, and whoever lives and believes in me shall never die.*
>
> *I am the way and the truth, and the life, no one comes to the Father but by me.*
>
> *Come to me all who labour and are heavy laden and I will give you rest.*[1]

So, in addition to claiming to be God's Son, Jesus also claims that we can only know God and be reconciled with God through him, and that, in fact, he is the only way that we humans can come close to God. Thus, we see Jesus emerging as the mediator between God and humankind. The one human being who knows God, and through whom God was revealed to humankind, and through whom the world was reconciled with God.

The other unbelievable claim Jesus made was that he could forgive sins. For the true Jewish believer that was something only God could do. Nevertheless, this is exactly what he claimed he could do, and he set out to prove it to his followers and detractors as reported in the following story:

> *And suddenly some people brought him a paralytic stretched out on a bed. Seeing their faith, Jesus said to the paralytic, "Take comfort my child, your sins are forgiven." And now some scribes said to themselves, "This man is being blasphemous." Knowing what was in their mind Jesus said, "Why do you have such wicked thoughts in your heart?" Now which is easier to say, "Your sins are forgiven" or to say, "Get up and walk?" But to prove to you that the Son of Man has authority on earth to forgive sins — then he said to the paralytic — "get up, pick up your bed and go home." And the man got up and went home.*
>
> — *Matthew 9, The New Jerusalem Bible*

The story ends with Matthew's observation that a feeling of awe came over the people who had witnessed this and they praised God for giving such authority to human beings.

In addition to describing himself as the Son of God, Jesus also repeatedly speaks of himself as a servant who has come to serve humankind. First he identifies himself with the suffering servant as described by the prophet Isaiah some 500 years before and as quoted in the previous chapter:

> *He is despised and rejected of men;*
> *a man of sorrows and acquainted with grief.*
>
> — *Isaiah 53, The King James Bible*

Jesus repeatedly told his hearers that he had come to serve humankind and that his followers must do the same. The clearest demonstration of this servant function is probably given in the story of Jesus washing the feet of his disciples. Since the people of Jesus' time generally wore only sandals, and since the roads were often very dusty, it was the custom of people to wash their feet, or have them washed by a servant, before they sat down to eat. Needless to say that the washing of feet was not done by the highest ranking servant. In the story by John, it is Jesus who kneels down to wash the feet of his disciples and, when they object, he tells them that unless he serves them, they cannot be his disciples. He then says to them:

> *Do you understand what I have done to you? You call me Master and Lord, and rightly; so I am. If I, then, the Lord and Master, have washed your feet, you must wash each other's feet. I have given you an example so that you may copy what I have done to you.*
>
> — *John 13, The New Jerusalem Bible*

Elsewhere Jesus emphasizes his servant function when he says:

> *Anyone who wants to be great among you must be your servant, and anyone who wants to be first among you*

> *must be slave to all. For the Son of Man himself came*
> *not to be served but to serve and give his life as a ransom*
> *for many.*
>
> — *Matthew 20, The New English Bible*

Of course, the full servant function of Jesus finds its culmination in his life and death through which he restored the relationship humankind had with its Creator at the beginning of time.

Considering what Jesus said about himself, it is no wonder that in almost 2,000 years since Jesus lived on earth, an unending stream of books and articles has been written about the true nature of Jesus. The early church tried to find a formula that would satisfy the many different aspects of Jesus' being. In the creed of Nicea, they stated that Jesus was in fact an integral part of God and therefore God himself. However, since one of the basic tenets of the church was then, and is now, that there is only one God and Creator, they formulated the doctrine of the Holy Trinity in which the one God is assumed to have three different natures: God, the Father; God, the Son; and God, the Holy Spirit.

A close scrutiny of the gospels shows, however, that nowhere did Jesus ever make such a claim and neither did the writers of the epistles including Paul. Probably one of the clearest statements about the nature of Jesus can be found in the first letter from Paul to his co-worker, Timothy, where Paul writes:

> *For there is only one God and one mediator between God*
> *and humanity, Christ Jesus, **a human being himself**, who*
> *offered himself as a ransom for all.*
>
> — *1 Timothy 2, The New Jerusalem Bible*

Another indication of the true humanity of Jesus may be found in Paul's letter to the Romans where he makes a comparison between the fact that sin came into the world by one man, Adam, and similarly grace and salvation came through another man, Jesus Christ. If Paul had believed that Jesus was

234

divine and an integral part of God, he never could have made such a statement.

So then, who do we say Jesus is? Summarizing what he said about himself, we find:

On the one hand, he was fully human:

- •he was born; he lived for some thirty years among us and then he died;
- •he had human emotions — he laughed, he wept, he was angry; but
- •he did not sin and, in fact, he was the human being we should have been;
- •he came as a servant to serve humankind.

On the other hand, he was the Son of God and so acclaimed by God;

- •he was the Messiah for whom Israel had been waiting for centuries;
- •he was so close to God that God gave him powers far beyond that of a normal human being;
- •after he died, God raised him from the dead and made him sit "at the right hand of God";
- •he was God's chosen vehicle to bring us the message of God's love and the forgiveness of our sins;
- •he was the mediator who reconciled us with our Creator.

If we consider all this evidence it is not surprising that the early church went so far as to declare that Jesus must be more than just a human being and must be divine as well.

Today, many Christians believe that this went too far. They believe that Jesus was a very special human being, but fully human nevertheless. In his book, *Jesus, The Evidence*, Ian Wilson pointed out that there is no evidence that Jesus ever made the claim that he was the personification of God. At the end of the book, he nevertheless asks the question, "Was Jesus so completely a vessel of God, the living, breathing word of God, that to all intents and purposes God was speaking through him, and *was* him?"[2] (My italics)

So, in summary, we may be able to say that Jesus was so close to God that for all practical purposes we can consider him part of God. The only comparison that comes to mind, and which may come near to describing this relationship, is that of a landholder with a large number of tenants who adopts a child from one of his tenants as his son. Later, when the child grows up, the landowner and his adopted son become so close that he gives him increasing authority over the running of the estate. Eventually, the adopted son knows exactly what his father would have done in any given situation and the father gives him authority to even forgive the tenants their debts. In the end, as far as the tenants are concerned the adopted son *is* the landowner. In fact, the son can say that he and the father are one, and if the landowner makes the further stipulation that the tenants must deal with the son only, the son can claim that, "No one comes to the father but through me." Despite this close relationship, the son never will *be* the real landowner; the latter will always retain his final authority and there will always be things the landowner alone will decide.

So it is with Jesus. He did not know everything. For instance, when the disciples asked him about the time of his second coming, he answered: "But as for that day and hour, nobody knows it, neither the angels in heaven, nor the Son, no one but the Father." (Matthew 24)

In closing, we repeat what the two creeds we mentioned at the beginning of the chapter say about Jesus:

> *I believe in Jesus Christ, his only Son, our Lord.*
>
> — *The Apostolic Creed*
>
> *We believe in God, who has come in Jesus, the Word made flesh, to reconcile and make new.*
>
> — *The United Church of Canada Creed*

Jesus' Teaching About The Holy Spirit

Both creeds continue, after expressing their faith in Jesus Christ, with a statement about the Holy Spirit. The Apostolic Creed states simply:

236

"I believe in the Holy Ghost."
The new creed is more specific. It states:
"We believe in God
Who works in us and others by the Spirit."
Some people may find the idea of the Holy Spirit being an essential part of God difficult to understand. But, in fact, it is one of the more logical concepts surrounding the mystery of God's true nature. It is, I believe, a very natural consequence of our faith in a personal God who is concerned with people's lives. If you accept as fact that God exists and is acting through people to make his/her love and concern felt in this world, then you must also accept the fact that God must have a medium or a vehicle to communicate with people and to make them aware of what is expected of them. It is this means of communication, this presence of God with us and within us, that we call the Holy Spirit or God's Spirit. It is this Spirit which is the intermediary through which God makes things happen. For instance, it was through this Spirit that God created the world and all that is in it, as described in the first two sentences in the Bible which read as follows:

> *In the beginning God created the heaven and earth. And the earth was without form and void, and darkness was upon the face of the earth. And the Spirit of God moved upon the face of the waters. And God said let there be light, and there was light.*
>
> — *Genesis 1, The King James Bible*

Thus the story of creation, as relayed to us in the first chapter of Genesis, stresses that it was God's Spirit and God's word that created all things.

A similar reference to God's word which makes things happen can be found in the gospel according to John when he begins his account of Jesus' life and teaching with these words:

> *In the beginning was the Word: the Word was with God and the Word was God. He was with God in the*

237

> *beginning. Through him all things came into being, not one thing came into being except through him.*
>
> — *John 1, The New Jerusalem Bible*

In the Jewish tradition, words once spoken were identified so closely with the person that they were almost considered synonymous. Thus, in this passage from John, the term "Word" is used to identify God or God's Spirit. The Word was God and it was through this Word, or this Spirit, that all things were made.

It is this same Spirit which descended on Jesus at the beginning of his ministry as reported by the gospel writers:

> *When Jesus was baptised and was praying, heaven opened and The Holy Spirit descended on him in bodily form like a dove, and there came a voice from heaven saying, "You are my Son; today have I fathered you."*
>
> — *Luke 3, The New Jerusalem Bible*

At the same time Jesus repeated many times that he was able to do the things he was doing only because the Holy Spirit was working these things through him.

Towards the end of his ministry, Jesus told his disciples that after his departure God's Spirit would descend on them. Anyone, who has any doubt about the actual power of the Holy Spirit, has only to read what happened to the disciples after they received this Spirit to make their doubt completely disappear. The story, as told in the Acts of the Apostles, recounts how a small group of disillusioned and fearful people were, after they received the Holy Spirit, suddenly changed into fearless, eloquent and inspired preachers. The apostle Peter, a simple fisherman, who could probably neither read nor write, and who had just recently sworn that he did not know Jesus, stood up in front of large crowds and gave a most eloquent and well reasoned account of the Good News that they were bringing to the world.

It was this bunch of unlikely to succeed, ordinary people who, guided by the Holy Spirit, left their homes and travelled through the entire known world of that time to proclaim the message of Jesus. In doing so they changed the world and the world has never been the same since.

We believe that this Spirit of God is with us today, just as it was with the early followers of Jesus. As the United Church creed expresses it: "We believe in God who works in us and others by the Spirit." It is this Spirit which makes us overcome doubt and makes us continue to try to follow in Jesus' footsteps no matter how many times we fail. It can, and does still, change people overnight as it did the disciples some 2,000 years ago. C. S. Lewis in his book, *Surprised by Joy*, tells how he finally came to accept God. In his account of the final event, one can almost feel the presence of an external force that makes him make this final step. As he reports it:

> *In the Trinity Term of 1929 I gave in, and admitted that God was God, and knelt and prayed; perhaps, that night, the most dejected and reluctant convert in all England ... a prodigal who is brought in kicking, struggling, resentful, and darting his eyes in every direction for a chance to escape.*[3]

Today, with all the problems that face the human race, we need this Spirit more than ever. Without that Spirit guiding us to take action to help level the inequalities that beset human-kind and to help overcome all the potential dangers contained in the unbridled application of science, our world may be doomed. So, today, more than ever, we need this Spirit and we should pray for this Spirit to become part of us and guide us in our lives. Because it is this Spirit which is, in fact, God with us.

What Jesus Taught Us About Our Importance

There is probably no single aspect of human life that causes greater anxiety and anguish among human beings than the feeling that they are of no importance and that their existence is meaningless. As Dr. Scott Peck put it in his book, *Further*

Along The Road Less Travelled: "There is nothing that holds us back more from mental health, from society, and from God than the sense we all have of our own unimportance, unloveliness and undesirability."[4] That this feeling is not new, and has been around for a long time, is evident from the world's literature in which this feeling of meaninglessness is repeatedly used as a major theme. It is probably most eloquently expressed in one of the lesser known books of the Bible, Ecclesiastes, written by a person known as the "Speaker" or the "Preacher," a king in Jerusalem. He writes:

> *Emptiness, emptiness, says the Speaker, emptiness, all is empty. What does man gain from all his labour and his toil under the sun? Generations come and generations go, while the earth endures forever. The sun rises and the sun goes down; back it returns to its place and rises there again. The wind blows South, the wind blows North and round it goes and returns in full circle. All streams run into the sea, yet the sea never overflows; back to the place from which the streams ran they return to run again. I have amassed great wisdom more than all my predecessors on the throne in Jerusalem; I have become familiar with wisdom and knowledge. So I applied my mind to understand wisdom and knowledge, madness and folly, and I came to see that this is also chasing the wind. For in much wisdom is much vexation, and the more a man knows, the more he has to suffer.*
>
> *So I said to myself, "I too shall suffer the fate of the fool. To what purpose have I been wise? What is the profit of it? Even this, I said to myself is emptiness. The wiseman is remembered no longer than the fool, for as the passing days multiply, all will be forgotten. Alas wisemen and fools die the same death!" So I came to hate life, since everything that was done here under the sun was a trouble to me; for all is emptiness and chasing the wind.*
>
> — *Ecclesiastes 1, The New English Bible*

No doubt this outpouring of the king reflects in many ways the thoughts and misgivings we have from time to time. Yet he was a great king and had achieved many things and had acquired much wisdom, but none of it seems to have helped him to find meaning in his life or give him a sense of self-worth.

At the time this "Preacher" was writing these outpourings of utter frustration, people still thought that they were unique and that the earth was the center of the universe. But even that was taken away, when over the years it became increasingly clear that, astronomically speaking, human beings were not that important at all, and that we were not located anywhere near to the center of the cosmos. The earth turned out not to be the center of our solar system; and our solar system turned out to be not anywhere near the center of our galaxy; nor did our galaxy turn out to be anywhere near the center of the known universe. In addition, it was discovered that there were millions of galaxies and that most of these were much larger than the one inhabited by humankind.

These discoveries have not tended to increase our sense of our own importance; on the contrary, it reduced our importance within that universe, in a physical sense, to absolutely nothing. It is no wonder that it took humankind some time to adjust to this steep decline in its apparent importance in the universe. Within this context, what a human being is left with is that it is born, it lives for some time and then it dies — period, end of story. It is this feeling of the meaninglessness of our existence that many people find very hard to live with and leads some people to such despair that they take their own lives.

Fortunately, despite what we may think once in a while, this evaluation of our situation could not be further from the truth. We are not without importance; we are not a speck in the universe; our lives are not meaningless and useless. On the contrary we are so important that we can call the creator of the whole universe, our Father/Mother. This Parent tells us that we are its children and that it knows us so well that it calls us by name. Any parent knows how important the well-being of his or her children are in their lives. From the moment they are born, the major concern for the true parent is for their children. Even when the children have become adults, the parent is still filled with worry and concern not only for their own child but, if there are any, for the grandchildren as well. It is a concern that a father or mother will never be able to drop. It is there for the rest of their lives.

If we can believe that the Creator of the universe cares for us in the same way, then we are obviously talking about an entirely different human being than that insignificant person whose life is without meaning and substance, so eloquently described by the "Preacher." We are suddenly talking about a person who operates in an entirely different reality, a person who lives on an entirely different plateau.

It is something like suddenly finding out that you are not a common citizen but that in fact you are of royal blood. Your outward appearance does not change, but you are suddenly a changed person, you are a somebody, you are a prince or princess. This is but a very pale comparison to what happens to us when we come to believe that we are so important in the sight of God that s/he calls us his/her children. We suddenly change from an ordinary citizen to a person of royal blood. A human being with no future, with no importance, is suddenly transformed into a person who is the child of the "Most High," and who has a glorious future ahead of him or her. And, just as the prince and princess derive their special importance solely from the fact that they are the son or daughter of a king and queen, so do we receive this position of special importance, not from our own attributes or special abilities, but simply from the fact that we are the children of the living God.

In the previous sections, I have quoted a few instances in which Jesus refers to the importance human beings have in God's eyes, such as when he says that the hairs on our head are counted; that if God so clothed the wild flowers, that are here one day and are gone the next, how much more will God look after us. The point Jesus makes, time and time again, is that we are known to God personally and that we are not an insignificant speck of humanity lost among the billions of others.

One of the important messages contained in the creation story, as it appears in the first book of the Bible, is that God put humankind in charge of the new creation or, as expressed in the old translation of the Bible, that humans were to have dominion over it. The writer of Psalm 8, who starts off by expressing how insignificant he feels, then changes course completely when he recalls that God has made humans a little less than gods and has put them in charge of God's creation. He writes:

When I look up at the heavens, the work of thy fingers, the moon and the stars set in place by thee, what is man that thou shouldst care for him? Yet thou hast made him a little less than a god, crowning him with glory and honour. Thou makest him master over all thy creatures; thou hast put everything under his feet: all sheep and oxen, all the wild beasts, the birds in the air and the fish in the sea, and all that moves along the paths of ocean. O Lord our sovereign, how glorious is thy name in all the earth!

— *Psalm 8, The New English Bible*

The special task assigned to us, as described in this psalm, puts a great deal of responsibility on our shoulders and has far reaching consequences for the human race. It means, for one thing, that God will hold us responsible for what we do with and to this earth. For instance, it means that our creative ability must always be guided and constrained by that responsibility.

The fact that God has put us in charge also means that we cannot count on God stepping in whenever we mess things up. For instance, if we make the earth unlivable through nuclear explosions, through pollution or through unrestrained genetic engineering, we should not expect God to suddenly come to our rescue and straighten things out for us. On the contrary, God will expect us to clean up the mess ourselves no matter what the cost may be in human misery in the meantime. We will return to this subject in the next chapter when we discuss what God demands from us, and how we should respond to the challenges we are facing.

While it is true that these responsibilities, which God gave us, add a great deal of meaning to the existence of the human race in total, it does not help us with our own personal feelings of insignificance. This feeling of insignificance, of being such a small part of God's universe, this feeling that our lives do not count, was countered by Jesus a number of times. He reminded his disciples, and through them reminds us, that our lives should not be lived in isolation, and that we, small as we may be personally and as the church, nevertheless must give direction to this world. In particular Jesus tells us that we must be like:

> *A light on a hill, that can be seen from afar and that no matter how small it is, still can give direction to the people that see it.*
>
> — *Matthew 5:13*
>
> *The salt of the earth, a little bit of which makes a large amount of food taste better.*
>
> — *Matthew 5:14*
>
> *The yeast in the bread, a little bit of which makes the whole loaf of bread rise.*   .
>
> — *Matthew 13:33*

In other words, Jesus makes it clear to us that although we personally may be one in six billion, or the church may have to retrench to much smaller numbers, our influence must be felt far beyond our immediate surroundings. Our Christian message must radiate from us and must transform the world like the salt and the yeast in the bread.

As humans we have a built-in tendency to compare ourselves with the high and mighty, the successful and the achievers of this world. Especially in this day and age, the women in our society often feel that they are not achieving what they are intellectually capable of. In many cases this may be true, maybe they could have achieved more in the outside world if they had not taken on the prime responsibility for the raising of their children. The fact remains, however, that no matter what value system we adopt, the raising of children is still the most important task parents take on, no matter how they organize this between themselves. It is a fact of life that parents when they get older will continue to ask themselves what they could have done better in raising their children. No career decision or any major decision will be questioned in later life as much as the decisions we made about the raising of our children.

In looking at what we are trying to achieve in this life, it may be well to reflect for a minute on those things that are really important in this life and those that are not.

In his teaching Jesus repeatedly, and sometimes angrily, rejected the idea that some people are more important than others because of their social status. In the Sermon on the Mount, Jesus speaks about:

How blessed are the poor in spirit;

How blessed are the gentle, and so forth.

Nowhere does he say anything about how blessed are the achievers. On the contrary, he told his disciples many times that whoever wanted to be first among them would be last, and that the last would become first. He talked about how difficult it is for a rich man (materially and mentally) to enter the Kingdom of God; he talked about us having to become like little children; he talked about us having to serve others and to become servants of our neighbours.

If we look at our importance, from that point of view, we get an entirely different picture of who is important and who is not. On this scale of importance many of our cherished ideas of what is important disappear completely. If we follow Jesus' teaching we get an important scale that looks something like this:

1. parenting, the upbringing of our children, teaching;
2. professions or jobs that put into practice love and concern for others without regard for themselves;
3. professions or jobs that seek to meet the basic needs of others;

    4. professions or jobs involved in creating things
       that are helpful in raising the standard of living
       of all people everywhere.

This list could go on and on, but it clearly indicates that the professions we most envy for their financial returns are not necessarily anywhere near the top of this scale. For instance, some of lowest regarded jobs, such as garbage collecting, would come very high on this list because they perform a most essential task without which modern society cannot function.

We must never forget that God has given us all different talents. Some of us are bright and some are not; some are creative and some are not. But we can all do the one thing that is more important than anything else and that is to show our love and concern for others. No matter what our intellectual, social or financial status is we can all do that. I have before mentioned my granddaughter who has Down Syndrome. She will never be a success in a material sense, but the love and affection she displays for other people make her one of the most successful people I know.

When we think about the individual importance we may have in this life, we also must remember that as individuals we can exert great influence for good or for bad. After all, all the significant changes in the world have come about by the efforts of individuals. Some years ago Dr. Best, the co-inventor of insulin, died. In one of the commentaries on the television, a reporter mentioned the astonishing fact that the discovery of insulin had saved more lives than were lost in the entire Second World War.

Or consider the young Jewish girl who was hiding in an attic from the Nazis during the war for three years. During her time in the attic she wrote a most moving diary. A story that was translated into all major languages and read by millions of people, and seen in theaters and on television by people around the world. It is quite possible that this girl, Anna Frank, will be remembered long after the memory of Hitler and Stalin have faded.

In conclusion, our importance as human beings derives from the simple fact that God has made us co-creators, responsible for the upkeep and well-being of this planet. Our importance as individuals comes from the fact that we must be like a light in the darkness, a light that gives direction to others. We must be like the salt of the earth that transform the lives of others. Our importance comes from the fact that we are called upon to serve our neighbours, a service that anyone can provide. But most of all, our importance derives from the fact that we are children of the living God, the Creator of the universe and all that is in it, and that this God, unbelievable as it may seem, cares for us individually.

What Jesus Taught About The Meaning Of Life

After discussing in the previous chapter the importance of each individual in God's creation, we must now look into the question of what meaning our lives have, or stated differently, "Why are we here?" In his book, *Jesus Rediscovered*, Malcolm Muggeridge writes:

> *The most interesting thing in the world is to understand what life is all about. This is the only pursuit that could possibly engage a serious person and of course it is a continuing pursuit.*

> *As I have realized the fallacy of all the materialist philosophies and materialist utopias, so I have come to feel more and more strongly that the answer to life does not lie in materialism. In seeking other transcendental answers I have inevitably and increasingly been driven to the conclusion, almost against my own will, that for a Western European, the only answer lies in the person and the life and teaching of Christ. Here and only here, the transcendental answer is expressed adequately and appropriately.* [5]

In essence Mr. Muggeridge is saying that the only worthwhile pursuit for humans is to seek a meaning to life, and that he somewhat reluctantly has found that only in the person, life and teaching of Jesus Christ.

In his book, *The Meaning of Life at the Edge of the Third Millennium*, Leonard Swidler starts his first chapter with the question, "Does life have a meaning?" Since he considers a reply of, I don't know, to be basically unsatisfactory, there are, according to him, only two ultimate answers to the question: "Yes, there is," and "No, there is not." He goes on to say:

> *Now, to say that our whole life is without meaning simply means that we are unable to relate reality as we experience it to ourselves so as to see its purpose.*
>
> *Hence, to claim that life has meaning is to imply that it has a certain direction.*[6]

So, in trying to find meaning to life, we seek in effect answers not only to the question, "Who am I?" but also to the question, "Where am I going? and "What is my ultimate destination?"

All religions from the beginning of time have grappled with these questions and, depending on their starting point, have come up with different answers. An interesting point to note about these questions is that they are really spiritual questions, because if you do not believe in God the question is really meaningless. If you truly believe that you came here purely by accident, that the qualities and abilities you have can only be the result of a long process of natural selection and continuous evolution, then the answers to our questions are very short indeed.

- What is the meaning of life? None! We are here purely by accident.
- What is our importance? None! We are one out of 6 billion people with not the slightest individual importance.
- Where are we going? Nowhere! Life on this earth will eventually come to an end and that will be the end of our civilization and all our striving.

As Christians we believe that God is in control and has created this world. If you believe that, then it is a very normal question to ask yourself and to ask your Creator, "Why did you create me and the world around me?" and "What is my ultimate destination?" These are of course not very easy questions to answer, and even our creeds do not specifically answer these questions in so many words. Neither will you find an explicit answer in the Bible. To assist us in finding an answer, I believe it will be helpful if we look at what we know about God and about ourselves:

•First, we know that God has created us and everything else as well, and that we have been given certain abilities.

•Second, we know that God loves us to the extent that when we did not follow the rules set for us, God sent the Son, Jesus Christ, to forge a reconciliation between us.

•Third, we know that God wants to be approached by us in the same way as we approach our earthly parents; in other words, we can consider ourselves to be God's children.

Of course, this does not tell us why God had these children in the first place. I believe that to find a reasonable answer we must look at the first chapter of the very first book of the Bible. We acknowledge that the book of Genesis does not give us a factual description of how the world was created and that it was never intended to do so: Rather, we believe that Genesis was written to tell us some very important things about ourselves. In the very first chapter it tells us:

> *And God said, let us make man in our image after our own likeness to rule the fish in the sea, . . . So God created man in his own image, in the image of God he created them; male and female he created them.*
>
> — *Genesis 1, King James Bible*

This is really a most astonishing statement: We are created in God's image! To make sure we get the point, that statement is repeated not less than four times in this brief passage.

I think the message is clear. We are not here by accident, and we do not have the abilities we have by accident. We are here and we have the abilities we have because God very purposely created us in this way. What is even more astonishing, these passages seem to say that we are somewhat like God! That is something so amazing that it is almost impossible to grasp the full meaning of it. What can it possibly mean, that we are somewhat like God, the Creator and the Sustainer of all the universe? I believe it must mean at least the following:

•First, it must mean that we can *think and reason* like God can, but unlike the rest of creation;

•Second, it must mean that we can *distinguish between good and evil*, again like God can but unlike the rest of creation;

•Third, it must mean that we have a *free will* which gives us the ability to make choices, to choose between good and evil, again not like anything else in creation;

•Fourth, it must mean that we can *respond to God* and can *communicate* with God; in particular that we can respond to God's love and to the love of other people;

•Fifth, it must mean that we can *create*, maybe not create things out of nothing like God can, but nevertheless create.

In short:

> we can think;
> we can distinguish between good and evil;
> we have a free will — we can choose between good
> and evil;
> we can create;
> we can respond to God; and
> we can communicate with God.

That is what I believe it means to be created in God's image.

If we look at all this evidence, it is very clear that God created us with a special purpose in mind. Since we were created with all these abilities, I believe we can only come to one conclusion: We were created so that God could have a relationship with a free and intelligent being with whom God could meaningfully communicate. This is a rather fantastic claim, quite unbelievable really. Think of it for a moment. The Creator of everything created this whole universe we live in, including all the stars and galaxies, just so that human beings could develop who could be companions to God.

It is interesting to note in this context that in *Before The Beginning*, Ellis expresses a similar idea when he makes the statement that "the universe exists in order that humankind can exist"; and that "this is done so that unselfishness and love may make itself manifest."[7]

To some, it may seem pretty far-fetched that God created all these billions of stars and galaxies just so there would be an opportunity for one solar system to be formed in which the conditions would be just right for life to develop. Strange as this may seem at first, it appears to be a fact of life that much of nature follows that same pattern of great abundance just so that one event can take place. Take for instance a flowering shrub or tree: Annually they will produce thousands, if not millions, of seeds just so that at the very best one seed in every ten years or so will take root to replace the original tree when it dies. Or, consider the human body which is estimated to have some 75 trillion cells (that is 75 followed by 12 zeros), and each of these cells is probably a more complicated mechanism than any of the stars. In other words, we should not get overly impressed with the abundance of stars or the immensity of the universe because our own body appears to be far more complicated than the whole universe of stars and galaxies put together.

In any case, out of this great abundance of stars, as far as we can tell at this point in time, there is only one star with a solar system where the conditions are just right for the development of living matter. It is from these originally very simple living cells that humans evolved — the ultimate objective of the whole creation process. No doubt, since we cannot think at the level at which God thinks, this is probably a very simplistic way of putting it, but nevertheless from a human point of view it covers all the known facts.

Also, accepting the fact that we were created to be God's companions makes sense out of a few things that otherwise do not make much sense. First of all, it makes sense out of the fact that we are created in God's image and all that that entails. Why would God want to do that if it were not to have some relationship with us? After all, in order to have a relationship with someone, one must be able to communicate and one must have something in common. Without these two conditions a meaningful relationship is impossible.

Secondly, accepting that God created us for companionship makes some sense out of the fact that God created us with a free will, so that we can choose to either have that close relationship or not. After all a relationship cannot flourish if there is no choice involved and if it is not freely entered into. We humans select the people we want to have a relationship with, the people we want to have as our companions, on the basis of people who can think for themselves and who are compatible with us. We certainly do not select mechanical dolls or puppets. Well, neither does God!

Thirdly, accepting that God created us for companionship also lifts a bit of the mystery of why God sent Jesus Christ. Having created us for companionship and having given us the necessary free will, and humans having used that free will to go in the wrong direction, it is not surprising to see that God made one supreme effort to regain and re-establish that relationship. In earthly terms we might say that, after having gone to all this length, God was not going to give up on the chosen companions that easily.

Let us think for a moment about the life and death of Jesus in a slightly different way than we are used to. Maybe, in addition to giving humans an opportunity to turn around and to learn about God first hand, Jesus in his capacity as the Mediator also came to find out what life really was like for God's chosen companions living under the sway of evil. As we have said before, a true mediator can only be effective and impartial if he is intimately familiar with the conditions of both parties. So, Jesus came to live on earth like a fully-human being:

one who suffered; one who knew joy; one who experienced the full range of human emotions. He even experienced the three things we most often hold against God: the experience of unheard prayer, of pain and suffering, and the feeling of being abandoned by God. Jesus had the experience of unheard prayer when, in the Garden of Gethsemane, he asked three times to be spared the cross; the experience of feeling abandoned by God when he cried at the cross, "My God, My God, why have you forsaken me?"; and the experience of pain and suffering when he died on the cross.

Last of all, accepting that God created us to be God's companions makes sense out of the fact that there is a life after this one that is eternal. After all this life is short, and God certainly cannot have meant to have fellowship with beings that are here today and gone tomorrow. Thus, this definition of the meaning of our lives points to a continued existence of God's designated companions after their earthly existence has come to an end. I am convinced that the ultimate meaning of our lives lies not in our existence in this world but in that of the world to come, and it is in this world to come that we will finally and completely know what the meaning of our existence on earth was and what it will be in the future.

Maybe, the ultimate meaning of our life is best expressed in the assertion of the Eastern Orthodox Church which states:

The world was created from nothing by the sole will
of God — this is its origin. It was created in order
to participate in the fullness of the divine life — this
is its vocation.

In summary then:

Why are we here? Certainly we are not here by chance. On the contrary, we are created in God's image so that we can be true and meaningful companions to God for all eternity.
What is our importance? We are God's chosen companions: We are sons and daughters of God, Creator of heaven and earth.
Where are we going? We are going to a place where we will be truly God's companions forever.

Finally, to answer that question we ask ourselves when we are completely discouraged by the problems and difficulties of our daily lives,

What is the use of it all? The use of it all is that we are on our way, on the way to becoming truly human as we were meant to be. Created in the image of God, we are on the way to a life the richness of which we cannot even imagine today, a life as God's chosen and eternal companions. What greater destination could anyone want?

What Jesus Taught About Life After Death

This section could equally well be called, "What Christians Hope For" or even more positively, "What Christians trust will happen at the end of time." Life after death is what we hope for, in the sense that we are looking forward to it and trust in God's promise that this new life will become a reality sometime in the future. The two creeds that we quoted at the beginning of this chapter speak of life after death in slightly different terms.

The Apostolic Creed states:

"We believe in the resurrection of the body and in life everlasting."

The second creed reads:

"In life, in death, in life beyond death God is with us. We are not alone. Thanks be to God."

Although stated somewhat differently, the meaning of the two is clearly the same, death is not the end but a new beginning.

The concept of life after death is, of course, crucial to the whole Christian faith: Without it, the life and death of Christ makes no sense and is of no value to humankind. As Carl Braaten wrote in his book, *The Future Of God*, "The starting point of our Christian belief is not at the beginning but at the end."[8] In other words, if we do not have a belief in eternal life, the whole New Testament and all the teachings of Jesus lose their significance. Without our personal resurrection into a new life, the resurrection of Jesus becomes meaningless.

254

Without this resurrection, the Christian has nothing to hope for but an inglorious end of the world, most probably by our own hand. To quote the apostle Paul:

> If there is no resurrection of the dead, then Christ cannot have been raised either, and if Christ has not been raised, then our preaching is without substance, and so is your faith.
>
> — 1 Corinthians 15, The New Jerusalem Bible

The idea of a soul or spirit surviving the death of the body has been with us from the beginning of time. Even the very earliest records we have of human life on earth show that people buried their dead with ceremonies and rituals which would, in their way of thinking, ensure the survival of the spirit. In *A History of Religious Ideas*, the author Mircea Elida writes:

> *Belief in survival after death seems to be demonstrated, from the earliest times, by the use of red ocher as a ritual substitute for blood, hence as a symbol of life. The custom of dusting corpses with ochre is universally disseminated in both time and space, in Europe, Australia and in America . . . A fortiori, belief in survival is confirmed by burials; otherwise there could be no understanding the efforts expended in interring the body.*

Thus it would appear that the idea of a soul or a spirit which survives the destruction of the body is an almost integral part of the human psyche. To the extent that it is feasible to use the customs and rituals of our primitive and unsophisticated forebears as an indicator, it appears that it is in the nature of humans to assume that the end of life on this planet is not the end of life itself.

As Christians, we believe in an eternal life, but the only thing we know about the condition of that future life is that it will be in close communion with God. In other religions there are similar beliefs about a life after death, but they do not include belief in a close relationship with the Creator of the

255

universe. (See Appendix 1 entitled, "Brief Summary of the Other World Religions and the Major Similarities and Differences with the Christian Religion.")

As was to be expected, the idea of a life after death was completely unacceptable to the critical and materialistic thinking of the scientific age. In that way of thinking, the only thing that exists or is real is made up of atomic and, later, of subatomic particles — nothing else is considered to be real. The idea of a soul or a spirit, which could not be described in terms of particles, made no sense to the scientifically minded. Similarly, medical science had no use for it because it could not be located anywhere in the body.

At the same time, the concept of a heaven had no place in the universe of students of astronomy who are accustomed to describing the universe in terms of stars, galaxies and quasars. The first Russian astronauts declared with some satisfaction, after returning to earth from their first space flight, that they had not been able to find the slightest sign of the existence of a heaven anywhere. They obviously believed that this profound observation would reinforce the Communist dogma that God, and therefore heaven, is a figment of the Christian's imagination. Little did they realize that their ability to travel in space reinforces one of the Christian tenets, namely that we are created in the image of God and are to function as co-creators with God. As such, we are urged to explore the earth and its immediate environment, while at the same time taking full responsibility for the continuing viability of the earth to support both its natural environment and its population.

However, the purely materialistic thinking of the early scientific age has had to make way for a much wider concept of what nature is and what it consists of. It is clear from modern scientific discoveries that the world is not made up of infinitesimally small ping-pong balls, but that all matter in the end is nothing other than little blocks of energy. Furthermore, the behavior of some of the most elemental particles are not following the materialistic concept of cause and effect, but are behaving in a quite random manner and are, in fact, influenced by the presence of the observer. This has led the two writers, Augros and Stanciu, in their book, *The New Story of Science*, to go so far as to state, "Physics in the twentieth century has gradually replaced materialism with the affirmation that *mind* plays an essential role in the universe."[9] I have already quoted Polkinghorne in chapter one as saying, "The physical universe seems to be shot through with signs of *mind*." At the same time, modern research of the brain has increasingly led to the conclusion that there is something that is called *mind* that is external to the body, something that is part of a human being but is not part of the human body.

Thus, it appears that science, forced by evidence coming from different directions, is now coming to the conclusion that the previous materialistic concept of the world is no longer tenable and other concepts of a more spiritual nature must be considered. In particular, it must consider the existence of something that may be called mind or spirit: something that does not consist of matter and is not tied to the physical body. If that concept is accepted, then the survival of the non-physical part of a human being, after the destruction of the physical body, should be acceptable in principle, at least, to any thinking person.

Possibly, in a reaction to the completely materialistic view of the early days of scientific discovery, the last century has seen a great increase in the popularity of parapsychology with its spiritualistic theories and practices. In general, these theories are all based on the belief in the existence of a mind or spirit detached from the body which survives death, even to the extent that some believe that the spirit of a dead person can, under certain circumstances, freely communicate with living persons. There are many different aspects of parapsychology that could be of great interest, and possibly of great benefit to society, but its practice is so riddled with fraud and deception that it is impossible to make use of the implications that some of these findings may have on our understanding of the working of the universe.

For our purpose, we shall only mention two phenomena which seem to have at least some credibility and which have been the subject of scientific scrutiny. If their claims could be substantiated, both would show that there is something which is operating outside the physical body that might be called mind or spirit. The first phenomena is called extrasensory perception or ESP. As the name implies, it is the ability to transfer information from one person to another without the use of our normal senses. Some of these phenomena seem to have come close to scientific verification such as telepathy by which thoughts are transferred from one person to another, sometimes over great distances, without the use of speech or any other direct physical links.

The other phenomena, that falls in this category, is clairvoyance, the ability to experience things that are happening far away or to become aware of events that have happened in the past. Most people seem to have had some experience with this type of phenomena. However, when we start considering clairvoyance, which claims to be able to see things that will happen in the future, we are entering a different scenario all together. If this were ever proven to be factual, we might have to change a few well-cherished ideas, because, if correct, it could mean that the future is fixed and that nothing can change the course of events from their ordained path. In other words, our belief in a free will would turn out to be a figment of our imagination. Few people will believe that this is true. If there is any clairvoyance of the future at all, it may be that we see the future as it would be if we did not take any corrective action. For instance, some people claim that they have had a vision of the aircraft, in which they were supposed to fly, crashing into a mountainside. As a result they cancelled their flight plans, and when an accident actually did happen they felt that clairvoyance saved their lives. In actual fact, it is much more likely that with plane loads of more than 400 people, there is at least one person on each flight who has had some premonition of something going wrong with the plane. So, if there is an accident, there is likely to be at least one person who will come forward and claim to have had a clairvoyant experience predicting the accident.

Interesting as the study of these phenomena may be, a Christian should not look upon parapsychology or ESP as proof that there is a mind, soul or spirit that survives death.

Before we leave the subject, however, we must briefly mention one human experience which some might want to use to prove that life continues after death and which has been given wide publicity lately. This phenomenon, the near-death experiences of people who have been clinically dead and who later revived, seems to have occurred to many people in the past and in many different cultures, but it is only recently that people have come forward to describe what they experienced. Almost all, who have had this experience, describe the same scenario. With the exception of a few, they all relate how they experienced a wonderful feeling of an all-surrounding love and beauty. It is interesting to note that these experiences were basically the same for religious and non-religious people. All report that they were profoundly changed after they returned to full consciousness and to their normal lives. Dr. Carl Jung, the famous psychiatrist and psychologist, who had a near-death experience himself, wrote later: "What happens after death is so unspeakably glorious that our imagination and our feelings do not suffice to form even an approximate conception of it." Similarly, Dr. E. Kübler-Ross, who was one of the first to write about the life after death experiences of her patients, mentions in her book *On Life After Death* that not one of her patients who had an out-of-body experience was ever again afraid to die.[10]

There is no doubt that the experiences are real enough, but there are a great many possible explanations that have little to do with survival of a spirit separate from the human body. Also, it should not be forgotten that these are near-death experiences and, therefore, by definition are not necessarily any indication of what happens after a real death. Just the same, the revelations of the near-death experiences are an exciting new development in our investigation of the human mind.

The observations of the people who had a near-death experience seem to have some similarity to the experiences communicated by dead people through the intermediary of a "medium." In the book, *We Are Not Forgotten, George Anderson's Message of Hope from the Other Side*, the authors, J. Martin and P. Romanowski, report how some of the spirits of the dead were apparently able to communicate with their close relatives through the medium of George Anderson. In answer to questions about God, these "spirits" answered in such terms as, "They have seen God in the sense of light" and, "God is, in my opinion, the complete essence of all that is beautiful, positive, uplifting, joyful. Every positive vibration is God"; in answer to the question, "Who is in charge?" the reply was, "God rules through the essence of complete love and understanding so pure and so right we cannot help but obey or follow."[11]

Most people will probably deny that such communications are possible and, therefore, that the testimony received through these sources has no value. Nevertheless, I believe that we should not off-hand discard the possibility that the dead can communicate with those left behind. At least we should, I believe, keep an open mind.

In any case, it is clear that, at this stage of our development and at this point in time, we can only accept the survival of the spirit separate from the body, and the existence of an eternal life after death on faith and trust. In faith and trust in God who has promised us, through the prophets of the Old Testament, and through the apostles of the New Testament, that there would be a new heaven and that we would live there in perfect harmony with God forever.

Of course, the first real proof that the spirit can survive the death of the body came from the resurrection of Jesus. If we can accept that as factual, then the survival of our own spirit and soul is much easier to accept. We have described in previous chapters why we believe this to be true. In this place it may be helpful to quote John Stott who listed in his book, *Basic Christianity*, the four things that prove to him that the resurrection of Christ was real and factual. He makes the following list:

- the body was gone;
- the grave clothes were undisturbed;
- the Lord was seen; and
- the disciples were changed.[12]

Naturally, the first three items on the list do not have any significance to a non-Christian who does not believe that the Biblical accounts have any validity. However, as pointed out before, the last point cannot be denied by even the most sceptical person as it is a historically known fact.

Jesus' own testimonies about the life to come, all relate to, or are connected with, our concept of God as a loving parent who provides for its children. John quotes Jesus as saying:

> *Do not let your hearts be troubled. You trust in God, trust also in me. In my Father's house there are many places to live in; otherwise I would have told you. I am now going to prepare a place for you, and after I am gone and prepared you a place I shall return to take you to myself, so that you may be with me where I am.*
>
> — *John 14, The New Jerusalem Bible*

Before that, John reports Jesus as saying:

> *I am the resurrection. Anyone who believes in me, even though that person dies, will live, and whoever lives and believes in me will never die.*
>
> — *John 11, The New Jerusalem Bible*

It will be noted that the first quotation also includes a reference to the second coming of Jesus. Jesus told his disciples that towards the end of time, when life as we know it will cease, he himself will return in glory. In some of his teachings, and more so in the letters written by his apostles, it is intimated that this second coming was to occur at least within the lifetime of some of the people present. One of the most vivid descriptions of this future event can be found in the gospel according to Mark where he reports Jesus as saying:

261

> *But in those days, after the time of distress, the sun will*
> *darken, the moon will not give its light, the stars will be*
> *falling out of the sky, and the powers in the heaven will*
> *be shaken. And then they will see the Son of Man com-*
> *ing in the clouds with great power and glory. And then*
> *he will send his angels to gather his elect from the four*
> *winds, from the ends of the world to the ends of the sky.*
> *... But as for that day and hour, nobody knows it,*
> *neither the angels in heaven, nor the Son; nobody but*
> *the Father.*
>
> — *Mark 13, The New Jerusalem Bible*

Thus Jesus makes it very clear that he, at this stage, does not
know when this second coming will take place, although in
a previous passage he is quoted as saying that this would happen before this present generation would have passed away.
Despite Jesus' statement that he, himself, did not know the
time of his second coming, people, over the centuries, have
tried to predict the time when this would happen by making
all kinds of far-fetched interpretations of some of the imagery
found in the prophetic books of Daniel and Revelations. They
seem to think that God, for some strange reason, has left hidden clues about this date in these writings, even though Jesus,
who is God's Son, was not made aware of this during his
sojourn on earth. In any case, regardless of the timing, we can
be sure that the end of the world will come and that life on
earth, as we know it, will cease to exist.

The all important question we must ask ourselves is, "What
will happen then?" For people who believe that there is no
other life than this one, there is nothing to look forward to
other than total oblivion. For the Christian, on the other hand,
there is the hope and trust that this end will be the beginning
of the next stage of our existence. One may reasonably ask
what kind of existence that will be. Again, as many times before, we must say that from our earth-bound perspective it
is impossible to comprehend what God, whose mind works
on such an entirely different plane, has in store for us. Will

our continued existence be a purely spiritual one, or will our new life more resemble the present one? It is not difficult to find indications of both in the Bible. In any case it is clear that our bodies will be transformed from the present temporary state to one that is permanent and incorruptible. To quote Hans Küng in his book, *Eternal Life*:

> *All we know is that there will be,*
>   *•a life that is eternal,*
>   *•a justice which is all encompassing,*
>   *•a freedom which is perfect,*
>   *•a love that is infinite,*
>   *•a salvation which is final.*[13]

But above all, life will be in close communion with God as described in the last book of the Bible:

> *Then I saw a new heaven and a new earth. The first heaven and the first earth had disappeared now, and there was no longer any sea (symbol of evil). I saw the holy city, the new Jerusalem, coming down out of heaven from God, prepared as a bride dressed for her husband. Then I heard a loud voice call from the throne "Look, here God lives among human beings. He will make his home among them; they will be his people, and he will be their God, God-with-them. He will wipe away all tears from their eyes; there will be no more death, and no more mourning or sadness or pain. The world of the past has gone."*

— *Revelations 21, The New Jerusalem Bible*

From time to time, one hears the remark by some scoffers that an eternal existence, with as the only diversion the perpetual singing of hymns of praise to God, is such a boring prospect that they would rather forego the experience. Obviously, they assume that our continued existence will be governed by the same desires and appetites that rule our earthly life. If there is one thing we can say with complete certainty about the life hereafter, it is that that will not be the case. Our earthly bodies will have disappeared and with it the bodily functions and desires. As a consequence, life after death will be entirely different from that which we are experiencing today. In fact, I believe the real existence in the New Jerusalem will be so different from our earthly existence now that it is simply beyond the imagination of our human minds. It is such a glorious future that has been promised us that we look forward to it with great anticipation, knowing that we will not be disappointed.

Our Communication With God

1. Introduction

Prayer, or communicating with God, is probably one of the most misunderstood aspects of the Christian's life. For many, it is no more than a litany of requests for God to take action on; but, as the title indicates, prayer is not a one-way process. In fact, praying is essentially a form of communicating which is a two-way process: It is a dialogue between God and humans.

For some people who are more mystically inclined, prayer is simply being open to God and that can best be done in silence. This is how Thomas Keating put it in his book, *Invitation To Love, the Way of Christian Contemplation*:

> *Silence is God's first language, everything else is a poor translation. In order to hear that language, we must learn to be still and to rest in God . . . God is communicating, not to the senses or to reason, but to our intuitive faculties.* [14]

This is probably one of the most surprising statements about prayer that I have ever read: God communicating with us not through our senses but through our intuitive faculties! Most of us are bound to have a problem with a prayer that is completely silent; we are more inclined to present God with a long shopping list of our, including the world's, concerns and needs, and wait for a response that we can register with our minds. Maybe the reason we often do not hear God's response is that we are not open to that kind of answer. Maybe we should end every prayer with a period of silence to give us time to absorb the message God is sending us through our intuition.

Most of what follows in this chapter is about the spoken prayer, but we should never forget that prayer is a two-way street and that we should take time to listen in silence to God's response and, according to Keating, we should do this not only with our senses but also with our intuition.

During Jesus' life on earth he was in almost constant contact with God. All the gospels are full of references to Jesus praying: He kept, as it were, an open line to God. In some ways, this is similar to what a personal representative of a president does when he is sent on a special mission. For this representative to be effective he must stay in constant contact with his home base, not only to be given instructions, but also to get encouragement and support especially so if the mission is a difficult and lonely one.

It is clear from reading the gospels that Jesus very much needed a similar daily contact with the Source Of His Being to draw the necessary strength from that Source so that he would be able to complete his mission. Jesus told his disciples to do the same and to approach God very much like he did: They could approach God as young children approach their parents. They come to their parents to tell them about their pains, hurts and disappointments, fully expecting that the parents can fix whatever the problem may be.

This invitation to communicate (hear and speak) directly with God is almost unbelievable. Emil Brunner in his previously quoted book, *Our Faith*, makes the remark that the fact we can do this is, at the same time, most daring and most humbling. Daring, in the sense that it takes a real leap of faith to believe that God, the Almighty, will actually listen to us individually. Humbling, because it means that we have to admit that we are not all self-sufficient and we need to ask for God's intervention.[15]

Over the years there has been a great deal of discussion on how and for what we should pray, and what we should expect from God as a result of our prayers. To get some insight into this, this chapter has been divided into a number of sections as follows:

- •What Jesus himself prayed for and about;
- •What Jesus said about prayer in general;
- •What Jesus taught his disciples to pray for;
- •What our response should be when our prayer is not answered in the way we wanted it to be.

The chapter concludes with a number of examples of prayers by some famous people and by some not so famous.

2. What Jesus Prayed For

Jesus' prayers were of course very private and we do not know exactly what Jesus said in his prayers except in a few isolated cases in which he prayed aloud for all people to hear. The best known of his prayers is also the most agonizing prayer, and it is reported exactly the same in the first three gospels. It is the one prayer most of us can identify with, not only because it concerned a very human situation, but also because it was a prayer that was not answered; just as many of our prayers appear not to have been heard and not to have been answered. The particular prayer I am referring to is Jesus' prayer in the Garden of Gethsemane just before his crucifixion. Jesus obviously knew what was about to happen to him and, being fully human, he was afraid. So he prayed to God asking if he could be spared the ordeal that lay ahead of him. While praying for this, he nevertheless added at the end of his petition, "Not my will but your will be done." (Luke 22)

That Jesus felt the full weight of his torment is clear from the fact that he repeated this prayer three times. While he was suffering these torments, he asked his disciples to stay awake and, as it were, share this burden with him, and to reassure him with their presence. However, even this comfort was denied him because the disciples, being tired, found it impossible to stay awake. When Jesus came back the last time and found them asleep again, he made this revealing statement:

> *Stay awake, and pray not to be put to the test. The spirit is willing enough, but human nature is weak.*
>
> — *Mark 14, The New Jerusalem Bible*

It is clear from this statement that Jesus himself had just experienced how weak human nature could be. Jesus had obviously been tempted, like we are often tempted, to take the easy way out and not complete the difficult tasks we have to face in our lives. In the end, however, Jesus did not take any shortcuts and he completed his mission in its entirety, from his death on the cross to the resurrection on Easter morning.

The other petition Jesus made publicly and openly was when he asked God to forgive his tormentors when he said:

> *Father forgive them, because they do not know what they are doing.*
>
> — *Luke 23, The New Jerusalem Bible*

The only longer prayer we have of Jesus is recorded in the gospel according to John. In actual fact, that prayer is more like a general conversation he is having with God. It does, however, include a number of petitions, all of them about the future of his disciples:

> *Holy Father, keep those you have given me true to your name, so that they may be like us. . . .*
> *I am not asking to remove them from this world but to protect them from the evil one. . . .*
> *May they all be one, just as, Father you are in me and I am in you.*
>
> — *John 17, The New Jerusalem Bible*

It is interesting to note that Jesus in this prayer, and also in the prayer he taught his disciples, asks for protection from the "evil one." It is something that we should never forget: Jesus found it so important to pray for protection from the influence of Satan that he repeated it in all his prayers we know about. It is obviously something we should not forget to do in our own prayers because, if his disciples needed this protection when Jesus was still with them, then surely we are in even greater need of it today.

3. What Jesus Said About Prayer In General

During his ministry, Jesus made a number of observations and remarks that are of great significance in our search for an appropriate way to approach God in our own prayers. First of all, he said that we should be aware that God knows our needs long before we pray for them. Second, he tells us to be persistent and not to lose heart. To illustrate this he tells his disciples the story of the unjust judge. The unjust judge refuses to hear the complaint of a widow but, because she keeps pestering him, he finally gives in to hear her case. Jesus then makes the following comment:

> *You notice what the unjust judge had to say? Now will not God see justice done to his elect if they keep calling him day and night even though he still delays to help them? I promise you, he will see justice done to them, and done speedily.*
>
> — *Luke 18, The New Jerusalem Bible*

Third, he tells his disciples time and time again that God will hear and answer their prayers if they approach him in complete faith. This promise has and is still causing much distress to a great many Christians whose urgent and persistent prayers have not been answered as he promised. The apostle Mark quotes Jesus as saying:

> *Have faith in God. In truth I tell you, if anyone says to this mountain, "Be pulled up and thrown in the sea" with*

no doubt in his heart, but believing that it will happen,
it will be done for him. I tell you therefore everything
you ask and pray for, believe that you have it already
and it will be yours.

— *Mark 11, The New Jerusalem Bible*

In the gospel of Luke, Jesus is quoted as follows:

So I say to you: Ask, and it will be given to you; search,
and you will find; knock and the door will be opened to
you. For everyone who asks receives; everyone who
searches finds; everyone who knocks will have the door
opened. What father among you, if his son asks him for
a fish, would hand him a snake? Or if he asked for an
egg, would hand him a scorpion? If you then, evil as you
are, know to give your children what is good for them,
how much more will the heavenly Father give the Holy
Spirit to those who ask him.

— *Luke 11, The New Jerusalem Bible*

These quotations are so specific and so clear in their intent that it begs for an explanation why people's prayers are
not always answered. We will come back to that later in this
chapter but, for our present purpose, it is sufficient to know
that Jesus told us to pray with faith and, if we do that, God
will hear us and act upon it.

4. How We Should Pray

During his ministry, Jesus was asked repeatedly how we
should pray. He replied by giving us the prayer that ever since
has been known as "The Our Father" or the "Lord's Prayer."
Jesus said to pray as follows:

Our Father who art in heaven,
Hallowed be your name,
Your Kingdom come,
Your will be done on earth as it is in heaven.

> *Give us this day our daily bread,*
> *Forgive us our trespasses,*
> *As we forgive those who trespass against us.*
> *And lead us not into temptation,*
> *But deliver us from evil.*
>
> *For yours is the kingdom and the power and the glory.*
> *Forever and ever.*
> *Amen.*
>
> — *Matthew 6, The King James Bible*

Since this is the prayer that Jesus taught us, it may be well to spend some time analyzing it, so that we may use it as a guide for our own prayers. First of all, it is obvious that Jesus did not mean this to be a cast-in-stone standard prayer that everyone should use on every possible occasion. Rather, I believe it is meant to show us what is and what is not important in our own communications with God.

First there is the address acknowledging God's closeness to us by using the father image:

"Our Father who art in heaven,"

followed immediately by the element of praise,

"Hallowed be your name."

This is followed by the expression of hope for our future:

"Your Kingdom come,"

and by an expression of faith in God's plan for us.

"Your will be done...."

It is only after this that we find the first petition to meet our own physical needs:

"Give us this day our daily bread."

It is maybe significant that only after having asked for our daily sustenance, that Jesus asks for the forgiveness of our sins:

"Forgive us our trespasses,"

followed by a request for strength to do the same to others,

"As we forgive those who trespass against us."

The prayer then ends with two requests for not being put in situations which tempt us to do wrong things:

"Lead us not into temptation,"
and to keep us from falling into the clutches of Satan,
"But deliver us from evil."

The last part of the Lord's Prayer as printed on page 270 is not actually found in the scriptures, but was later added and became part of the liturgy of the church and has always been considered as an integral part of this prayer. It is obviously meant as an expression of praise and thanksgiving at the end of the prayer:

"For yours is the kingdom, the power and the glory.
For ever and ever.
Amen."

Most prayers since then have ended with this expression of "Amen," which literally means "that it may be so."

The Lord's Prayer, as we have seen, only includes one petition for our physical well-being. The reason for this may be that, just before Jesus taught his disciples this prayer, he had told them that God knew their needs long before they prayed for them. In any case, it is clear from this example that our prayers should include a section of praise and thanksgiving, as well as a petition to God to be granted forgiveness for the things we have done wrong.

Of course, this does not mean that we cannot approach God with our everyday concerns and problems. On the contrary, Jesus encouraged his disciples to lay all their problems and concerns at his feet, as long as we remember that God knows our concerns already and, that at best, we are reminding him/her that we have these problems. Maybe the best way to illustrate the fact that God is ready to listen to our everyday, earthly concerns, is to look at what problems Jesus dealt with when he was on earth:

•People asked him to cure their sick, both the physically and the mentally sick, and he cured them all provided they came to him in faith. This sickness did not necessarily have to be life-threatening: For instance, he cured Peter's mother-in-law when all she had was a fever.

•His own mother asked him to do something about the wine supply at one of their friend's wedding. And Jesus, in order not to cause the bridal pair embarrassment, did change water into wine.

•Jesus calmed a storm when his disciples, even with him aboard, were afraid that they might sink. When they expressed their concern to him, Jesus calmed the storm.

•When a crowd of people had followed him to an isolated place, where there was no food to be obtained, Jesus took pity on them and fed them.

Looking at these examples of how Jesus answered this wide ranging list of everyday problems people brought before him, it is clear that we also should not be afraid to approach God with our ordinary concerns either.

5. Our Response To Unanswered Prayer

As we saw in the previous section, we have this repeated assurance that God will hear and act upon our prayers when we pray in faith. But we all know from bitter experience that God does not always answer our prayers. Sometimes, and for some always, we feel that we are talking to an empty heaven and that there is no one who listens to us. Many people have lost their faith as a result of this seemingly absent God, because they feel that when they called for help God was not there: God did not do what s/he had promised to do, and s/he left them desolate without any indication that they had been heard.

As we have said, Jesus made these very specific statements about the fact that God would hear us if we prayed in faith. With some thought, it is clear that we cannot take this to be literally true for all the petitions in all the prayers which are made everyday. For example:

•There are obviously many situations in which different people ask for the opposite thing to happen. Some might ask for rain, while others might ask for dry weather, depending on what is important for them at any given time.

•There are equally obvious prayers that are improper. Prayers that if they were answered would do harm to others. For instance one might pray that a threatening hurricane will be diverted from its path and strike somewhere else.

•There are also many instances in which we ask for something, and it later turns out that it was a very good thing that our request was not granted. For example, we may pray to get a certain job, or a certain position, only to find out later that the granting of this wish would have ended up in disaster because the demands made on us in that position were completely beyond our capacity.

•There are many instances when we pray for something to happen, knowing full well that the outcome is already determined except that we do not know the outcome. For instance one might, and many probably do, pray earnestly to God that the outcome of a biopsy test may be favourable, knowing full well that they are too late with their prayer, because the outcome of the test cannot be changed.

•Furthermore, if we believe that God has a plan for this world, then it is most likely that if we ask for something that is contrary to that plan, it will not be granted.

We can probably classify the answers we have received to our prayers in the following three categories:

1 — Yes, God has answered our prayer to the letter;
2 — No, God has not answered our prayers in any way we can discern; and
3 — God has answered our prayers, but in an entirely different way than we had asked.

The Bible, and the history of the church, are full of prayers that were answered by the Creator exactly the way they were asked. Thus, you might say that in these instances, God changed the course of events at the request of a mere human being. That is a pretty daring and far-reaching statement to make. However, if we believe that God does answer our prayers then that is exactly what happens.

While, no doubt, it is true that God has and does answer some of our prayers, the fact remains that a survey today would almost certainly show that the answers to our prayers fall mainly in the third category: That is, our prayers are answered but in an entirely different way than we had originally asked for. For instance, we may have asked to pass an exam but, despite our prayer and our hard work, our request may not have been granted causing us to question God's fairness. Yet, years later, we may come to realize that this failure did, in fact, put us on a career path which much more suited our abilities.

At this point, it is also well to remember that God acts in this world almost entirely and exclusively through people and not through direct divine intervention. We are co-creators with God, and we are the hands and feet with which God acts today in this world. So, if our prayers are heard today, they will almost certainly be answered through the intervention of other human beings. Harold Kushner in his book, *When Bad Things Happen To Good People*, quotes the theologian, Jack Reimer, as saying:

> *We cannot merely pray to you, O God, to end war, for we know that you have made the world in a way that man must find his own path to peace within himself and his neighbour.*

> *We cannot merely pray to you, O God, to end starvation, for you already have given us the resources with which to feed the entire world if we would only use them wisely.*

> *Therefore we pray to you instead, O God, for strength, determination, and will power, to act instead of just to pray, to become instead of merely to wish.*[16]

In short, we should ask God not so much to perform miracles on our behalf, but to change people so that they may perfectly follow in Jesus' footsteps. That is, to start living in accordance with the rules God gave us and, more specifically, to love our neighbours as ourselves. If all of us managed to do that, the world would change and life on earth would be transformed. For instance, the reason for many of our prayers would disappear because if we lived in accordance with that rule:

War and all kinds of conflicts would disappear;

Hunger and starvation would disappear;

Crime would disappear;

Discrimination of any kind would disappear;

Mistreatment of one human by another would disappear, and so forth.

Having said all this, we are still left with the personal tragedies of life — the incurable illnesses, the fatal accidents, the lasting unemployment. Maybe we have prayed without giving up hope; maybe we have prayed with all the faith and trust we can muster, and still God does not seem to hear us. In that situation, it does not help us in the slightest to know that God acts through human beings, or that God sometimes answers our prayers in mysterious ways. What we feel we need is for God to work a miracle: What we need is for God to come to our rescue or to that of a loved one, now. If that cry for help is not answered, what do we do and how do we respond then?

To some extent, the answer to that must be found in what happened to Jesus when God did not answer his prayer in the Garden of Gethsemane. Jesus obviously had faith that could move mountains; he did not give up easily but repeated his prayer several times, but his prayer was not answered just the same. In a similar way, Paul, the apostle, obviously had some physical ailment or condition that gave him great discomfort. He prayed that God would cure him of this, but his request was not granted. In the second letter to the Corinthians, he wrote:

> *I was given a thorn in the flesh, a messenger from Satan to batter me and prevent me from getting above myself. About this, I have three times pleaded with the Lord that it might leave me; but he answered me, "My grace is enough for you."*
>
> — *2 Corinthians 12, The New Jerusalem Bible*

For us the lesson is clear. God does not always answer our prayers the way we want, just as he did not answer Jesus' prayers the way Jesus asked him to do. It is clear that God did not deviate from the chosen path and, if God had, the world would be different from what it is today. There would not be the complete reconciliation with God that we have now, and which we will see in its full realization in the life to come.

So, we must conclude that there are many instances in which our requests cannot be met because God's plan is different from ours, no matter how much pain and distress this may give us.

However, there is one thing we can count on. The same that was given to Jesus when his prayer was not answered. That is, that God will give us the strength and endurance to bear the pain and misfortune. In the case of Jesus, he was able to fulfill his destiny and he was given the necessary strength to endure, even to the extent that he was able to pray for his executioners. Similarly, I believe that God will give us the strength to bear the emotional and physical stress to which we may be exposed. Harold Kushner writes as follows:

> *We don't have to beg or bribe God to give us strength or hope or patience. We need only turn to him, admit that we cannot do it on our own, and understand that bravely bearing up under long-term illness is one of the most human, and one of the most godly, things we can ever do. One of the things that constantly reassures me that God is real, is the fact that people who pray for strength, hope and courage so often find resources of strength, hope and courage that they did not have before they prayed.* [17]

I believe that this experience is shared by many. It is the way in which God answers our prayers, when for some reason, that we may never understand, God cannot grant us the request we have made.

In summary then, there are a number of things we can say about prayer:

a) Prayer is a way of communicating with God: It is a two-way street, we must speak to God and we must listen to God's response.

b) God may be communicating with us not so much through our senses as through our intuition.

c) Although God knows our needs before we pray for them, nevertheless God wants to hear from us.

d) God will always hear our prayers, but will only answer them in the way we have prayed for, if it fits within the overall plan for us and the world.

e) If God does not grant us our request for release of pain and suffering, God will give us the necessary strength and fortitude to bear that pain and suffering.

f) We should not be discouraged when God does not answer our prayers immediately, but we should persist and not give up.

g) Our prayers can change things. God sometimes does change the course of our lives; and our future is not cast in stone.

h) If we pray in faith, we can do great things, things that we are unable to accomplish without it.

i) God answers our prayers today mainly through the acts and actions of other people and seldom through direct intervention.

I believe it is appropriate to close this section on prayer with the invitation which Jesus made to all of us:

> *Come to me all who labour and are overburdened, and I will give you rest. Shoulder my yoke and learn from me, for I am gentle and humble in heart, and you will find rest for your souls.*
>
> — *Matthew 11, The New Jerusalem Bible*

6. Some Examples Of Prayers

Outside of The Lord's Prayer, probably the most famous prayer is that attributed to St. Francis of Assisi. By all accounts Saint Francis was as close to a real saint as anyone can come in this world. He lived in Italy around the year 1,200. He gave up all his possessions and devoted himself entirely to the service of the sick and the poor. His prayer very much reflects his sense of need to help others:

> *Lord make me an instrument of your peace*
> *Where there is hatred, let me sow love,*
> *Where there is doubt, let me sow faith;*
> *Where there is despair, let me sow hope;*
> *Where there is darkness, let me sow light;*
> *Where there is sadness, let me sow joy.*
> *O, divine Master grant that I may not so much seek*
> *to be consoled, as to console,*
> *to be understood, as to understand,*
> *to be loved, as to love.*
> *For it is in giving that we receive;*
> *it is in pardoning that we are pardoned;*
> *it is in dying that we are born to eternal life.*

As a prayer, what stands out above all is that he is not asking anything for himself other than gifts and abilities to help others.

An entirely different prayer comes from a young Ghanaian Christian. It is concerned with the workings of the Holy Spirit. It is reprinted from the Oxford Book of Prayer:

> *On your last day on earth you promised to leave the Holy Spirit as our present comforter.*
>
> *We also know that your Holy Spirit blows over this earth. But we do not understand him. Many think he is only wind or a feeling.*

Let your Spirit break into our lives. Let it come like blood into our veins, so that we will be driven entirely by your will.

Let your Spirit blow over wealthy Europe and America, so that men there will be humble. Let him blow over the poor parts of the world, so that men there need suffer no more. Let it blow over Africa, so that men here may understand what true freedom is.

There are a thousand voices and spirits in this world, but we want to hear only your voice, and be open to your Spirit.[18]

A prayer by a Muslim convert, reproduced from the same source reads:

O God, I am Mustafah, the tailor, and I work at the shop of Muhammed Ali. The whole day long I sit and pull the needle and the thread through the cloth. O God you are the needle and I am the thread. I am attached to you and I follow you. When the thread tries to slip away from the needle it becomes all tangled up and must be cut so that it can be put back in the right place. O God, help me to follow you wherever you may lead me. For I am really only Mustafah, the tailor, and I work at the shop of Muhammed Ali on the great square.[19]

Another prayer that is familiar to many people is that by the American theologian Reinhold Niebuhr. It is probably best known because it was adopted by Alcoholics Anonymous in their struggle against alcoholism:

God, give us grace to accept with serenity the things that cannot be changed, courage to change the things that should be changed, and the wisdom to distinguish the one from the other.

I believe that it may be fitting to close this section on prayer with the words God instructed Moses to use in blessing the Israelites:

> *The Lord bless you and keep you.*
> *The Lord make his face to shine upon you and be gra-*
> *cious to you.*
> *The Lord turn his face towards you and give you peace.*
>
> — *Numbers 6, The New International Version*

I hope that this blessing may be yours as well.

9

What God Demands From Us Today

Introduction

In the Old Testament, God had given the people of Israel a basic set of rules to live by. If anyone had asked a Hebrew the question, "What does God demand from you today?" he would have answered by quoting the Ten Commandments, the basic set of rules God had given to Moses, as reproduced on pages 165 and 166. This set of rules is as relevant today as it was then; in fact, it is still the cornerstone of the justice system of approximately one third of the world's population. But these rules are almost all negative as they tell us what not to do. When Jesus came, he turned this around and restated these rules in their positive form. When asked, how people should live, he answered with this well-known interpretation of the law:

You shall love the Lord your God with all your heart, with all your soul, with all your mind and you shall love

> *your neighbour as yourself. Everything in the law and*
> *the prophets hangs on these two commandments.*
>
> — *Matthew 22, The New English Bible*

The challenge, which has faced the world ever since Jesus made this statement, is to interpret this command for the situations and conditions as they exist at any given point in time. The situations we find ourselves in today are different in many ways from those that prevailed during Jesus' lifetime, but the adherence to the principle of loving God and your neighbour is today as important and as essential for the building of a just society as it was then.

It may be interesting to quote at this point a follower of Confucius, Mo Tzu, who made this statement 500 years before Jesus:

> *Therefore, all the calamities, strifes, complaints, and*
> *hatred in the world have arisen out of want of mutual*
> *love.... How can we have this condition altered? It is*
> *to be altered by the way of universal love and mutual aid.*
> *But what is the way of mutual love and mutual aid? It*
> *is to regard the state of others as one's own, the houses*
> *of others as one's own, the persons of others as one's*
> *self.... When all the people in the world love one*
> *another, then the strong will not overpower the weak,*
> *the many will not oppress the few, the wealthy will not*
> *mock the poor, the honored will not disdain the humble, and the cunning will not deceive the simple. And it*
> *is all due to mutual love that calamities, strifes, complaints, and hatred are prevented from arising.*
>
> — *Quoted in K. L. Reichelt's book, Meditation and Piety*
> *in the Far East.*[1]

Mo Tzu's stress on mutual love and mutual aid are very close to what Jesus told us to do when he said that we must love our neighbour as ourselves.

However, in today's society we not only function as independent entities who can make decisions on our own without further reference to others, but we are also a part of an integrated society that acts on our behalf collectively. For most of us this means that we are citizens of a country; members of churches, synagogues, temples and mosques; and all types of other organizations which affect not only our own lives but those of others as well. Regardless of what type of organization we belong to, once we have joined it we are automatically responsible for what these organizations are doing or what they are not doing. In the following pages I will describe what I believe God demands from us today, at this point in time, and under our present circumstances:

- collectively as a citizen of a country;
- collectively as a member of a church; and
- individually as a member of our society.

In reflecting on this we should remember that we are God's hands and feet on earth, and that God acts today mainly through us, people like you and me. This has probably never been more clearly expressed than by Teresa of Avila, a Roman Catholic nun, who lived in Spain from 1525 to 1582:

> *Christ has no body now on earth but yours; yours are the only hands with which he can do his work, yours are the only feet with which he can go about the world, yours are the only eyes through which his compassion can shine forth upon a troubled world. Christ has no body now on earth but yours.*

In the previous chapter we mentioned the new creed at present in use in the United Church of Canada. That creed includes, in a very abbreviated form, the things God demands from us both as followers and co-creators. In the first instance, this creed reminds us that God calls us to be the church, and it then spells out in more detail what is required from us, namely:

> to celebrate God's presence;
> to love and serve others;
> to seek justice and resist evil;
> to proclaim Jesus, crucified and risen, our judge and
> our hope.

In the following pages, this list will be used as a guide in discussing the things God demands from us in the three situations in which we find ourselves. In doing so, we should remember what Jesus said about serving God through people in need, when he discussed the day of judgement with his disciples:

> *I was hungry and you fed me, thirsty and you gave me drink; I was a stranger and you received me in your homes, naked and you clothed me; I was sick and you took care of me, in prison and you visited me.*
>
> *The righteous will then answer him, When, Lord, did we ever see you hungry and feed you, or thirsty and gave you drink? When did we ever see you a stranger and welcome you in our homes, or naked and clothed you? When did we ever see you sick or in prison, and visit you?*
>
> *The King will answer back, I tell you, indeed, whenever you did this for one of the least important of these brothers of mine, you did it for me!*
>
> *— Matthew 25, Good News For Modern Man*

What God Demands From Us Collectively

In Chapter 6, I mentioned some of the collective sins for which we, as citizens of this world, must assume responsibility: They include the waging of war and the continued existence in today's world of starvation, hunger and poverty. At first glance it may appear that there is very little that we can do individually to prevent these calamities: Nevertheless, collectively we are responsible and it is our duty to make every possible attempt to make the rules God gave us effective in these situations. Nothing could possibly be more opposed to God's will than people killing people, often using the most atrocious means; or of people dying of hunger in some corner of the world while there is a surplus of food elsewhere.

Today, we are becoming increasingly aware that collectively we must assume responsibility for what is happening to our environment. It is clear, from what we said before, that humankind has a very specific set of duties and responsibilities for the world in which it finds itself. God clearly put us in charge of this earth, and it is for us to ensure that we treat the earth so that its continued ability to support life is not put in jeopardy, which means that it is our obligation to:

- carefully marshall all the resources of this earth so that future generations have enough food, energy, etc. to sustain life on a meaningful level;
- prevent further pollution from making the earth uninhabitable not only for ourselves but also for the animal world for which we are responsible;
- prevent science from creating situations which put the continued existence of this world at risk, either by genetic manipulations or by uncontrollable chemical reactions.

The first step towards taking responsible action on all these problems is to recognize that they are problems, and that there is no one else but us to deal with them. To recognize, in effect, that we will be held accountable for the conditions under which other people live and for the way we exercise our stewardship of this earth.

At the end of this chapter, a list is presented of all the manmade environmental problems we have created for ourselves and for our children, and for which collectively we must accept responsibility. The frightening thing about this list is that almost everyone of these problems was created by us within the last 50 years. Also, unfortunately, we are probably right now in the process of creating other problems of which we are not even aware, and which could have long-term cumulative disastrous effects on the well-being of our children and grandchildren, and which may even threaten the continued existence of life on this earth.

Maybe, the time has come for us to use the criterion, for making decisions regarding future technological developments, that was used by the native Indians of North America. They would ask themselves, when making choices, what effect their decision would have on people living seven generations later. If we did that, we would be much more careful in going ahead with some of the developments of which we have no idea what their long-term effects on people and the environment will be.

As individuals, in a democratic society, we can only make our wishes felt by submitting our views to the people we have elected to make these decisions for us. In other words, we must actively take part in the political life of the country. The problem is, of course, that there is never any one party that comes even near to attempting to put into effect the requirements of God's simple law. Maybe there are some political organizations that at least give lip service to the law of loving your neighbour, but I do not think that there is any political party anywhere that would put in its book of rules the commandment to love one's enemy.

In some parts of the world there are political parties affiliated with specific churches. But even these parties have great difficulty living up to their commitments in today's complicated world. They, and most other parties, are all for fighting starvation and reducing poverty. The big question they face is: How do you do this without giving up programs that are more popular with the general public which elects them? The question is then one of priorities and, as history shows, it is very difficult for any political organization to put the concern for others ahead of the party's own need to survive. As I am writing this, there is a small item in the newspaper about strikers in a defense industry in France, who are protesting against the fact that the production at their facility is being cut down because of the easing of international tensions. In other words, they are striking because they feel that their factory should continue to produce war machinery at great cost, that is both useless and superfluous, so that they can maintain their jobs. This is actually happening at a time of unprecedented starvation and poverty elsewhere in the world. Clearly here is a case of wrong priorities.

One other area of concern which we collectively must start to address is the population explosion which is taking place mostly in the underdeveloped countries. In large part, this increase in population is the result of better hygienic conditions, safer water supply and better medical services, which have made it possible for large numbers of children to survive their infancy and for older people to live longer. No doubt this is a great humanitarian achievement, but at the same time it has caused a very rapid growth in world population. There are predictions today that the world population will double in the next 50 years to 11 billion people. This is a most serious situation that the world at large cannot ignore. If not checked in time, it will lead to suffering on a scale never even envisaged before. Especially since the amount of available arable land is decreasing alarmingly, both through desertification and through urban sprawl. Unless the countries with excessive growth rates find a way to stop this growth, or unless entirely new sources of energy and food are found, the world's people will face starvation on an unprecedented scale. The ironic situation might then arise that all our advances in hygiene, in medicine, in agriculture, and in science, have led to far greater suffering on this earth than would have been the case if we had simply remained in the Stone Age. Clearly, collectively, we have a responsibility to see that this will not be so.

A case in point is the epidemic proportions taken on by AIDS, especially in the countries of Southern Africa. The fact is that in some of these countries more than 60 percent of the men and women are testing HIV positive and, because of lack of even the most elementary facilities to cope with this problem, most are destined to die under the most horrible conditions. Even if a cure to AIDS is found, it is very unlikely that people in the worst affected countries will be able to afford these drugs. The only hope is that the rest of the world, if only for reasons of self-interest, will make these drugs or vaccines freely available and set up appropriate facilities to oversee their distribution. Despite this present high death rate, the population of these countries is still expected to increase because of the high birth rate. Thus, in spite of all our inventions, all our miracle drugs, all our international aid, we still have:

- •continued starvation, hunger and poverty for many people;
- •millions of people, both young and old, dying of treatable diseases under appalling conditions;
- •a future which portends even greater poverty, because of the still growing population and the continuing depletion of the natural resources of this earth.

Clearly, God's command of loving your neighbour as yourself is not being applied here with any effectiveness. Having worked in many of these countries on development projects, I realize that there are no easy solutions, no easy cure-alls. At best, we seem to be able to help alleviate the conditions during the most serious emergencies, such as the starvation crises in Ethiopia, Somalia and the Sudan. But this is not enough. If we consider these people to be our neighbours, and they are, then we must come up with something better — with solutions that are of a permanent nature. Clearly with our scientific and technological abilities, it is our responsibility to see that these God-given abilities are applied to these problems, rather than to developing the most effective ways in which to kill our fellow human beings.

Of course, we are not only responsible for what happens in other countries, but we are also, and often more directly, responsible for what happens in our own countries. The fact that today we have foodbanks, that we have increasing numbers of people who are homeless and must live on the streets of our cities, is unacceptable and against our Christian principles, and it is also against the most basic principles of our democratic way of life. Collectively, we simply must find a way of conducting our affairs that assures everyone a decent standard of living, and that means that people should not have to stand in breadlines or have to sleep on the streets of our cities.

Now that communism is for all intents and purposes dead and buried, it is our responsibility to make sure that unbridled capitalism does not take over and cause an even greater gap to arise between the rich and the poor. John Kenneth Galbraith, the well-known economist, warned the world against complacency now that, as he said: "Capitalism stands alone, triumphant in the world." In a recent article he wrote: "There is a grave problem of social injustice and political danger, and the sources lie in the economic system. We must identify the flaws and shortcomings of capitalism and move to correct them."

Obviously, if this avowed supporter of capitalism can see the dangers ahead, we better heed his warning and change our system in such a way that the shortcomings of that system are rooted out so that all people can enjoy a standard of living that is compatible with their human dignity.

What God Demands From Us As A Church

1. To Be The Church And Celebrate God's Presence

Using the creed mentioned before as a guide, the first demand made on us is to celebrate God's presence or, said differently, to worship God. On reading this, the question naturally comes to mind, If God is so almighty why does he/she want to be worshipped by his/her own creation? And, if we think of this worship as a TV spectacular, this first demand certainly does not make much sense. But, if we think of worship as a human response to God's love, the whole practice takes on a different meaning. It is in the sense of giving thanks and giving praise as a response to what God did for us, that we find the true significance of all the worship as practiced in the Christian Church.

One other question which is often raised concerning worship is, Why do we have to worship in a church; can we not give thanks and praise alone by ourselves? The answer to that question is that no doubt you can give thanks and praise privately but, if you have found something precious, you want to share your luck and good fortune with your friends and other like-minded people. In the same way, as Christians, we want to give thanks and praise not only by ourselves but also with others who have similar thoughts, beliefs, and experiences. An example may illustrate this better than words.

At the end of World War II, my family found itself in the middle of the frontline, the German army on one side and the British army on the other. Both were shelling the no-man's land in-between at regular intervals. During one of the quiet intervals we managed to escape to a nearby town that had been liberated sometime before. When a few days later the end of the war was announced, the town became almost instantly a milling, shouting, crying and singing mass of people, civilians and Allied soldiers alike. Suddenly the immediate danger to life was over and all rejoiced and celebrated together, talking and shouting to each other, often without understanding one word the other person was saying. The point I want to make is that they did not do their rejoicing and celebrating alone by themselves. On the contrary, people poured out of their homes and onto the streets, not only in that small town but also in London, New York, and all over the world, people celebrated together. People who had never spoken together, had never acknowledged each other's existence, danced together. They wanted to rejoice together because they all shared the same wonderful experience: They were saved — a nightmare had come to an end.

So it is with the worship in the church. If you are really convinced that Jesus was the Son of God, and that he put the world right again with God; that evil has been overcome; and that, as God's children, we have a future which goes beyond this life, then you too want to give thanks and praise together, just as was done when the war came to an end and the world was suddenly transformed from a world at war to a world at peace.

2. To Love And Serve Others

Just as it is the duty of every Christian individually, so it is the duty of the Church as an organization, to demonstrate that love and concern for others and to transform that concern into effective action. During the long history of the Church, that concern has not always been visible in a tangible form. For instance, the very poor labour conditions during the early days of the industrial revolution; the child labour in the mines and factories; and other unbearable conditions of existence were tolerated by the Church without effective protest far too long. It was socialism, and to some extent communism, which led the way in forging reforms and not the established churches.

As noted in the previous section, the Church today faces the issues of poverty and starvation in many underdeveloped countries. And, although the Churches are doing their share in the direct alleviation of emergency situations, the Church must take a more defined stand and proclaim that the conditions as they exist today are not acceptable to a Christian society, and that lasting remedies must be found regardless of the cost.

Similarly, the Church has a message to bring on the subject of prejudice, particularly racial discrimination. If we are all children of the same God, and therefore all brothers and sisters, then any discrimination of a person on the basis of skin pigmentation or sexual orientation is against the fundamentals of our belief and is not to be tolerated.

One of the problems the Church has to face is the fact that the established churches have been very much the church of the middle-class and the well-to-do throughout the ages. This has caused the Church to be very cautious in condemning practices that were and are, by any standard of Christian behaviour, unacceptable. For instance, a demand by the Church for better living conditions for the working-class during the early years of the industrial revolution would have upset the establishment of which the Church was very much a part. Thus, the Church often found itself on the side of the oppressors rather than in the forefront of those seeking much needed changes in social and economic conditions. It is the challenge for the churches of today to learn its lessons from the past and to apply the principles it stands for in both the local and the international arena, regardless of who will be upset and regardless what the immediate economic consequences will be.

In South America, the apparent acceptance by the official church of the social conditions of the poor and hungry has led to a revolution in the religious life in some of these countries. It has resulted in the emergence of a whole new theology, Liberation Theology, as well as the emergence of an entirely different style of congregational life in the so-called "base communities." Liberation theologists point out that for most of us the Bible has been used to support and strengthen our way of life; but for them the Bible is a book that challenges accepted values and calls for revolutionary change. They point out that our actions fall short of the Bible's radical demand for justice for all. Harvey Cox, the well-known author of *The Secular City* wrote recently:

> *In story after story and teaching after teaching, Jesus insists that God gives the Kingdom to the poor because they have nowhere else to turn, not because of their doctrinal orthodoxy or moral purity.*[2]

In the base communities, members support one another in striving for justice and in offering an abundant community life for all. They are working for both social transformation and effective evangelism. As such, they consider themselves to be the church in action, and no doubt they are. Both the liberation theology and the base communities have increased the social awareness of the church at large and have in many ways transformed the religious life in South America. Their example and leadership in this type of social ministry is beginning to have a profound influence on the way the mission of the church is perceived in other parts of the world as well.

As was pointed out in the section on our collective responsibilities, the so-called victory of capitalism over communism does not mean that our capitalist system is flawless. On the contrary, capitalism has the inherent potential for the emergence of great injustices if left unchecked. I believe that now that communism is no longer a viable alternative, the Church at large should take on the responsibility of becoming the watchdog of our system and point out where injustices are occurring. The church is probably the only organization in the world today that can take on this responsibility. It can speak out impartially and it must do so without fear of losing supporters: All it has to do is to see what is happening to people and judge whether that treatment is in agreement with what Jesus taught.

For this to be possible, the Church must organize itself so that it can speak with one voice. It must point out the inequities that exist and it must demand that corrective steps be taken. It must point out that there are enough resources available to make it possible for every person to live a life that is in keeping with its human dignity. It must demand that ways and means be found to guarantee a more equal distribution of the resources of this world between all its citizens and eventually between all people in the world. Only in this way can the Church claim that it is living up to its responsibilities and is meeting the demand of its own creed "to love and serve others."

3. To Seek Justice And Resist Evil

Many people, Christians and non-Christians alike, will have very little problem in acknowledging that "to seek justice and resist evil" is a good thing to do. The problem we all face is how we can do this effectively. When is justice being done, or not being done, and when is something evil, and by what standards do we make this distinction? Today, we all must face questions such as, what is evil and when is justice served in situations such as abortion, euthanasia, degrading poverty, accumulation of great wealth, etc.

Within today's society, with its emphasis on science and technology, the list of issues on which the Church must speak out increases daily. To name just a few:

293

•The issue of whether there is ever any justification for using atomic and chemical weapons. Despite seeing the effects of the atomic bombs on Japanese cities, the world has come perilously close to doing just that in the last few decades.

•The issue of genetic engineering — How far can the world let scientists go before putting a stop to the tinkering with our genetic heritage?

•The issue of the new reproductive technologies — When do these new methods become morally and economically unacceptable?

•The issue of long-term energy consumption and conservation. How long can we continue our reckless depletion of the world's natural resources?

•The issue of the uneven use of the world's natural resources, with 20 percent of the world's population using 85 percent of these resources.

•The issue of the environmental problems caused by deforestation, and the use of some chemicals that destroy the ozone layer which protects us from the effects of direct radiation by the sun.

The list goes on and on. If the church is alive, there is no way in which it can remain silent on these issues, because it is these issues which are going to determine whether, in the long run, there is going to be any life on this earth at all.

While these problems must be faced by every person individually, I believe that it is the Christian Church, hopefully in cooperation with the other religions, which must take the lead in defining a responsible stand on these issues. In fact, it is hard to find any other organization in the world today that is willing and able to take on this crucial task. If for no other reason, I believe the main-line churches not only have the responsibility but, because of the resources available to them, have a clear obligation to investigate, analyze and explain and, in the end, recommend appropriate action. For it to do so, the Church must have knowledgeable lay people who can make the necessary evaluations of the economic and social costs and benefits of these programs to humankind. But, above all, they must be capable of stating these benefits and costs in terms that the average person can understand. In other words, the Church must have the best technical advice possible. Anything that is not done in accordance with the highest technical and scientific standards will backfire when it is exposed as such. Neither the Church nor, humanity at large, can afford for this to happen.

So, for the Church to effectively seek justice and resist evil in these areas of concern, it must assume a new role, that of scientific interpreter of the facts as they relate to these life and death issues. This is something completely new to the Church, and it will have to be very careful indeed in assuming that responsibility, but there is no other way that it can meet its obligations. For the Church not to speak out on these issues, which could affect life on earth forever, would be to shirk its greatest responsibility not only as caretaker of this earth but also in its obligation to be God's Church and to resist evil. Surely, here is a field in which the various churches can cooperate and take joint action so that they can be heard as one voice.

4. To Proclaim Jesus, Crucified And Risen, Our Judge And Our Hope

This is the last task listed in our creed and, from the point of view of the Church, probably the easiest to agree upon, especially since most people find it difficult to do this on a personal level. But even here, there is the question how to best do this and where. In the past, almost all churches interpreted this command to mean that they should go out to the Third World and take the Christian message to the "heathens abroad." There is no doubt that missionaries made great contributions to the spreading of Christ's message across the world, but, as could have been foreseen, the end result was often different from that expected. As soon as you tell a person, who is ruled by foreigners, that he is essentially the same as the person who rules over him, and that you are actually brothers, you can expect that person to begin to question what that other person is doing, telling him what to do.

So, the missionaries through their preaching and teaching, not only laid the foundations of the young churches, but also bred a very fine crop of revolutionaries and freedom fighters. The effect of this can be seen today most clearly in Africa, where a large percentage of the leaders of the newly independent countries were educated in missionary schools. Not only they, but also the other educated people in these countries, almost invariably started their education in missionary schools often located in remote and isolated places. During interviews I conducted recently with engineering graduates in a Southern African country, almost all the graduates had started their schooling in missionary schools and, in many instances, had continued their education in secondary missionary schools as well.

Today, however, all the former colonies have become independent, and naturally their churches and school systems have too from the missionary societies that supported them in the past. The young churches are standing on their own feet and are mostly doing very well. But even today, after so many years, the leaders of these churches still voice, once in awhile, their resentment about the fact that they were governed for so long from abroad and were kept dependent on the foreign churches long past the point that this was necessary. So, the role of the overseas missions has changed and today is mainly limited to providing much needed teachers, doctors and technical advisers. It is through them that the older churches in the developed countries now must fulfill their mission abroad, not by preaching but by serving.

While most churches made great efforts in missionary work overseas, very little was often done about bringing Christ's message to the people in their immediate vicinity who had never heard this message. The need for doing this is clear from the sharp decrease in Church membership over the last decades. This has inevitably led to the situation that there are increasing numbers of people in our Western society who have never heard Christ's message and, unless the church does something

296

about this, will never hear it during their lifetime. Therefore, they will not even be presented with a choice whether to accept or reject Jesus' message.

While the membership in the mainline churches has decreased in all Western countries, there has been a growing influence on the mind of young people by non-conventional religions. New Age movements have sprung up all over North America and Europe, some, to our way of thinking, with the weirdest ideas. However, whatever we may think of these movements, one thing is clear: The adherents of these cults and sects did not find in the established churches what they were looking for. Thus, the Church has obviously fallen short in its task to "proclaim Jesus, our judge and our hope" to these people.

It is clear that as a Church we must again begin to place greater emphasis on evangelism and outreach to people who have never heard the message or, having heard it, have forgotten or misunderstood that message. Many people will have seen and heard Billy Graham on the television or may have seen and heard him in person. There is no doubt that Rev. Graham is proclaiming "Jesus, crucified and risen, our judge and our hope" to a very large audience. His example and that of others have shown us that, with the new technologies now available to us, it is possible to effectively proclaim the gospel to large numbers of people simultaneously. Unfortunately, it has also shown that the same media, in the hands of less scrupulous evangelists, can be equally well used to mislead and distort God's message. It is for us to find ways of using these new media effectively and responsibly in our task of proclaiming the risen Christ to the world.

There are many indications today that, despite the decreasing membership in the established churches, there is a growing search by many people for values and for a meaning to life. Recent polls have shown that between 60 and 70 percent of the people in North America believe in the existence of God and in a life hereafter, but only a fraction of these attend worship services with any regularity. If these figures are correct, then the Church is obviously falling far short in its task of proclaiming Jesus, crucified and risen. At least, it is not convincing these people to join a Christian community. No doubt, some people feel uncomfortable in the Church with the way the worship services are conducted; others may feel that the Church does not take an active stand on social issues and does not reach out to people in need; yet others may feel that the institution of the Church is outmoded and that we need a new form of spirituality. Whatever the reason, it is the duty and obligation of the Church to overcome these resistances and, in the end, the Church can only do that by proclaiming the Christian message. In other words, it is our obligation to tell the world the good news that death has been overcome; that we are reconciled with God; that we can look forward to a life that is eternal and that will have a richness that is beyond our wildest imaginations.

It is difficult to close this section on what we should be doing as a church without mentioning the work and life of The Church Of Our Saviour in Washington, D.C. This church which was started shortly after the end of World War II, is still very small with less than 150 members. But their influence goes far beyond that suggested by their numbers. The reason for this is that this church has an extraordinarily strong commitment to both study and action. In fact, members must every year recommit themselves to both their faith and work; each member must carry out an important function in one of their mission groups; and members must make a financial commitment of at least ten percent of their income. Because of this strong commitment of time and money, they are able to achieve the most remarkable results. Each mission group consists of a small number of members, who are committed to the group's particular project, plus some people who are not yet ready to make such a complete commitment. The result is that they are able to operate with this small number of people some 30 mission projects, ranging from communities for the homeless and sick, to soup kitchens, low-cost housing, rehabilitation centers for alcohol and drug abusers, etc.

There are other groups within the world church that are making similar commitments. The example of this particular group shows what a dedicated church can achieve when it is fully committed to carrying out Christ's command to love and to serve.

What God Demands From Us As A Person

1. General Introduction

In the end, the Church is made up of individuals, people who lead a life of their own outside the confines of the Church and within the world. So what is required of us as individuals living in a fast-changing world? In principle, the answer to that question is very simple and has been given in these pages time and time again, "We are to love God and love our neighbour as ourselves." This is a very simple rule — a very general rule! In some ways the Christian religion has its greatest difficulty right there. We have no set of rules that we must follow, nothing but the command to love and serve others. Each one of us must find the right interpretation of that basic rule in any given set of circumstances.

As we have seen in the Old Testament, God gave the Jews a set of rules, the Ten Commandments, which they were told to obey. In general, we still believe that these rules should be adhered to today, but these rules were relevant to the situation as it existed 3,000 to 4,000 years ago.

Today we live in an age that continually forces us to make decisions in an entirely different environment. For instance, at a recent meeting of young adults, a young girl raised the question of sex and sexual norms. "Surely," she said, "you must be able to give us some hard and fast rules instead of just saying that your conduct must be based on the command to serve God and love your neighbour as yourself." Unfortunately, that is not possible in today's world where young people often have to go through long periods of adolescence before they can economically afford to get married, and where new birth-control methods have made it possible to live together without having the immediate responsibility for a growing family. I believe the question, like so many similar questions, cannot be answered in one way that is valid for all people under all conditions and circumstances. Rather, we must decide in each case what we should do using the general rule that Christ gave us as our guide. That gives us great freedom, but like all freedoms it gives us great responsibilities as well. As professing Christians we must show our faith through our actions. Others, outside the Church, will judge the Church and what it stands for by the actions of the Christians they know. As a well-known hymn says, "For They Will Know That We Are Christians By Our Love." All who say that they are Christians will automatically be judged by others using higher standards of measuring behaviour than a person who does not make that confession, and rightly so. For example, in his book, *Social Ministry*, Dieter Hessel quotes K. Underwood as saying, "To claim to be Christian who loves God and neighbour and not to attempt to be an effective person in the formation of just social policies, is to talk nonsense in the modern world."[3] Gandhi, probably the best known Hindu of our time, is reported to have said to someone who asked him what his message was, "My life is my message." And, so it should be for the Christian.

A few decades ago, existentialism was one of the favoured philosophies. People like Jean-Paul Sartre, Albert Camus and others wrote novels about the awful feeling of emptiness in the universe that had nothing to offer but final oblivion of the human race. Since, according to their philosophy, there is nothing to hope for, nothing to guide us, all people must make their own way and live their life as they see fit. But, existentialists say, responsible people will conduct themselves in such a way that they can be an example for others to follow. In some sense, this is very much like the Christian's attitude: We also believe that we should be living lives that are examples for others. But, we have the added concern that our behavior will be used by others to judge the effectiveness of not only our Christian faith, but also that of Christianity in general.

As we did, when we discussed what God demands from us as a Church, we will again use the responsibilities listed in our modern creed as a guide for our discussions on what God demands from us as an individual.

2. To Celebrate God's Presence

First of all the creed says that we must celebrate God's presence. As an individual we can do that in many ways. We can do it at home, in the Church, in the car or in nature. It is something that we can do at almost any time and in any place. It should include above anything else an expression of our thankfulness and praise for all that God has done for us. We should express that appreciation not only for the personal blessings we have received, but also for the beauty of nature, for the majestic clockwork of the movement of the stars in the heavens and the magic of the sub-atomic world. No matter who we are, no matter what our mental capabilities are, we can all celebrate God's presence in this way. All we have to do is to be aware that God is with us; that nothing in the universe can separate us from that presence; and to express our appreciation for that presence. That is what I believe it means to celebrate God's presence.

3. To Love And Serve Others

As said repeatedly before in these pages, Jesus' message to us was to live a life of love — to love God, to love our neighbour and to love even our enemy. The message is simple, but to actually live such a life is difficult for most of us. Most people, who are not retired, must work in a workplace to make a living. That workplace may make demands on us that are not always conducive to putting this command into effect. Maybe our work is repetitive, such as working on an assembly line, but even there we have contact with co-workers, with people who may need our help.

Maybe our work is that of a high pressure salesman: Even in that situation we must find a way to express our concerns for others. Even if we find it impossible in our work situation to apply the rule of loving and serving others in a meaningful way, there are still all the hours of leisure time we have to comply with God's demands regarding our relationships with other people. Maybe you feel that you have enough problems of your own and do not want to become embroiled in the problems of other people. You may feel so, but it is also true that often the most effective help comes from people who have wrestled with the same problems you have. A clear indication of this effectiveness is the increasing numbers of self-help support groups that are springing up all over the country. They are effective because they bring people together who can share their experiences, their hurts and their pains, and their successes and failures in dealing with their particular situation.

Maybe you find it difficult to think of something constructive to do which effectively demonstrates your concern for others. If so, you only have to think of all the lonely and sick people there are in this world, people without relatives, old and abandoned in homes and institutions. Most likely they are not the type of people that you particularly want to spend time with — maybe they are too old, too cranky, too unbalanced, too demanding, too critical, too smelly, too snoopy, etc. No doubt each one of us can find many reasons why not to stretch out our hand to someone. But, if we have these reasons, then most likely others have exactly the same feelings and nothing will be done. Jesus did not say that you must help this good-looking girl, or that important fellow, or that charming old couple. No, he said, "Unless you have done it to any of these little ones or to the least of these ones, you have not done it unto me."

Again, you do not need a lot of talent to do this; anyone can stretch their hand out to someone in need. For instance, a person with learning disabilities often can put us to shame and do this far better and more naturally than the people with dignities to maintain, people who are afraid that their approach will be rejected, people who are afraid of being made a fool of, and so on. My little granddaughter, the one who has Down Syndrome, can give all of us a lesson. She does not make any judgements; she is not thinking about her dignity when she goes to all kinds of people and hugs them without discrimination and in that way is a joy to many.

Jesus' command was to love your neighbour as yourself. When the people around him asked, "Who is my neighbour?" Jesus gave them the parable of the Good Samaritan. The message of that parable is very clear: Your neighbour is the person in need around you. Not only your family, not only your friends, not only the people next door, but anyone who asks for your help. That includes those people who you see need help but do not ask for it. It is our responsibility to recognize that need of our neighbour and to put into effect the command of God, to love and to serve.

Obviously, we cannot respond to every demand that is made on us or every need we see, that would be impossible and would soon reduce our effectiveness to do anything. But if we do nothing, if we cannot think of anyone to whom we have stretched out a helping hand lately, then there is surely something wrong with the way we live our lives; because no matter where you find yourself, there are people who need a helping hand. It is clear, that if we find ourselves in that situation, we must start to rethink our commitments and our priorities, and change our life in such a way that we have time to "love and to serve."

4. To Seek Justice And Resist Evil

On a personal basis, we find it often difficult to meet that requirement although we probably all agree that it needs doing. In fact, it is a sort of motherhood statement: Everyone is for it, but the problem is how to put it into effect in today's world.

As with all other requirements, we can start off by applying them in our own personal family life in the way we treat our spouses and in the way we treat our children and close relatives. Also, we can start applying it in our workplace. To seek justice and resist evil there may not always be as easy as applying it in our own homes, but if we are to live up to our Christian responsibility we must do so. It may require us to take stands that are not popular with our unions, our co-workers, or our superiors. It is easy to see from today's newspapers that many people find it very difficult to apply the principles of resisting evil particularly in the workplace. For instance, the wrong-doings, recently disclosed in our financial institutions and in government agencies, could not have happened if there had not been a large number of people in these organizations who knew about these irregularities but who did nothing to remedy it: In other words they did not resist evil and seek justice.

One of the areas where we must seek justice and resist evil is in the field of abuse and violence, and not only the violence in the streets but also the violence and abuse in the family. Abuse of women and children seems to be rampant everywhere and in every social milieu. It is our duty as Christians to fight this evil wherever we find it. Again, we must start in our own homes, in our own companies, and even in our own churches. Violence of any form cannot be tolerated, and we must fight it with all the means at our disposal.

Probably the greatest influence we can exert in seeing that justice is being done is by ensuring that we have a responsible and honest government. And, if it so happens that the government we elected does not follow through on its promises, we, in a democratic society, have the right and the duty to let that government know that they are not meeting their commitments. The feeling that we may have of not being important enough to be listened to is, in most cases, more a cop-out than a true reflection of the actual situation. In a democratic society, where our government is elected and must be re-elected to stay in power, any elected person is by the very nature of this process extremely sensitive, probably too sensitive, to criticism by even a very small group of well-informed and vocal electors. A good case in point is the consumer protest against increasing violence in the daytime television programs. Everyone seems to finally agree that the increasing violence on our streets is partially the result of the steady diet of murder, rape, and other violence that our children are exposed to on TV as they grow up. A well-published boycott of the products of the companies that advertise on these programs, by a relatively small percentage of concerned consumers, would very quickly put a stop to these excesses.

So, to seek justice and resist evil at the personal level we must first apply it within our own immediate range of influence, that is in our families and in our businesses and in our workplaces. Beyond that we must see that it is being done at the local, provincial, state and federal levels. Contrary to what many people may think, we are not powerless and helpless: We have a great deal of power to force changes when we see that our government is not seeking justice and resisting evil. But, to do so, we must protest in cooperation with like-minded people, either in the church or through other organizations that have been especially formed for that specific purpose.

5. To Proclaim Jesus, Crucified And Risen, Our Judge And Our Hope

As said before under the section on what the church should be doing, if we take our faith seriously we will want others to know about it as well. How to do that is not always easy for most people. However, the findings of a survey quoted previously, indicating that a great majority of the people interviewed do believe in the existence of a God and in the existence of an after-life, should make it easier to talk about the subject. Especially since there exists, at the same time, among many people, a feeling of purposelessness and lack of direction. It is for the individual Christian to help others to move from the belief in a vague and distant deity to the faith and trust in a loving God who cares for each one of us personally.

The problem is how to do this without making one sound like a "holier than thou" person and thus alienating people. We can, of course, respond to direct questions about our faith, but in today's society it is very rare that people ask questions of this type directly: After all who wants to admit that they find life meaningless and have lost all sense of direction. Even if we were asked direct questions, we would probably have great difficulty in putting our convictions into words or explaining our faith in such a way that makes sense to the other person.

In any case, regardless of our ability to convince by words, we should be able to convince people by the way we live our lives — the way our life follows the example set by Jesus Christ. As someone said, it is our lives that are the most potent signs of Christ in any generation, stronger certainly than miracles or arguments or decrees.

The rise of the early Christian Church was to a very large degree due to the fact that the apostles and early followers stood out from the crowd and were easily recognizable, because of the way they lived their lives. They lived their faith for everyone to see, and they were willing to die for their convictions and many of them did.

In that respect, the Christian of today can learn something from the use of television commercials. The commercials are full of people trying to tell us that they have tried this or that product, and that it is better than the other products on the market. Someone told them about the good qualities of this product, so they tried it and their teeth are whiter, their wash is cleaner, their headache is gone, and so forth. All this advertising money is spent, because the agencies know that there is no better way to sell their products than by showing and quoting satisfied customers.

I believe, that as Christians, we should show that same evidence of a "good product," by showing the difference that our faith makes in our lives, so that others can see that we have something special that they also may want to have. So, in the end, we proclaim Jesus crucified and risen by the way we live his command to love our neighbours as ourselves; by the way we treat adversities in our lives; and by the way we project ourselves to others as a joyful people, people who have a set of marching orders and know where they are going.

Alternatives For The Future

It may be helpful to close this chapter, on what God demands from us today, with what we believe the future of this earth could be if we applied the principles Christ taught us, and what it will be if we continue on our present path of self-destruction.

As far as we can see into the future today, always remembering that the president of IBM predicted in the late 1940s that there would be place in the U.S. for only two or three electronic computers, it would appear most likely that the following will happen:

1 — further automatization and further computerization of many ordinary human activities;

2 — decreasing employment in industry and agriculture, and increasing employment in the service and leisure sectors of the economy;

3 — increase in leisure time; shorter work weeks and earlier retirement; possibly, continued high unemployment worldwide;

4 — increasing influence of the electronic media on people's lives everywhere;

5 — increased loss of privacy through the link-up of electronic data banks;

6 — further increase in world population, both through birth and by the gradual increase in average age;

7 — decreasing percentage of the population supporting increasing percentage of dependents;

8 — further developments in genetic engineering, probably culminating in the increased use of cloning;

9 — increasing intervention in the natural process of human genetics, for example, choosing the gender of off-spring;

10 — increasing utilization of artificial intelligence in the decision-making process;

11 — increasing understanding of the workings of the universe and of the nature of things;

12 — increasing understanding of the workings of the human body and especially of the human brain/mind;

13 — decrease in the availability of natural resources, and decrease in the availability of agricultural land;

14 — increased use of atomic energy, hopefully using the almost pollution-free fusion process;

15 — increased proliferation of atomic weapons, in some cases to countries with very unstable and unreasonable governments;

16 — increasing formation of large, international economic units;

17 — increased difference in lifestyles between the highly industrialized and the less-developed countries;

18 — increased international awareness of the dangers of the effects of pollution on life on earth;

19 — despite this, there is likely to be increased pollution of the world's water, land, air and atmosphere because of the high financial costs associated with the prevention of further pollution and the clean-up of the effects of past pollution;

20 — great difficulties in disposing of atomic weapons and atomic wastes which will make nuclear accidents and nuclear pollution a real and continuing threat to humanity for many years to come.

Looking at this list of potential developments, it is clear that we as a society, with the technology available today and potentially available to us in the future, have an almost unlimited capability to improve human existence and to bring human life to its fullest potential. On the other hand, as the list clearly indicates, we also have an almost unlimited capability for evil and for the destruction of life.

I believe that the future course of human existence will be determined to a very large extent by the choices we make today, and by the choices we must make in the near future. As said before, the choices we make will, to a considerable extent, depend on the value system we live by. From looking at the capabilities we have now, and the additional ones we will likely have in the future, it is clear that we will have a number

of opportunities unequalled in the history of the human race.
I believe they will include the following:

a) an unequaled opportunity for world peace —
For the first time in decades, we have the opportunity
to live without the threat of major wars. Also, since
there are no major ideological differences between the
superpowers, it is possible for the United Nations to
become an effective world government.

b) an unequaled opportunity to do away with hunger and
poverty worldwide —
This is probably the first time in the world's history
that we can produce enough food for all and that we
have the capability to distribute it to the most remote
and inaccessible places in the world.

c) an unequaled opportunity for the full development of
human potential —
With today's mechanization of almost all human physical work, it is possible to produce all basics needed for
human existence in a relatively small percentage of
available human time. Thus, if organized properly,
there is the possibility for everyone to be freed of the
necessity to work long hours to earn a basic living, and
to use this time to develop the self to its highest potential through active participation in the arts, philosophy,
social programs, etc.

Unfortunately, as we all well know, there is also the potential of using these opportunities in the wrong way. Today, we
have the possibility:

a) to destroy the earth —
For the first time in human history, we have the potential to end all life on this planet. It is possible to do it
through atomic warfare, or we can do it through unrestrained pollution and the consequent destruction of
the environment.

b) to have worldwide starvation —
With the almost inevitable further polarization between
the poor and the rich, both locally and internationally,

there is a very distinct possibility that starvation by a large part of the world's population will become an accepted way of life.

c) to destroy all human values and freedoms —
With the communication systems available to governments, large industries and criminal cartels, it is possible for these institutions to completely control our lives and our human value system, and thus make human existence intolerable and even make us live in fear for our lives.

So, we have these six possibilities, and at this point in time, it is by no means clear in which direction we are moving. The way to full development of the physical and spiritual human potential or the way to self-destruction.

Jesus said, "I have come that men may have life, and may have it abundantly" (or, in all its fullness). (John 10:10) It is obvious that if we choose the way to that abundant life or to full development of the human potential, we must make changes in both our way of thinking and in the way we are doing things. To focus our attention, I have listed below some of the questions we should ask ourselves. These questions have been posed both in the general and in the specific, because some of these questions are mostly relatively easy to answer in general but are much more difficult to agree upon in some of the specific instances. The way we answer these questions, I believe, will to a large extent determine the future of human development, and maybe even the future of our planet.

Some of the questions we might ask ourselves on a national basis are:

1 — Do the citizens of every country have the right to receive adequate food, shelter and medical attention?
Even if their government is repressive and spends a large part of the available resources on armaments?

2 — Does a country have the right to defend itself if it is attacked?
Even if this means using chemical and atomic weapons?

3 — Does every country have the right to fully develop its natural resources?

Even if this means that it causes harm to the world's ecosystem?

4 — Does every country have the right to freely export its products?

Even at a price below its production cost?

5 — Does every country have the right to freely adopt whatever type of government it wants?

Even if that means that some minority rights are being suppressed?

6 — Does every minority group in a country have the right to separate and form an independent state?

Even if the resulting state is not an economically viable unit?

Most of the basic questions we are probably inclined to answer in the positive, while we are probably more inclined to answer the specific cases in the negative. If anything, it shows that we cannot just follow general principles blindly, but that we must, at all times, be vigilant that we do not make terrible mistakes by simply following those generally accepted principles regardless of the circumstances.

On a more personal basis, we have an even longer list of potential problem areas, including some of the following:

a) Does everyone have the right to receive adequate food, shelter and medical attention?

Even if a person is not willing to work for it?

b) Does everyone have the right to receive wages that place a family above the poverty line?

Even for the lowest paying and simplest jobs?

c) Does everyone have the right to work as long as s/he wants above the retirement age?

Even if that means that others go without work?

d) Does everyone have the right to have as many children as they want?

Even if they cannot support them?

e) Does everyone have the right to choose an university education if capable?
Even if there is not likely to be work in the profession of their choice?

f) Does everyone have the right to accumulate great wealth?
Even if it is at the expense of others?

g) Does everyone have the right to vote on all issues?
Even if they are not capable of understanding the issues?

As I said before, I believe that the future of the world will depend very much on how we, in the industrialized world, answer these and other questions of a similar nature. Also, we must ask ourselves about our willingness to give up certain of our privileged positions to make it possible for this world to become a better place to live in for all its inhabitants.

As Christians, we have no choice: We are bound by Christ's demand to love our neighbour as ourselves, even if that neighbour is an enemy. That essentially leaves us with only one problem to solve, and that is how to interpret that command in each specific case. Looking at the lists above, it is easy to see that different people will interpret their responsibility in different ways. Nevertheless, we must face that difficulty and use our judgement to decide what God demands from us in each specific instance. I believe that it is important that in doing so we realize that, at this point in time, there is only one institution in the world that can provide a value system for answering these questions. That institution, organized religion in all its multiple forms, is the only institution that has not only the capability, but in most cases also the inherent obligation to provide guidance to the people who must deal with these problems.

For me, that religion is the Christian religion; for others it is Islam, Buddhism, Hinduism, Bahai, etc. Today, regardless of which religion we support, it is of the utmost importance that we make our views known, and that we apply the value system that is the result of our religious beliefs to the problems that face the world today. If we fail to do so, we can expect the worst, simply because there is no other acceptable value system available.

So, the future is in our hands. Today, we still can make choices, something that may not be possible in the future, because the choices we make today may set the world on a path which may be irreversible.

The good news for today is that we are co-creators with God and as such we have a task to fulfill: We are responsible for the preservation of this earth and for the spiritual and physical well-being of all its inhabitants.

Table Of Environmental Problems And Concerns

A — Nuclear
- (1) the destruction of existing nuclear weapons
- (2) the prevention of further nuclear proliferation
- (3) the dismantling of obsolete nuclear stations
- (4) the storing and destruction of nuclear wastes

B — Climate
- (1) the destruction of the ozone layer
- (2) the greenhouse effect — danger of global warming and potential melting of the polar icecap
- (3) desertification, mainly in Africa

C — Chemical and Industrial Pollution
- (1) the destruction of all chemical weapons
- (2) the pollution of rivers and lakes; acid rain
- (3) the pollution of the oceans
- (4) deforestation and inadequate reforestation
- (5) the pollution of the air through car and industrial emissions
- (6) the accumulation of garbage, farm wastes and chemical wastes
- (7) oil spills from tankers and sabotage (Kuwait's oil lakes)

D — Natural Resources
- (1) the depletion of all natural resources
- (2) the ongoing destruction of arable land
- (3) the ongoing destruction of wildlife habitat

E — Population
- (1) the population explosion and the environmental problems created by it

10

Where Do We Go From Here?

I started this book with a discussion of what life is like if we do not accept the concept of a God who has created and maintains the universe we are living in. If there is no God, there can be no real future and our world will eventually come to an end like a wound-down clock.

I then went on to describe what the Christian religion teaches about the existence of God, God's message of love for us, and the importance humans have in God's universe.

Personally, I believe that there is no contest if the choice is between these two alternatives: on the one hand a winding down universe with no real future, and on the other hand a transformation into a new world that is eternal and in which we will live a life that is beyond our wildest imagination.

So, you ask, what are these basic beliefs of yours that lead you to think that this glorious future will eventually become a reality? The answer is simply this. I have come to believe and accept the following:

- There is a God, who is Spirit, but whom we may approach as our Father/Mother, who is the Life Giver and has created the entire universe.
- The main quality of this God is that s/he is not some vague force or remote disinterested mind, but the personification of love who cares for us personally.
- This God created humans in his/her image, giving them a free will, to love or to hate, to do right or to do wrong, to accept or to reject God.
- God created humans to be his/her companions, not only in this life but also in the life hereafter.
- God most clearly revealed him/herself through the Son, Jesus Christ who, by entering life at our level and living a life like ours, became the true mediator between God and his/her people who of their own free will had separated themselves from their Creator.
- This Mediator also showed us how we should live our lives and what God demands from us as companions and as co-creators.
- As humans we have an importance that transcends our human frailty and impermanence, simply because we are the eternal companions of the Creator of this universe.
- As a result of this, we have an unimaginable, indescribable future ahead of us as the chosen, eternal, companions of God the Creator.

Recent polls have shown that the greatest majority of people in the western world believe in the existence of some sort of Supreme Being — someone who is in charge. To some extent, this is probably caused by the fact that in the last decades there have been a series of scientific discoveries that have tended to confirm the possibility that such a Supreme Being or Creator might exist. To mention a few:

- most recent scientific discoveries seem to indicate that the universe is filled with what might best be described as "Mind," in other words, with something that is not material but spiritual in nature;

•the apparent confirmation of the theory of creation which postulates that the universe started at a fixed point in time;
•the increasing evidence of the existence of a human mind, or spirit, which survives death.

These developments don't prove that God exists, they merely prove that our universe is not just an assembly of material building blocks, but that it has a far more spiritual nature than we would have ever dreamed of, even a few years ago. They certainly do not show that the God of the Christian religion exists. That, I believe, will never be subject to verification but must always remain a matter of faith and trust.

I assume that the readers who have reached this point in the book can basically be divided into the following four categories:

•people who are convinced and confirmed Christians now;
•people who once were Christians, but are not so now;
•people who subscribe to other religions;
•people who are complete newcomers to any type of religion.

For the first category of readers, this book has, hopefully, been an interesting review of their own faith.

For the second category, I hope that this book will generate a sense of having lost something precious that they once had. I hope the book will make them rethink the basic reasons for their loss of faith, and that they will consider making an effort to retrieve what they have lost.

For the third category, I hope that you have found the book interesting. If it leads you to wanting to share in this faith, so much the better. If not, I hope you will remember Gandhi's words as quoted in Appendix 1, ''Our inward prayer should be that a Hindu become a better Hindu, a Buddhist become a better Buddhist, a Muslim become a better Muslim, and a Christian become a better Christian.''

For the last category, those with no church affiliation at all, I hope that reading this book has opened your eyes to the things you might be missing. The remainder of this chapter is especially addressed to you.

The question you may be asking yourself after having reached this point is: Do we need this religion any longer? Has the world not outgrown the need for this "safety net" of a loving Father/Mother and the concept of love as the motivating force which should govern our actions? I have dealt with this question in other chapters, but I believe the question is important enough to attempt to answer it once more.

Looking at the world today, it is increasingly clear to me that we need to adopt a value system for the world to live by that does away with the terrible injustices which are so evident in our world today. The situation in our "modern" society concerning war, poverty, starvation, crime, etc., is so bad that every person of good will must be appalled and must surely agree that this cannot be allowed to continue. At the same time, corruption and wrongdoing in the political and business sectors of our society are rampant. In a recent newspaper, the results of a survey about the attitude of business people towards ethics in their work were discussed. According to this survey, most business people were aware that there was something like business ethics, but most said that they would put profits before ethics, and many of those interviewed said that they considered business ethics a joke.

It is obvious, that with this attitude, we cannot expect much leadership from this important segment of our society to fight for a more just and equitable society.

It is clear to me at least, that, if we want to find a way to remove the injustices and reduce the wrongdoings that are so rampant in our society today, we must find a value system that, if adhered to by all, will do just that.

As I wrote in the previous chapter, I can think of only one institution that has a value system which has the potential for doing this. That institution is organized religion. More specifically, for me that religion is the Christian religion; for others it may be Islam, Buddhism, Hinduism, Bahai, etc. I firmly believe that, at this point in our history, the only way we will get a morally acceptable society is by adopting an universally acceptable value system that makes us use our physical and spiritual resources for the betterment of society and not for its destruction.

So, I think it is important, even crucial, for the continuation of our civilization that we adopt a set of values to live by which can be generally accepted regardless of race or religion. For me, that set of values is most adequately represented by the simple Christian message that all our behavior — personal, political, business, etc. — must be governed by the concept of love and compassion for our neighbour. It is for this reason that I think the answer to the question "Do we need this religion any longer: Has the world not outgrown this concept?" is a most positive "Yes, we need it today more than ever before." It is for this same reason that I believe it to be important that you, the reader, become involved in the life of some Church or affiliated organization.

The question then is: How can someone, who has not been brought up in the Christian tradition, learn more about its values and perhaps even become part of this religious life?

As I have said before, the Christian message is contained in the writings of the Bible, but for a person not familiar with it, it can be a very difficult book to understand. The Old Testament contains great wisdom, and makes very interesting reading if only for its literary and historic value, but it is not a book that is likely to inspire anyone to become a Christian. I believe that it is more likely that anyone looking for inspiration will find it in the books of the New Testament. This part of the Bible contains the message of Jesus as reported in the gospels of Matthew, Mark, Luke and John, and in the interpretation and application of that message in the letters sent by the early apostles to the young churches of Asia Minor and Europe. It is the message contained in these books which we believe can transform the world of today.

For a person not familiar with the Bible, I would recommend that he or she start reading one of the gospels. I would suggest Matthew followed by John. Regardless which gospel you select, I would recommend the use of a good Bible commentary, such as Barclay's, to help in explaining some of the circumstances surrounding the gospel stories and to clarify some of the wording. After these, I would recommend reading The Acts Of The Apostles, followed by one or two of the letters of the apostles, such as, The First Letter of John and Paul's Letters to the Romans and the Corinthians.

For a person who is searching for understanding and inspiration, it may be helpful to read some of the experiences of others who have found new meaning to life. I would recommend some of the books written by Malcolm Muggeridge. In the foreword of his book, *Jesus Rediscovered*, he writes:

> *All this book represents is the effort of one aging twentieth-century mind to give expression to a deep dissatisfaction with prevailing twentieth-century values and assumptions, and a sense that there is an alternative — an alternative propounded two thousand years ago by the Sea of Galilee and on the hill called Golgotha.*[1]

The other thing a searching person might do is to seek affiliation with one of the churches. That is, of course, easier said than done, because of the fact that there are so many of them. As a quick guide, there are basically three main types of churches — the Roman Catholic Church, the Greek Orthodox Church and the Protestant Churches.

Within the Protestant Church there are a great many different denominations; the difference between them is mainly a matter of emphasis. Some are very fundamentalistic as they believe that every word in the Bible is literally true; others are more evangelical; some are more liberal and yet others are more middle-of-the-road. Also, today, there are churches for the gay community, and then there are churches in which the services are conducted in other languages. The choice between these churches is mainly a personal one and depends very much on your own preferences.

Probably the best way to choose a church is to talk to friends or acquaintances who are active members of a church, or talk to ministers of various denominations. They will be very pleased to talk with you. I would think that even a short conversation with a minister, or one attendance at a Sunday morning worship service, will tell you very quickly whether this is what you are looking for or not. Depending on the church you choose, it may very well be that you find the way they do and say things uncomfortable. If so, choose another one, because not all churches have the same mannerisms and ways of conducting services or of approaching strangers. Some you will find very welcoming, while in others the people will be more reserved and wait for you to approach them.

One way of selecting a church is by looking at what they are doing to express their faith in effective action within the community at large. If they are a caring, involved congregation, they may be the church you want even if, in the beginning, you are not all that comfortable with the way they are doing other things. Also, it could be very helpful to join a study group or a confirmation class for older people. Probably one of the quickest ways of getting to know a church is to participate in one of its programs, even if you are not too sure that you want to commit yourself wholeheartedly to that church and its teachings.

At all times, it is good to remember that the people you will meet will be, for the most part, very ordinary people: They certainly are not going to be saints, although you may find some that come close to that. Most of them will be struggling with their own faith, their own commitments, and the way they can most effectively reflect their faith in their everyday life. The only difference between them and the other people you know will be that these people know what they should be doing, even if they do not always do so. They know where they are going and they have guide lines to follow; they know that whatever happens to them, they can always be sure of God's presence; and they can always be sure of their ultimate destiny. Hopefully, you will find that is something worth having.

The good news for today is that regardless who you are, or what your problems are, you are loved. In life, in death, in life after death, God is with you. You are not alone. Thanks be to God.

Postscript

During the years this book took form, many changes have occurred in the world's political, economical, social and scientific conditions. As a result of these developments I have been making changes to the text almost continually. But, not only have changes taken place externally, I myself have changed as well. New discoveries and new ways of thinking have changed my outlook and have given me new insights and new understanding. No doubt, similar changes will continue to take place in the future. So, I expect that this book, as it now stands, will lose some of its currency in a relatively short time. Because of this, it is my intention to periodically review the contents and, if the changes I would want to make are numerous and fundamental enough, I will republish the book. In doing so, I hope to take into account the comments and criticisms of you the reader. Therefore, if you have any comments, please feel free to send them to me at the address below. I will try to acknowledge all contributions and send a copy of the

Good News For Today

republished book to those contributors whose comments have been included in the new version.

Please address all comments and inquiries to the author at:

5380 McLeod Street
Beamsville, Ontario
Canada, L0R 1B2

Appendix

Brief Summary Of The Other World Religions
And The Major
Similarities And Differences With The Christian Religion

1 — Introduction

The Christian Church has always believed that the only way to God is through Jesus Christ, the Son of God, who revealed God to us humans and who was the mediator between God and humankind.

There are indeed many passages in the Bible indicating that Jesus is the only mediator and that there is no other way to God than through him. If we take this literally, this would mean that all other religions are wrong and mistaken and that their teachings are false and misleading. However, before we can make such a judgement, we must look at what it is that these other religions teach and whether their teachings are irreconcilably in conflict with the teachings of the Christian Church.

If we look at the world today, we recognize five major religions which together hold the allegiance of the vast majority of the religious people in the world. The adherents to these religions may not always be practicing members, but they live in communities and countries in which the basic concepts of these religions are the basis for the everyday conduct of life. In the order of their appearance on the world scene they are respectively: Judaism, Hinduism, Buddhism, Christianity and finally, Islam.

In a very general way, Judaism is concentrated today in the State of Israel and by people of Jewish descent in North America and Europe. It is estimated that at this time there are some 15 million practicing Jews in the world. This is a very small percentage of the world population, but their influence in world affairs is far greater than indicated by this percentage.

Hinduism is practiced today by the majority of the people in India, Nepal, Bali and large sections of China. It is estimated that some 500 million people in the world today are Hindus.

Buddhism is practiced today in Thailand, Burma, Cambodia, Vietnam, China, Korea, Mongolia and Japan. There are estimated to be a total of 1.2 billion Buddhists in the world today.

Christianity is spread mainly throughout the countries of Europe, including most of the Russian republics; North, South and Central America; most of the countries of Southern Africa; Australia and New Zealand; with minorities in most of the countries of the world. Christianity is nominally the religion of 1.8 billion people today.

Islam is practiced mainly in the countries of the Middle East, plus Pakistan, Bangladesh, Indonesia and the countries of Northern Africa. There are estimated to be a total of 750 million followers of Islam in the world today.

It is interesting to note that of the five religions, three — Judaism, Christianity and Islam — have a common root in the figure of Abraham. The other two, Hinduism and Buddhism, had their beginning in the same country, India, and have a common root in the old Hinduism of 2,000 B.C.

Also, of the five basic religions, three were started by historical figures — Buddha, Jesus and Mohammed. It is believed that not one of them was able to write (at least there is no record of any of them committing anything to paper); their message was in most cases committed to memory and carried by word of mouth for some time before it was written down. In all three cases the religions they founded spread rapidly after their death and then, some time later, reached a threshold after which the number of believers remained fairly constant, and this will probably remain to be the case for the foreseeable future. At this point in time, it appears highly unlikely that Christianity will make major inroads in Islam, Hinduism or Buddhism, and vice versa. Thus we must accept the fact that more than 65 percent of the world population lives essentially outside the influence of the Christian Church, and that the majority of the people in this world are not even aware of its basic beliefs. If anything, this percentage is likely to increase rather than to decrease.

The question we must ask ourselves then is: Given these facts, can we continue to maintain that the Christian way of salvation is the only way to God, or is there in the other religions also a way, maybe radically different from ours, to the God who created and is still creating Jews, Hindus, Buddhists, Christians and Muslims alike? In other words, is there a way that leads to God through Buddha, or Mohammed, as well as through Jesus Christ? This is a question that really touches all people in the world and for that reason has been the subject of intensive study by all the major religions. The conclusions vary widely, as could be expected, with some of the Hindu thinkers postulating the most positive response. The question can certainly not be answered in these pages. The only thing we can do is to briefly outline what these religions teach and point to the things they have in common and the things that separate them. In the following pages, a very brief summary is given of the teachings of the Hindu, Buddhist and Muslim religions; in the last section the differences and similarities are presented in a condensed form.

2 — Hinduism

Introduction

Most people, when they think of Hinduism, think of it as one unified religion; in fact, however, there is no such religion. What we understand by Hinduism is in actual fact a series of quite different religions which all have their origin in the old scriptures which appeared in the Indus Valley of India/Pakistan some 4,000 years ago. However, for the sake of expediency, I will follow the general practice and use the term Hinduism for all the religions which emerged over time from this one source. This source, the so-called Vedic literature, is considered to have come directly from the god Brahma, and is still considered to be sacred to this day.

It contains the belief that is central to the Hindu religion, namely the existence of a supreme god, Brahma, from whom everything emanates. At the same time, this literature refers to a great many other deities who are believed to be able to influence the lives of people on earth in both good and evil ways.

Later writings led to the establishment of the caste system which, while officially judged to be illegal in the India of today, is still a very powerful influence in Indian society.

In the last two hundred years, Hinduism has been increasingly exposed to western influences. This has not only brought traditional Hinduism in contact with new religious concepts, but also exposed the Hindu world to the critical thinking of a new scientific age. The result has been the creation of a number of reform movements which try to find a middle ground between the old beliefs and the concepts of modern scientific and social thinking.

While the basic concepts of Hinduism are generally considered to be foreign to the western way of thinking, many westerners have nevertheless been attracted to some of the ideas contained in this ancient religion. This has led to the establishment of many Hindu communities in the West, to the extent that today every major western city has at least one Hindu meeting place. Also, many of the old scriptures have been translated into western languages which has given rise to the appearance in these languages of such Hindu terms as yoga, karma, maya, and nirvana, to name just a few.

The Deities In Hinduism

The supreme God of the Hindus is Brahma, who is described in the Vedas in the following terms: He is the

Absolute, he is one and indivisible, he is unchangeable and beyond action and inaction, and he is beyond good and evil. Brahma is usually referred to as It or That rather than He or She. It is from Brahma that everything in this world has emerged, and it is the ultimate objective of every Hindu to finally merge with it again. The description of Brahma in one of the best known, early, sacred scriptures in Hinduism, the Bhagavad Gita, in a translation by Mohini Chatterji, reads as follows:

> *I shall declare that which is to be known; knowing which man attains deathlessness, the Supreme Brahma, having no beginning, and said to be neither subject to affirmation nor to negation. (Because he is above all attributes.)*

> *His hands and feet are everywhere; everywhere His eyes, heads, and mouths; His ears everywhere in the worlds; enveloping everything He dwells.*

> *Manifested in the operations of all organs and faculties, yet devoid of organs and faculties. Unattached, He supports all. Though devoid of attributes, He is the experiencer of all attributes.*

> *He is the within and without of all beings, moving and stationary. Unrealizable on account of his subtlety; though afar, He is near. (To the illuminated man who realizes Him as the true Self.)*

> *Though undistributed, He appears to dwell as distributed in creatures; the same that which is to be known is the supporter of creatures, is the devourer and producer.*

> *He is the light of lights, is said to be beyond darkness. He is knowledge, that which is to be known and that which is the ultimate end of knowledge, and is seated in the hearts of all.*

Thus the Hindu believes that Brahma is everywhere and in everything. This has led to the great reverence by the Hindu of everything living, an attitude which greatly affects the everyday life of the Hindu. It accounts for their vegetarianism, the cows wandering in the streets, the monkeys in the temples, and so forth.

Despite this pre-eminence of Brahma, it is interesting to see that in the daily life and worship of the Hindu, Brahma plays only a minor role. It is the other deities which are much more involved in their daily lives who receive most of their attention. It is their belief that there are literally millions of deities who are shaping their daily lives. The two that are the most important, Vishnu and Shiva, are often depicted in paintings as forming a sort of trinity together with Brahma.

Vishnu, the Preserver, is considered more to be the god of love and is believed to have taken on a physical form a number of times in the past to overcome evil. So far, it is believed, he has appeared nine times, the most important being Rama, of Ramayana fame, and Krishna.

Shiva, the Destroyer, is also the god of fertility. In pictorial form he is usually shown as dancing and having four arms. While Shiva is the destroyer, he is at the same time considered to be the creator because out of destruction and death comes rebirth and new life.

Outside of these two, there are perceived to be millions of other gods: There are the household gods, the village gods, the gods of trees, fire, rivers, etc. In general, although each Hindu is devoted to his own particular god, they are usually also devotees of Shiva or Vishnu. Furthermore, they never exclude either one completely from their devotions. This has had the fortunate result that there are not the deep divisions in Hinduism which so plague the Christian and Islam religions.

The Sacred Scriptures

Hinduism, like Christianity and Islam, has both its sacred scriptures, which are thought to have been directly inspired by God, and the writings which are not held to be sacred and which were mostly written much later, but which nevertheless have great authority because of tradition.

The oldest scriptures in Hinduism, dating back thousands of years, are the Vedas. They consist mainly of hymns dedicated to individual gods or goddesses. There are four Vedas, each consisting of thousands of hymns. The following hymn to Varuna, God of the Sky, gives some idea of the contents of these hymns:

> *If we have sinned against the man who loves us, have ever wronged a brother, friend or comrade,*
> *The neighbour ever with us, or stranger, O Varuna, remove from us the trespass.*
> *If we, as gamblers cheat at play, have cheated, done wrong unwittingly or sinned deliberately,*
> *Cast all these sins away like loosened fetters, and Varuna, let us be your own beloved.*

Following the Vedas in importance are the Brahmanas which are basically commentaries on the Vedas. In time, these were followed by the Upanishads. These are also comments on the Vedas but in the form of questions and answers. The following conversation between a father and his son, named Svetaketu, is an example of the type of message that is contained in these hymns:

> *... Whatever these creatures are here, whether a lion, a wolf, a boar, a worm, a midge, a gnat, a mosquito, that they become again and again. Now that which is that subtle essence, in all that exists has itself. It is the True. It is the Self, and thou, O Svetaketu, art it.*
> *"Please, Sir, inform me still more," said the son.*
> *"Be it so, my child," the father replied. "Fetch me thence a fruit of the banyan tree."*
> *"Here is one, Sir."*
> *"Break it."*
> *"It is broken, Sir."*
> *"What do you see there?"*

> *"Not anything, Sir."*
> *The father said, "My son, that subtle essence which you do not perceive there, of that very essence this great banyan tree exists. Believe it my son. That which is the subtle essence, in it all that exists has its self. It is the True. It is the Self, and thou, O Svetaketu, are it."*

There are also the twelve books of ordinances by the semi-divine hero Manu, who in these highly revered books gives instructions on how to live. The following is a short passage from one of his books:

> *Wound no others, do no one injury by thought or deed, utter no word to pain thy fellow creature. He who habitually salutes and constantly pays reverence to the aged obtains an increase in four things: length of life, knowledge, fame and strength. Depend on no other, but lean instead on thyself. True happiness is born of self-reliance. By falsehood a sacrifice becomes vain. One should speak truth, and speak what is pleasant; one should not speak unpleasant truth; one should not speak unpleasant falsehood. This is fixed law.*

Outside these three sacred scriptures, there are innumerable commentaries, poems, dramas and epics that are part of the rich heritage of the Hindu world. To the western world the best known of these epics and dramas are the Ramayana and the Mahabharata. The Ramayana tells the story of the great battle fought against evil by the god Rama and his wife Sita. They eventually won this battle with the help of the monkey god, Hanuman. (This is the reason the Hindus treat monkeys in a special way, even today.)

The Mahabharata again involves a war, this time between two princely families. The main characters in this epic are the prince Arjuna and the god Krishna, who appears in the form of Arjuna's charioteer. The epic is very long; however, there is one section, the Bhagavad Gita, which has been translated in many languages and is probably the best-known Hindu writing outside India. It consists mainly of long discourses between Krishna and Arjuna.

These two epics are considered essential to an understanding of the Hindu religion, and parts of them are learned by heart by the devout Hindu. They have been said to contain India's message to humankind. Also, these two epics are held by some to be the cement that holds the vast world of Hinduism together, despite differences in caste, location and language.

For a westerner, it is interesting to note that for the Hindu it is the message in these stories that is important and not its authenticity. For example, from the Hindu point of view, it is not at all important whether Jesus actually ever existed as a living person. For them the message contained in the books of the New Testament is what counts. In fact, they go so far as stating that myths are far more important than, so-called, historical facts.

The Creation Story

As said before, the Hindu believes that everything was created by Brahma and that everything emanated from it. There are a number of creation stories in the Vedas. The following is a passage out of the Hymn of Creation from the Rig Veda. It is not always clear what is meant exactly in some of the passages; also the last sentence is for most of us an enigma and does not make it any easier to understand the message this hymn is intending to convey:

> *At that time there was neither nonexistence nor existence; neither the worlds nor the sky, nor anything that is beyond. What covered everything, and where, and for whose enjoyment? Was there water, unfathomable and deep? Death was not there, nor immortality; no knowing of night or day. "That One Thing" breathed without air, by its own strength; apart from it, nothing existed.*

> *Darkness there was, wrapped in yet other darkness; un-*
> *distinguished, all this was one water; the incipient lay cov-*
> *ered by void. "That One Thing" became creative by the*
> *power of its own contemplation. There came upon it, at*
> *first, desire which was the prime seed of the mind, and*
> *man of vision, seeking in their heart with their intellect,*
> *found the link to the existence in the nonexistent. There*
> *were begetters, there were mighty forces, free action here*
> *and energy up yonder.... The gods are later than this*
> *creative activity; who knows, then, from where this came*
> *into being? Where this creation came from, whether one*
> *supported it or not, He who was supervising it from the*
> *highest heaven, He indeed knows; or He knows not!*

There are other creation stories in the Vedas, the following one includes a passage on which the caste system is based.
The quotation is from the Hymn to Perusha which is also found
in the Rig Veda:

> *When they divided Perusha, how many portions did they*
> *make? What do they call his mouth, his arms? What do*
> *they call his thighs and feet? The priests were his mouth,*
> *of both his arms were the warriors made. His thighs be-*
> *came the merchants, from his feet the workers were*
> *produced. (The four castes) The moon was gendered from*
> *his mind, and from his eye the sun had birth. Storms and*
> *fire from his mouth were born, and winds from his*
> *breath. From his naval came mid-air, the sky was*
> *fashioned from his head, Earth from his feet, and from*
> *his ears the regions. Thus they formed the worlds.*

Some Basic Hindu Beliefs

As indicated before, Hinduism is unbelievably complicated,
confusing and sometimes contradictory, especially to our
western way of thinking with its emphasis on logic even in religious matters. Because of the many different beliefs and practices, it is difficult to generalize and present a coherent and

general set of beliefs that all Hindus accept. I believe that the following are more or less universally accepted by most Hindus:

- Brahma, The Absolute, is the Creator of everything and it has the power of life and death.
- The power of life of Brahma is manifested in the creation of the universe. It takes the form of Maya, the material world we perceive to exist around us.
- Maya is a projection of Brahma; it is not synonymous with Brahma; it is temporary and has no real meaning.
- Everything that lives and breathes has a soul, Atman.
- Each soul, while it exists in Maya, is trying to be reunited with Brahma in Nirvana.
- The process by which one gains access to Nirvana is through the successive reincarnations into higher levels of the caste system.
- When a Hindu reaches this stage of self-realization, one flows back into Brahma losing one's personality and one's individuality: In fact, life for the Hindu is finally over.
- The higher levels in the caste system are attained by following one's duties (dharma) which are associated with one's particular caste. These duties must translate into works (karma) of a moral, social and religious nature.
- If one falls short in the duties one is supposed to perform in this life, one will be reborn into a lower caste, possibly even as an animal.
- Suffering in this life is attributed to bad works (bad karma) from a previous incarnation.
- There are four ways to integration and union with Brahma, each consists of a system of training both body and mind:
  there is the way through knowledge (jnana yoga);
  there is the way through love (bhakti yoga);
  there is the way through work (karma yoga); and
  there is the way through psychological exercises (raja yoga).
- There are four permissible goals in life:

to seek pleasure and especially love;
to seek power and accumulate material possessions;
to follow the religious and moral laws; and
to attain liberation and salvation.

Of course, it is the latter two, and more specifically the last one, which should be the final objective of all Hindus.

New Forms Of Hinduism

Probably the best-known and most influential forms of Hinduism in North America are offshoots from the school of Vedanta. The followers of this school of Hinduism believe that Brahma has incarnated himself in human form a number of times in the past. For instance, they believe that Christ and Buddha were incarnations of Brahma. The latest incarnation was that of Sri Ramakrishna. He lived in the middle 1800s and taught that all religions are basically the same. He practiced Hinduism, Christianity and Islam, and he claimed that he had received visions of God in each one of these religions.

Ramakrishna also taught that the outward form of any religion is unimportant compared to the unity they express inwardly. According to him, a truly religious person can pass through these outward forms to experience reality which is always and everywhere the same.

Aldous Huxley, the writer-philosopher, was a follower of Ramakrishna. He proclaimed that it was perfectly possible to remain good Christians, Hindus, and Muslims, and yet be united in full agreement on the basic doctrine of the "Perennial Philosophy."

The most revered and influential Hindu of modern times was no doubt Mahatma Gandhi, who led the independence movement in India. His message of non-violence inspired people worldwide, including some of the leaders of the civil rights movement in the USA such as the Rev. Martin Luther King. In his book, *The Story of my Experiments with Truth*, Gandhi wrote the following:

I came to the conclusion long ago, after prayerful search and study and discussion with as many people as I could meet, that all religions are true and, also, that all had some errors in them; and that whilst I hold by my own, I should hold others as dear as Hinduism; from which it logically follows that we should hold all dear as our nearest kith and kin and that we should make no distinction between them. So, we can only pray, if we are Hindus, not that a Christian should become a Hindu; or if we are Muslims, not that a Hindu or a Christian should become a Muslim; nor should we even secretly pray that anyone should become coverted; but our inward prayer should be that a Hindu should be a better Hindu, a Muslim a better Muslim, and a Christian a better Christian. That is the fundamental truth of fellowship.[1]

Thus, at least in Hinduism, the opinion has been expressed that all religions have so much in common that it is reasonable to assume that they must be manifestations of one and the same Supreme Being.

Similarities And Differences

Because of the many different schools in Hinduism, it is difficult to point to similarities and differences between Hinduism and Christianity that are true for all Hindus. The major similarities, the things I believe Christianity has in common with the Hindu religion, I have summarized below as follows:

1 — Both believe in one God who created the universe.
2 — Both believe that humans should live moral lives and should be unselfish in dealing with their neighbours.
3 — Both believe that we have to account for the things we do in our lives.
4 — Both believe in an afterlife in which we are joined with God, although not in the same way.
5 — Modern Hindus can accept Jesus as an incarnation of God, but not as the only incarnation.

Against these things we have in common there are a number of things that tend to separate us, including the following:

a) The Hindu believes that the world God created is not real and is essentially an illusion.

b) A Christian believes in a rebirth into an eternal life but not in a series of rebirths into an earthly existence.

c) For a Christian, that new existence will be in the presence of and in close communion with God. For a Hindu the final rebirth leads to complete oblivion.

d) Christians cannot accept the caste system nor can they accept the position of women in the Hindu society.

e) Christians believe that they cannot work their own salvation because they can never be good enough to do so — they need Jesus as an intermediary. Hindus believe that through good works and good living they can eventually work their own salvation.

f) In the Hindu religion, suffering is considered to be the result of bad karma in previous incarnations. In the Christian religion, suffering is considered a part of life and is not the result of an individual's sins or mistakes, but it has its basic origin in the continuing rebellion of humankind against God, its Creator.

3 — Buddhism

Introduction

Buddhism was founded by Siddhartha Gautama, a Hindu, who could not find the salvation he was seeking in the practice of Hinduism. Gautama was born in the year 563 B.C. in what is now Nepal. His father, who was very wealthy, surrounded the young man with great luxury and tried to shield him from the unpleasant aspects of human life. He was happily married to a beautiful woman by which he had a son. Despite his father's preventive measures, he saw, at the age of 29, some of the uglier aspects of life such as sickness, suffering and death. This so affected him that he left his family and became a wandering monk in search of enlightenment. He studied the old Hindu literature, but he could not find what he was looking for in its texts. Next he sought enlightenment in leading a very ascetic life and he almost starved himself to death, but that did not bring him any nearer to his goal either. After six years of searching in vain, Gautama sat down under a Bodhi tree and vowed that he would not leave that place until he had found the salvation or enlightenment he was looking for. Finally, after 49 days, he found enlightenment. It is claimed in some of the Buddhist writings that he at first wanted to enter into nirvana and keep the enlightenment he had found to himself. In the end, however, he decided that he must inform others as well about the insights he had gained. So he left his place under the Bodhi tree and went to Benares, the holy city of the Hindus, on the Ganges River. Here he taught his first sermons in a park outside the city and made his first converts.

For the next 45 years, he travelled across Northern India meditating and teaching. After he found enlightenment he was called by the name we generally use for him, Buddha, or the Enlightened One.

At first the new religion spread rapidly across India replacing the old Hindu religion. However, after some 300 years, a revised and more popular form of Hinduism began to erode the dominance of Buddhism in India. Later, after the rise of Islam, large parts of what are now Pakistan and India were invaded by Muslim armies and the population was forced to accept the Muslim religion.

Today, Buddhism is the main religion in Tibet, Burma, Thailand, Cambodia, Sri Lanka and to some extent in China and Japan, although in the case of China it is not entirely clear how much of the religion has survived the Communist regime.

Gautama never claimed that he was anything more than a human being who had attained enlightenment. He certainly did not claim that he was divine or that he was related to any deity in any form.

Good News For Today

Buddha, like Jesus and Mohammed, never wrote down any of his insights and teachings; they were passed on by word of mouth for hundreds of years before they were written down. The first written texts, written in Pali, appear to have originated around the first century B.C. or some 400 years after the death of Buddha.

The Basic Beliefs Of Buddhism

The enlightenment Buddha received he called the Middle Way or Middle Path — it is the path between asceticism and indulgence. As he taught his followers:

> *There are two extremes, brethern, that he who has given up the world ought to avoid. What are these extremes?*
>
> *A life given to pleasures, devoted to pleasures and lusts — this is degrading, sensual, vulgar, ignoble and profitless.*
>
> *And a life given to mortification — this is painful, ignoble and profitless.*
>
> *By avoiding these two extremes, brethern, I have gained the knowledge of the Middle Path, which leads to insight, which leads to wisdom, to knowledge and to supreme enlightenment.*

Later, in the same sermon, he presented the principle of the Four Noble Truths which are:
1 — Suffering is universal.
2 — The cause of suffering is craving.
3 — The cure for suffering is the elimination of craving.
4 — The elimination of craving can be achieved through the "Eightfold Path."
In his first sermon in Benares, Buddha elaborated on the Four Noble Truths as follows:

*This, brethern, is the **noble truth of suffering**: birth is suffering; decay is suffering; death is suffering; presence of objects we hate is suffering; separation from objects we love is suffering; not to obtain what we desire is suffering. In brief, the five aggregates that spring from grasping are painful.*

*This, brethern, is the **noble truth concerning the origin of suffering**: verily, it originates in that craving which causes the renewal of becomings, is accompanied by sensual delight, and seeks self-satisfaction, now here, now there: that is to say, craving for pleasures, craving for becoming, craving for not becoming.*

*This, brethern, is the **noble truth concerning the cessation of suffering**: verily, it is passionlessness, cessation without remainder of this very craving; the laying aside of, the giving up, the being free from, the harboring no longer of, this craving.*

*This, my brethern, is the **noble truth concerning the path that leads to the cessation of suffering**: verily, it is the noble eightfold path, that is to say, Right Understanding, Right Thought, Right Speech, Right Action, Right Livelihood, Right Effort, Right Mindfulness, and Right Concentration.*

Later, in the same sermon, Buddha explained in greater detail what he meant by these eight steps. The following is a summary of the meaning of each step as presented in the book, *Buddhism Made Plain*, by Antony Fernando with Leonard Swidler:

Right Understanding — Understand life correctly as transient, painful, and "selfless."

Right Thought — Think wholesome thoughts of detachment and good will.

Right Speech — Use speech correctly without resorting to talebearing, harsh words, gossip and lies.

Right Action	— Act correctly, abstaining from stealing, killing, and unchaste actions.
Right Livelihood	— Earn your livelihood without harming others.
Right Effort	— Strive constantly to keep your mind free from evil thoughts and filled with thoughts of detachment and friendliness.
Right Mindfulness	— Act mindfully, attentive to what you are doing each moment and conscious of the transience of life.
Right Concentration	— Train your mind to restfulness and insight by periods of meditation.[2]

It was Buddha's claim that by following this Eightfold Path one would be able to reach nirvana and get outside the cycle of death and rebirth.

In his teachings, Buddha accepted a number of Hindu insights, including the cycle of reincarnations and karma, the accumulation of good works. He did not accept the authority of the Vedic literature and consequently did not believe in a supreme being in any form, including Brahma. Nirvana for Buddha was to be released from the cycle of suffering and not a merging with the Brahma. He believed that a person must free himself of all worldly cravings and physical desires, only then could he come close to a true realization of the self and could he enter nirvana. Above all he advocated the renunciation of all human appetites and passions.

Buddha, most emphatically, rejected any idea of a caste system; instead he strongly believed that everyone had the same spiritual potential. His whole teaching is of a very practical nature, and he taught only what he believed to be essential for spiritual development — philosophical speculation and concepts were of no interest to him. For instance, in one of the discourses he is reported to have said:

Bear in mind what it is that I have elucidated and what it is I have not elucidated.

I have not elucidated that the world is eternal or, that it is not eternal.

I have not elucidated that the world is finite or, that it is not finite.

I have not elucidated that the soul and the body are identical.

I have not elucidated that the monk who has attained enlightenment exists after death nor that he does not exist after death.

And why have I not elucidated this? Because this profits not, nor has to do with the fundamentals of religion, therefore I have not elucidated it.

And what have I elucidated? Misery have I elucidated: the origin of misery, the cessation of misery and the path leading to the cessation of misery have I elucidated. And why have I elucidated this? Because this does profit, has to do with the fundamentals of religion, and tends to absence of passion, to knowledge, supreme wisdom, and nirvana.

One of the consequences of the renunciation of all desires, and the detachment from all earthly things, was that Buddhism became mainly a monastic religion. It was only in the atmosphere of the monastery, and by leading the life of a monk, that it was possible for the average person to come close to living a life that would lead to enlightenment. At the same time, the renunciation of all passion and attachments led to a very self-centered life for most Buddhists. It certainly does not encourage the practice of loving one's neighbour as one's self, because this love would lead to attachment and therefore to suffering.

The Two Main Schools Of Thought In Buddhism

Within a relatively short time after the death of Buddha, there began to appear a divergence of opinion among his followers regarding the interpretation of some of the things taught by Buddha. This difference in interpretation eventually led to the establishment of two basically different forms of Buddhism: Hinayana or the Lesser Vehicle, known as the Theravada, and the Mahayana or the Greater Vehicle. Within these two main streams there are a great number of other schools, some of them with concepts that appear to be far removed from the original teachings of Buddha.

The Hinayana school basically follows the principles as they were originally taught by Buddha. Buddha himself is considered a man with great insights, one that found enlightenment, but still a normal human being. They believe that there were many Buddhas before Gautama, and that there will be many to follow after him. The Hinayana believe that nirvana can only be obtained at the end of a long series of reincarnations and that the progression of human beings along the path of enlightenment depends on the performance of good works in the various incarnations. A good Hinayana Buddhist is a holy man, an arkat, who attains enlightenment basically for himself alone.

The Mahayana school has deviated considerably from this basic concept. To the Mahayana Buddhist an ideal Buddhist is a bodhisatta, a holy man, who when he is ready to enter nirvana postpones it, vowing that he will not enter nirvana until all are liberated. Thus this school of Buddhism is far less self-centered than the Hinayana who basically seek salvation only for themselves.

The Mahayana believe that in addition to the historical Buddha there is an eternal Buddha, a god who is a redeemer, a god to whom prayers can be addressed. This god they call the Amitatha Buddha, or the Buddha of the Eternal Light. This Buddha resides in a paradise much as the Christian heaven depicted in the Middle Ages pictures. The Buddha of Eternal Light sits on a throne of lotus leaves in the middle of this paradise. The way for a faithful to attain this heaven is through a life of faith and devotion. Thus the stress was removed from the obligation to do good works in successive incarnations. This idea is highlighted in the following quotation from one of the Mahayana texts:

> *Beings are not born in that Buddha country as a reward and result of good work performed in this present life. No, all men or women who hear and bear in mind for one, two, three, four, five, six, or seven nights the name of Amitabha when they come to die. Amitabha will stand before them in the hour of death, they will depart this life with quiet minds, and after death they will be born in paradise.*

This type of thinking was one of the great attractions for the common people and is believed to be one of the reasons for its quick adoption by many Buddhists across the world. Following is a poem by Hui Yuan describing the paradise as the Mahayana Buddhists depict it:

> *What words can picture the beauty and breadth*
> *Of that pure and glistening land?*
> *That land where the blossoms never wither from age,*
> *Where the golden gates gleam like the purest water ...*
> *The land where there are none but fragrant bowers,*
> *Where the Utpala lotus unfolds itself freely.*
> *O hear the sweet tones from hillside and grove*
> *The All-Father's praise from the throats of birds!*
>
> *There never was a country so brightened with gladness*
> *As the land of the Pure there far off to the West.*
> *There stands Amitabha with shining adornments, He*
> *makes all things ready for the Eternal Feast.*
> *He draws every burdened soul up from the depths*
> *And lifts them up into his peaceful abode.*
> *The great transformation is accomplished for the worm*

> *Who is freed from the body's oppressive sorrows.*
> *It receives as a gift a spiritual body,*
> *A body which shines in the sea of spirits.*

Some Mahayana sects, in addition to accepting the idea of a heaven for the righteous, have also adopted a concept of hell to which the soul of the evildoer goes after death.

In addition to these two strains of Buddhism, there are a number of others that are familiar to Western society at least by name. The best known of these is probably Zen Buddhism which is practiced mainly in Japan. The Zen Buddhists believe that enlightenment can come to a person only through very extensive meditation. They are a very austere group and live mainly in monasteries in Japan.

Similarities And Differences

As with Hinduism, there are so many schools of Buddhism that it is difficult to point to similarities and differences that are valid for the whole spectrum of Buddhist thought. In the case of Buddhism, this is further complicated by the fact that Hinayana Buddhism and Mahayana Buddhism are so different that they could be considered as two different religions, although originating from the same principles taught by Buddha. In the list of similarities and differences listed below, the two are therefore both represented:

1 — Both, Christians and Buddhists, believe that they should live a moral life. In Christianity, this is taken one step further in that it teaches to treat one's neighbour as one's self.

2 — We have in common with Mahayana Buddhism the belief that faith and devotion are an essential part of our religious life; although for a Christian, faith and devotion must be accompanied by good works, which are considered to be a natural result of faith and devotion.

3 — While Hinayana Buddhism rejects the idea of a Supreme Being, Mahayana Buddhism does have that concept, although their god does not appear to be associated with the creation of the world as in the Christian religion.

4 — With Mahayana Buddhism we have in common the belief in an afterlife, a heaven where we will live in the presence of God.

5 — In the eyes of the Buddhist, Jesus can be considered as one of the many Buddha's the world has known. At best, therefore, he is a teacher or an Enlightened One, but not an intermediary between human beings and God.

6 — For the Buddhist, suffering is the result of craving, if s/he can find a way to get rid of this craving s/he can get rid of suffering by entering nirvana. In Christianity, craving or selfishness is also considered the basic cause of many of humankind's sins, but it is the rebellion against God, the Creator, which is considered the underlying cause of all that is evil in this world.

7 — For the Buddhist, salvation or entering into nirvana is essentially a personal quest, one that can be achieved without the help or assistance of an intermediary between humankind and God. Christianity, on the other hand teaches that humankind cannot obtain salvation on its own but needs an intermediary between it and its Creator.

It is obvious from the above that Mahayana Buddhism is, in its basic concepts, much closer to Christianity than the Buddhism taught originally by Buddha and now continued by the Hinayana Buddhists.

4 — Islam

Introduction

The founder of Islam, Mohammed, was born in the year 570 A.D. in the city of Mecca, which is located in what is now called Saudi Arabia. He belonged to a fairly prominent family but became an orphan at an early age. When he was 25 years old he married a rich widow, 15 years his senior. Despite the difference in age, they appear to have been very happy together and they had several children, including one son, who unfortunately died at an early age. Mohammed, being financially independent after his marriage, spent a large amount of time in meditation, mostly in seclusion in the desert. After some time, he began to have visions of the angel Gabriel who, in one of these visions, commanded him to recite what the angel was telling him. It is interesting to note that Mohammed himself never wrote down any of these recitations, just as Jesus never wrote anything. The first recitation Mohammed received from Gabriel reads as follows:

> *Recite: In the name of thy Lord who created, created*
> *man from a blood-clot.*
> *Recite: And thy Lord is the most generous, who taught*
> *by the pen. Taught man that he knew not.*

> — *Koran, Surah 96* [3]

Over the next 23 years Mohammed continued to have these revelations and recited what the angel told him to say. These sayings were written down by his followers and, after his death, were collected in one book, called the Qur'an in Arabic and the Koran in English. The word Qur'an means simply — recite. The Koran has 114 chapters or surahs, some as short as 3 verses and others as long as 286 verses. Although the text of the Koran is sometimes confusing (see the quotation above), and sometimes contradictory (just as the Bible), the Muslims believe that the original text of the book is maintained in heaven and is therefore not to be questioned in any way. It should not even be translated for fear that some of the finer meaning might get lost in the translation process; this, of course, has proven to be untenable and there are now translations of the Koran available in every major language.

Mohammed attracted at first only a limited amount of support in Mecca, and his teachings were not accepted by the society of that city at large. Eventually he was even forced to flee the city. He finally settled in the city of Medina 400 kilometers to the north of Mecca. The date of his departure from

Mecca, 16 July, 622, is considered to be the start of Islam. It is this date which is used as the start of the Islamic calendar, and it is identified by placing the letters A.H. (the year after the hegira — flight) after the year. Mohammed was much better received in Medina, and eventually won over the town to his new religion. As a consequence of this, war broke out between Mecca and Medina which finally ended with the victory of Medina in the year 632 A.D. or 10 A.H. Mohammed died in Medina two years later at the age of 62.

After his victory, Mohammed declared the Kaaba, the large mosque in Mecca, which contains a large black meteorite and which was thought to have been built by Abraham and Ismael, as the most holy shrine in Islam and the center of the Islamic world. From then on, all prayers of Muslims the world over have been directed towards this mosque. That is why to this day Muslim visitors to the West will ask their host for the direction in which East is located, so that they can direct their prayers to Mecca.

Mohammed never claimed that he was in any way divine or even close to God. He was simply the Messenger: the prophet who brought the Koran to the world. In the Koran, there are innumerable references to the fact that he was simply a messenger and should not be idolized, as is shown in the following example:

> *We did not send you, Oh Mohammed, except as a mere bearer of good news, as well as a warner.*
>
> — *Surah 25, verse 56*

Although the Koran makes it very clear that the Koran is sufficient and not to be tampered with, soon after the Prophet's death publications began to appear with additional sayings of the Prophet and his early companions. They were eventually collected in six books called the Hadith (tradition). Of the six, only two are generally accepted as authentic and they have become the two most important books in Islam after the Koran.

Good News For Today

A saying in this book is called a Suma (custom). There are many Muslims today who completely reject the idea that even these two books of the Hadith have any validity. Over the years, many other writings by scholars, lawgivers, poets and ascetics have been added to the literature of Islam. Today, there are nearly as many divisions in Islam as there are in Christianity: The main difference is that the different ideologies in Islam have not caused the official divisions that plague Christianity. The main exception to this is the split between the Sunnis and the Shiites, and this division was originally caused, not by ideological differences, but by disputes over the true successor to Mohammed.

The Koran

As mentioned before, the Koran was written down not by Mohammed but by his followers. It was later assembled starting with the longest chapter and, thereafter, in descending order of the number of verses in each surah, so that the last surahs have only 3 or 4 verses. The first surah is an exception to this as it is only a few verses long, and is called the opener. It reads as follows:

> *In the name of God, most gracious, most merciful. Praise be to God, Lord of the universe; most gracious, most merciful; master of the day of judgement. You alone we worship; and you alone we ask for help. Guide us in the right path; the path of those whom you blessed; not of those who deserve wrath, nor the strayers.*

The second chapter or surah is 286 verses long and, like the other long verses, is a mixture of general teaching, of historical facts, instructions on how to live, etc. To give some idea of this, a partial list of subjects covered in this second surah is given below:

A description of the three categories of people.
An allegorical description of heaven and hell.
The stories of the creation of humankind and the
rebellion of the children of Israel.
A number of rules and regulations such as the pro-
hibition of sorcery, dietary regulations, rules of war,
menstruation, prohibition of usury, etc.
Instructions to pay alimony for widows and orphans.
And lastly a very practical admonition, namely to
write down monetary transactions.

For the average Christian, who only knows about Islam
from the daily newspapers — the revolution in Iran and its
many executions, the tyranny of Saddam Hussein in Iraq and
the kidnappings of innocent bystanders by Islamic fundamen-
talists in Lebanon — the reading of the Koran is a very revealing experience. The teachings of Mohammed, just like
those of Jesus, have been twisted by some of his followers to
defend, and even sanctify, the committing of the most horrible atrocities both against their fellow Muslims and against
Christians and Jews. This despite the fact that the Koran states
a number of times:

> *Those who believe, those who are Jewish, the Christians*
> *and the converts, any of them who believe in God and*
> *in the last day, and lead a righteous life, have nothing*
> *to fear, nor will they grieve.*

The main surprise in reading the Koran for the first time
is the realization how closely the ancestry of the Arabs and
the Jews is interwoven. As explained before, both the Arabs
and the Jews claim that Abraham was the founder of their
nation. The Koran proclaims:

> *Abraham was neither a Jew, nor a Christian, he was a*
> *monotheist Muslim, and never an idol worshipper.*

The Koran names the following books as inspired by God:

•the first five books of the Bible;
•the psalms of David;
•the Gospel of Jesus;
•the Koran, which is final, and it has the last word.

Furthermore, the Koran teaches that there were some 125,000 prophets before Mohammed of which 27 are named. The list includes: Adam, Noah, Abraham, Moses, David, Jonah, and finally the last one before Mohammed, Jesus of Nazareth. Of course, the Koran makes it very clear that Mohammed was by far the most important prophet, and that his teachings take precedence over and above any of the others.

The Five Pillars Of Islam

There are five basic duties the Muslim must perform; these are:
•The recitation of his statement of belief, the Shahadah: "There is no God but Allah, and Mohammed is his prophet."
•The second duty is that he must pray five times a day, facing the Holy Mosque in Mecca.
•The third duty is to pay alms, 2.5 percent of his wealth.
•The fourth duty is to observe the fast in the month of Ramadan.
•The fifth is the hajj or hadj, a once in a lifetime pilgrimage to Mecca.
A sixth has been added by some, which is the participation in any holy war, the Jihad, to defend Islam. Today, this duty is used by Islamic countries to whip up support for any war. For instance, during the Iran-Iraq war, both sides called the conflict a holy war, with the promise that any soldier upon his death on the battlefield would go directly to heaven.

In general, the first five duties are not too hard to keep for the average person, especially since the faithful can receive dispensation from them if there are valid reasons that s/he cannot keep them.

The Creation Story And The First Appearance Of Satan

The Creation story appears a number of times in the Koran. Chapter 23 contains the following description:

> *We created the human from a certain kind of clay.*
> *Then we created the drop into a clot;*
> *then we created the clot into a cartilage;*
> *then we created the cartilage into bones;*
> *then we covered the bones with flesh;*
> *then we turned him into a new creation.*
> *Most exalted is God, the best Creator.*
> *Then you will die.*
> *Then on the day of resurrection, you will be raised.*

In at least six places the creation story is linked with the emergence of Satan. In Chapter 38, it reads as follows:

> *Your Lord said to the angels, "I am creating a human from clay, once I perfect him and blow into him from my soul you shall fall prostrate before him." All the angels fell prostrate. But not Satan; he was arrogant and thus became a disbeliever. God said, "O Satan, what prevented you from prostrating before my creation?; are you too arrogant; or much too high?" He said, "I am much better than he; you created me from fire and created him from clay." He said, "Then you must get out, for you are rejected. You have deserved my curse till the day of judgement."*

It is interesting to note that according to the Koran, Satan is a fallen angel who disobeyed God because he did not want to pay homage to man. Thus, in the Koran, man is the indirect cause for the downfall of Satan.

The Position Of Jesus In The Koran

To the Muslim, Jesus is an important prophet, a messenger like Mohammed, except that Mohammed was the last of the messengers and the most important one. The story of Jesus' birth appears a number of times in the Koran. As in the Bible, the announcement of the birth of Jesus is preceded by the announcement of the birth of John the Baptist. In Surah 3:42, the story of the announcement of Jesus' birth follows very much along the lines of the story in the New Testament as can be seen from the following passages:

> *The angel said, "O Mary, God gives you good news: a word from him to be called Messiah, Jesus the son of Mary. He will be honorable in this life and in the hereafter, and one of those who are close to God. He will speak to the people as an infant, and as a man, and he will be righteous." She said, "My Lord, how can I have a son, when no man has touched me?" She was told, "God thus creates whatever he wills. To have anything done, he simply says, 'Be' and it is."*

Of course, the Koran absolutely rejects the idea that Jesus was the son of God. In Surah 4:171 it reads:

> *The Messiah, Jesus the son of Mary is no more than a messenger of God . . .*
> *Therefore you shall believe in God and his messenger, and do not say Trinity . . .*
> *God is only one God, much too glorious to have a son.*

The Koran rejects the crucifixion and the resurrection; instead the Koran proclaims that God raised Jesus and that he never actually died. In Surah 4:157 it reads:

> *And because they said, "We killed the Messiah, Jesus the son of Mary," the messenger of God. Indeed they never killed him; they never crucified him; but they were led to believe that they did. Those who dispute in this matter are doubtful thereof; they have no real knowledge; they follow only conjecture. They never killed him, for certain. Instead, God raised him towards him, and God is almighty, wise.*

In some ways this appears to contradict the claim that Mohammed was the greatest prophet. It would seem logical to assume that the one who was directly raised by God must be higher in stature than a person who died a natural death like Mohammed. Since the Muslims do not believe in Jesus' resurrection, they also must reject the idea of Jesus' sacrificial death and that Jesus has reconciled the world with God.

Similarities And Differences

Because Judaism, Christianity and Islam all trace their origin back to the history of Abraham and his family, the three religions have many things in common, probably more than what separates them, although the latter ones are more divisive. Some of the things they have in common are:

- Judaism, Christianity and Islam share the same belief in the one God, who has created the entire universe.
- All three accept that humankind was created separately and that it was the crowning point of creation.
- All three accept that God also created angels.
- All three believe in the personification of evil — Satan.
- All three believe that God revealed himself through the descendants of Abraham, although the Muslims will say that God revealed himself, not through Mohammed or Jesus, but through the Koran.
- All three believe in the resurrection of the body and in a life hereafter.
- All three believe that there will be some sort of accounting on how we have lived our lives.
- Similarly, all three believe that there will be a different sort of treatment in the hereafter depending on how life on earth was lived.
- All three believe in the historical Jesus. This, unfortunately, is the only thing about the person of Jesus the three agree on.

The points of major disagreement are:

- For the Jews, Jesus was not the long awaited Messiah; in their opinion he was at best a good teacher and an example to be followed.
- For the Christians, Jesus is the son of God, the one who reconciled the world with God and is so close to God that it is difficult to distinguish between the two.
- For the Muslims, Jesus is a great messenger and prophet, so great that God took him to himself/herself. They do not believe that he is the son of God, nor that he reconciled man with God.

The other essential difference between Christianity and Islam lies in the fact that sin in the eyes of Islam consists in not following the five basic rules. For the Christian, it is not living up to God's basic rule of loving God and your neighbour as yourself. To follow the five basic rules of Islam is not too difficult to do, but to live in accordance with the basic rules given by Christ is impossible for even the best of us. The result is that the Muslim does not need someone to intervene between God and himself/herself. By doing the right thing at the right time s/he is able to work his/her own salvation, a thing that is simply impossible for the Christian. Thus, the Christian needs a Saviour or Redeemer, someone who can put him/her right with God, while the Muslim has no need for such an intermediary.

5 — Similarities And Differences

As I said in the introduction, it is impossible from these very brief overviews to decide whether there is enough common ground to decide whether these religions could possibly be the manifestations of the same Supreme Being. All we can do at this point is to summarize what these religions teach concerning a number of points that are central to the Christian faith.

1 — The Belief In The Existence Of A Supreme Being

Christianity: There is one God.
Hinduism: There is one Supreme God, but there are many other gods as well.
Hinayana Buddhism: There is no God and no Supreme Being.
Mahayana Buddhism: There is one God, Amitatha Buddha.
Islam: There is one God, Allah.

2 — Who Created The World?

Christianity: God created both heaven and earth.
Hinduism: Brahma created the world, but it is an imaginary world and it is not real.
Hinayana Buddhism: Not sure, but the world is real.
Mahayana Buddhism: Not sure, but the world is real enough.
Islam: Allah created both heaven and earth.

3 — The Relationship Between God And Humans

Christianity: God is considered to be so close to humans that it can be compared with the relationship children have with their parents.
Hinduism: There is no close personal relationship between Brahma and human beings.
Hinayana Buddhism: There is no deity.
Mahayana Buddhism: One can pray to the Amitatha Buddha.
Islam: God is too great to have a direct relationship with humans.

4 — The Ultimate Destiny Of Humans

Christianity: A person's ultimate destiny is to live in close communion with God.
Hinduism: A person can finally merge with Brahma.

Hinayana Buddhism: A person can finally enter a state of complete oblivion.

Mahayana Buddhism: A person's ultimate destiny is to enter paradise which is seen as a garden of delight.

Islam: A person's ultimate destiny is paradise, which is seen as a place in which most physical desires of humans are met.

5 — The Path By Which This Ultimate Destiny Can Be Reached

Christianity: Through a life of faith and deeds, but a mediator is needed because humans cannot meet these requirements on their own.

Hinduism: Through a series of successively higher stages one must accumulate a store of good deeds. No intermediary is needed — a person can do it by himself/herself.

Hinayana Buddhism: Through a life of good works one can find enlightenment and enter nirvana, and no mediator is therefore needed.

Mahayana Buddhism: Through a life of faith and devotion to the Amitatha Buddha one can enter paradise and no mediator is needed.*

Islam: By following the five basic rules one will enter heaven eventually. No intermediary is needed — one can do it by himself/herself.

*In some schools, the excess of good works (karma) that a holy man has accumulated can be transferred to someone else. One can pray to the holy man and ask to be given part of that excess, and thus enter paradise with the help of someone else.

6 — The Position Of Jesus

Christianity: Jesus is the Son of God, the mediator between humankind and its Creator.

Hinduism: Jesus may be considered as one of the manifestations of Brahma. He was a teacher.

Hinayana Buddhism: Jesus may be considered as one of the many Buddhas the world has known. He was an Enlightened One, a teacher.

Mahayana Buddhism: Jesus was a person who had found enlightenment.

Islam: Jesus was one of the many prophets the world has known; he certainly was not the Son of God.

7 — The Origin Of Pain And Suffering

Christianity: Suffering and death entered the world when humans rebelled against God. Since then it has been a condition of life.

Hinduism: Suffering is a condition of life on earth.

Hinayana Buddhism: Suffering is the result of craving and can be overcome by getting rid of craving.

Mahayana Buddhism: Suffering is a condition of life.

Islam: Suffering and evil are caused by a fallen angel, Satan.

8 — The Obligation To One's Neighbour

Christianity: The natural fruit of love and faith in God is love for one's neighbour, including one's enemy.

Hinduism: A believer has certain moral obligations for other believers in his caste.

Hinayana Buddhism: The good works one must perform consist almost entirely out of rituals. One works his/her own salvation.

Mahayana Buddhism: A holy man dedicates himself to helping others to enter paradise.

Islam: One of the five obligations of the Muslim is to give alms, but there is no such obligation as to love your neighbour.

The most striking differences between Christianity and the other three major religions are:

•Christians acknowledge that humans cannot meet the requirements for reconciliation with God on their own; they need an intermediary between humankind and God to make that reconciliation possible.

•Christians believe that humans can have a personal relationship with the Creator, a relationship that is similar in nature to that between a child and its parents.

The four religions have in common a belief that a moral life here on earth is a prerequisite for entering a later life, although there are wide differences in opinion about the nature of this later life.

Endnotes

Chapter 1 — Why This Book Was Written

[1]Davidson, James Dale and Rees-Mogg, Lord William. *The Great Reckoning — How the World Will Change in the Depression of the 1990s*, (Simon & Shuster, New York, 1993) p. 498.

Chapter 2 — Life Without God

[1]Leakey, Richard. *Origins Reconsidered*, (Doubleday, Garden City, New York, 1992).

[2]Horkheimer, Max. *Eclipse of Reason*, (Oxford University Press, New York, 1947).

[3]Keck, Robert L. *Sacred Eyes*, (Knowledge Systems Inc., Indianapolis, 1992) p. 5.

[4]Casti, John L. *Paradigms Lost*, (William Morrow, New York, 1989).

[5]Toffler, Alvin. *Future Shock*, (Random House, New York, 1970).

[6]Küng, Hans. *On Being a Christian*, (Collins, London, 1977) p. 39.

[7]Polkinghorne, John. *reason and reality*, (Trinity Press Int., Philadelphia, 1991) p. 99.

[8]Davies, Paul. *The Mind of God*, (Simon & Shuster, New York, 1992).

Chapter 3 — The God Of The Christian Religion

[1]Brunner, Emil. *Our Faith*, (SCM Press, London, 1977) p. 39.

[2]Keck, *op. cit.,* p. 153.

[3]Küng, Hans. *Does God Exist, An Answer for Today*, (Doubleday, Garden City, New York, 1980).

[4]Isaacs, Alan. *The Survival of God in the Scientific Age*, (Penguin, Baltimore, 1966) p. 155.

[5]Davies, *op. cit.,* p. 232.

[6]Adler, Mortimer J. *How To Think About God,* (McMillan, New York).

[7]Küng, *op. cit.,* p. 102.

Chapter 4 — The Forces That Oppose God

[1]Camus, Albert. *The Rebel*, (Penguin, New York, 1968) p. 416.

[2]Polkinghorne, *loc. cit.*, p. 99.

[3]Keck, *op. cit.*, p. 34.

[4]Peck, Scott. *The People of the Lie*, (Simon & Shuster, New York, 1983) pp. 203-207.

[5]Keating, Thomas. *Invitation to Love*, (Elements Inc., Rockport, 1992) p. 136.

Chapter 5 — Jesus — Our Direct Link With God

[1]Avi-Yonah, M. and Kraeling, E. G. *Our Living Bible*, (McGraw Hill, New York, 1962) p. 247.

[2]Barclay, William. *The Daily Study Bible, The Gospel of Matthew*, (Saint Andrew Press, Edinburgh, 1975).

[3]Siegel, Bernie. *Love, Medicine and Miracles*, (Harper & Row, New York, 1985).

[4]Josephus, Flavius. Quoted by E. F. Bruce. *Jesus and Christian Origins Outside the New Testament*, (Eerdmans, Grand Rapids, 1974) p. 37.

[5]Stevenson, Kenneth and Habermas, Gary. *The Verdict of the Shroud, Evidence for the Death and Resurrection of Jesus Christ*, (T. Nelson, Nashville, 1990).

[6]Kennedy, James D. *Why I Believe*, (Word Incorporated, Waco, 1980) pp. 111-112.

Chapter 6 — The Things That Separate Us From God

[1]Soelle, Dorothy. *Suffering*, (Fortress Press, Philadelphia, 1975) p. 178.

[2]Stackhouse, Reginald. *How Can I Believe When I Live In A World Like This?*, (Harper Collins, Toronto, 1990).

[3]Ellis, George. *Before The Beginning, Cosmology Explained*, (Bowerdean Publishing, London, 1993) p. 122.

[4]Kushner, Harold S. *When Bad Things Happen To Good People*, (Schocken Books, New York, 1981).

[5]Beker, J. C. *Suffering And Hope*, (Fortress Press, Philadelphia, 1987).

[6]Soelle, *loc. cit.,* p. 178.

[7]Siegel, Bernie. *Peace, Love and Healing*, (Harper & Row, New York, 1989) p. 192.

[8]Kushner, *op. cit.,* p. 141.

[9]Küng, Hans. *Christianity And The World Religions*, (Doubleday, New York, 1986) p. 95.

[10]Küng. *Does God Exist?*, pp. 623-624.

[11]Bonhoeffer, Dietrich. *Letters And Papers From Prison*, (SCM Press, London, 1953) p. 21.

[12]Kushner, *op. cit.,* p. 128.

[13]Hillesum, Etty. *The Interrupted Life, Diary of Hetty Hillesum*, (Lester & Orpen Denny's, 1983) translated from *Het Verstoorde Leven*, (De Haan, Haarlem, 1983).

[14]Becker, *op. cit.,* pp. 89-90.

[15]Stackhouse, *op. cit.,* p. 92.

Chapter 7 — Humankind's Reconciliation With God

[1]Frankl, Victor E. *Man's Search For Meaning*, (Simon & Shuster, New York, 1959) p. 88.

Chapter 8 — The Essence Of Jesus' Teaching

[1]Stott, John. *Basic Christianity*, (Inter-Varsity Press, Downers Grove, Illinois, 1958).

[2]Wilson, Ian. *Jesus, The Evidence*, (Harper & Row, San Francisco, 1984) p. 184.

[3]Lewis, C. S. *Surprised By Joy*, (Walker & Co., New York, 1986) p. 337.

[4]Peck, Scott. *Further Along The Road Less Travelled*, (Simon & Shuster, New York, 1993) p. 98.

[5]Muggeridge, Malcolm. *Jesus Rediscovered*, (Collins, London, 1969) p. 158.

[6]Swidler, Leonard. *The Meaning Of Life At The Edge Of The Third Millenium*, (Paulist Press, New York, 1992) p. 2.

[7]Ellis, *op. cit.,* p. 127.

[8]Braaten, Carl. *The Future Of God*, (Harper & Row, San Francisco, 1969).

[9]Augros, Robert and Staciu, George. *The New Story Of Science*, (Random House, New York, 1987).

[10]Kubler-Ross, E. *On Life After Death*, (Celestial Arts, Berkeley, 1991).

[11]Martin, J. and Romanovski, P. *We Are Not Forgotten*, (Putnam, New York, 1991).

[12]Stott, *op. cit.*

[13]Küng, Hans. *Eternal Life*, (Doubleday, Garden City, New York, 1984) pp. 230-231.

[14]Keating, *op. cit., p. 90.*

[15]Brunner, *loc. cit., p. 39.*

[16]Kushner, *op. cit., p. 118.*

[17]*Ibid.,* p. 125.

[18]Appleton, George. *Oxford Book Of Prayers*, (Oxford University Press, New York, 1985) pp. 153, 88.

[19]*Ibid.,* p. 96.

Chapter 9 — What God Demands From Us Today

[1]Smith, Houston. *The Religions Of Man*, (Harper & Row, New York, 1986) p. 233.

[2]Cox, Harvey. *The Secular City*, (Beacon Press, Boston, 1988) p. 178.

[3]Hessel, Dieter. *Social Ministry*, (The Westminster Press, Philadelphia, 1982) p. 42.

Chapter 10 — Where Do We Go From Here?

[1]Muggeridge, *loc. cit., p. 158.*

Appendix

[1]Gandhi, Mahatma. *The Story Of My Experiments With Truth*, (Beacon Press, Boston, 1957).

[2]Fernando, Anthony and Swidler, Leonard. *Buddhism Made Plain*, (Orbis Books, Maryknoll, New York, 1985).

[3]The quotations from the Koran are from a translation by Khalifa Rashad, (Islamic Productions, Tuscon, Arizona, 1981).